In this ... to the
importa ... envi-
ronment ... which
limits ou ... ed, or
hidden f ... ergy,
food sec ... itical,
economi ... ation
of enviro ... hem.
The bool ... imics
that shap ... pand
the reade ... ed at
particula ... ower
leads to a ... and
will help f

The bc ... s of
environm ... g ... background but will also appeal
to social and political scientists who wish to look at the topic from this
different perspective. Although the book reviews and applies theoretical
concepts of scale and power, it limits the use of jargon and presents ideas
and information in a style accessible to a broad audience.

SHANNON O'LEAR is a Professor of Geography and Environmental Studies at
the University of Kansas. Her research has focused on energy, environment,
and politics in the South Caucasus. She has also published on environmental
terrorism, territorial conflict, and genocide. She teaches courses on environmental policy, environmental geopolitics, and on Russia and Eurasia. She has
won a prestigious W. T. Kemper Fellowship for her teaching and her work
with students. She is an active member of the Association of American

Geographers (AAG) and has served as President of the Political Geography and the Russian, Central Eurasian and East European specialty groups of the AAG. In addition to her teaching and research, Dr. O'Lear is active in outreach to encourage students to become more thoughtfully engaged in geography and environmental studies. She is highly respected by both faculty and students as an outstanding researcher, teacher, and mentor.

Cover image translation: the sign on the cover image in Hindi is a business address and reads as follows:
"Sunil Kakkar
Nigam Parshad (Vine [word unclear] 89)
Member of the permanent organisation D.N.Ni.
609, Gali Ket Wali [literally "the narrow lane with the ket"], Pahargunj"

ENVIRONMENTAL POLITICS: SCALE AND POWER

SHANNON O'LEAR

University of Kansas

CAMBRIDGE
UNIVERSITY PRESS

CAMBRIDGE UNIVERSITY PRESS
Cambridge, New York, Melbourne, Madrid, Cape Town, Singapore,
São Paulo, Delhi, Dubai, Tokyo

Cambridge University Press
The Edinburgh Building, Cambridge CB2 8RU, UK

Published in the United States of America by
Cambridge University Press, New York

www.cambridge.org
Information on this title: www.cambridge.org/9780521765763

First published 2010

Printed in the United Kingdom at the University Press, Cambridge

A catalogue record for this publication is available from the British Library

Library of Congress Cataloging-in-Publication Data
O'Lear, Shannon.
Environmental politics : scale and power / Shannon O'Lear.
p. cm.
ISBN 978-0-521-76576-3 (Hardback) – ISBN 978-0-521-75913-7 (Pbk.)
1. Environmental policy–United States. 2. Environmentalism–United States. 3. Environmental
protection–United States. I. Title.
GE180.O58 2010
363.7'0561–dc22
2010022748

ISBN 978-0-521-76576-3 Hardback
ISBN 978-0-521-75913-7 Paperback

This book is lovingly dedicated to Maeve and Cian, my bliss.
Knucks!

Contents

Acknowledgements

My first word of thanks must go to my students who, each semester, have challenged and inspired me to challenge and inspire *them* with innovative, humorous, and (they tell me) sometimes depressing insights about things they may not have thought about before. My Environmental Policy and Environmental Geopolitics classes, in particular, have road tested much of the material in this book. Graduate students in my seminar courses, through their work on an array of intriguing research topics, have expanded my knowledge considerably. I am grateful for their patient support throughout my focused effort on this book project and for their offerings of news items, humorous clips, and music. My colleagues in the Geography Department, the Environmental Studies Program, and the Center for Russian, East European and Eurasian Studies were accommodating and understanding about me undertaking this project without the benefit of a sabbatical. If at times I was less available than they might have liked, they were kind enough not to bring attention to it. Darin Grauberger and Eric Weber in Cartographic and GIS Services here in the Geography Department deserve recognition for their professional devotion of time and their diligent response to my enthusiastic requests for graphics.

Over the course of writing this book, I was fortunate to work with four outstanding undergraduate research assistants who energetically responded to my requests for seemingly random pieces of information. Theron Cook and Owen Patterson, Geography majors, worked on earlier portions of the book, and Jason Hering and Shane Johnston, Environmental Studies majors, worked with me in later stages of the book. I am grateful for their zeal and attention to detail. I appreciate Matt Lloyd, Christopher Hudson, Laura Clark, Penny Lyons, and Dawn Preston at Cambridge University Press for their stewardship that saw this book through to its timely completion and for responding to questions pertaining to the minutia that a project of this scope entails. I enjoyed working with all of the artists and researchers whose visual work appears in (and on) this book. I am honored that they have so graciously contributed their talents to this effort.

My deepest gratitude goes out to my colleagues and friends, Mariya Omelicheva, Steve Egbert, Bev Morey, and Masha and Jake Kipp who provided honest commentary and insight, a sense of humor, and chocolate throughout the writing process. Thanks are also due to the whole gang at Muncher's Bakery where I spent numerous hours while piecing together portions of this book (and *not* the romance novel that they imagined I was writing!). My family, long familiar with my passion for my calling, cheered me on from distant sidelines encouraging my progress. Throughout this process, Mark O'Lear was supportive and understanding as ever, and I am profoundly grateful for his unwavering friendship. Illuminating my work is the ever present memory of Wally Weir, my Zorba, who taught me to dance.

1

Introduction

Introduction

The cover of the 15th anniversary (June 2008) issue of *Wired* magazine says it all:

Attention Environmentalists:
Keep your SUV.
Forget organics.
Go nuclear.
Screw the spotted owl.
If you're serious about global warming, only one thing matters: Cutting carbon. That means facing some inconvenient truths.

In typical, edgy *Wired* style, several short commentaries explain how what we thought was good for the environment turns out to be all wrong. Organic food is often grown in energy-dependent greenhouses and requires extensive transport to market. Air conditioning generates less CO_2 than does heating. Urban centers are more energy efficient than suburban sprawl. Old growth forests do not have the same carbon sequestration capacity as do younger forests, and "pound for pound, making a Prius contributes more carbon to the atmosphere than making a Hummer, largely due to the environmental cost of the 30 pounds of nickel in the hybrid's battery" (p. 163).

 At the end of the section is a final, brief commentary titled "It's Not Just Carbon, Stupid." It would be easy to miss after all of the photographically rich challenges to green thinking, but this short piece is essentially a rebuttal to the central story. The author argues that focusing solely on greenhouse emissions is not a realistic way to understand environmental problems and that such a focus "blinds us to more sustainable, and ultimately more promising, solutions." Indeed, reducing humans' relationship with the physical environment to the cycle of a single gas molecule misses many of the political, social, and economic dimensions underlying predominant environmental narratives.

The objective of this book is to reconsider several, significant environmental issues by looking at two related aspects of each: the spatial scale at which these issues are generally discussed and understood and the politics that bring these issues to our attention or, in some cases, obscure them from our view. In each instance, the case will be made that the scale of the particular issue needs to be reconceptualized if we are to understand the issue more completely and develop more appropriate responses and adaptations. This book will demonstrate an explicitly geographic perspective by integrating concepts of spatial scale and power into the discussion of a selection of timely environmental concerns. Applying a geographer's sense of scale and power helps us to understand the complexity of environmental issues while at the same time highlighting ways in which spatial scales of our narratives about and of our responses to environmental issues are not necessarily well matched to the problem.

What is the environment?

To clarify the point of departure for this book, it is helpful to consider the title. The word "environment" is used in so many contexts that its intended meaning is not immediately clear. We hear about businesses that care about the "environment," we know people who are "environmentalists," we hear about "environmental change" in the news. We can think of the environment as the physical realm from which we draw resources to sustain our lives and our societies, but we have also created understandings of what the environment is and what our relationship to it is. Where is the environment, for example, in an aquarium? People visit an aquarium to see exotic fish and, presumably, to learn about the places from which those fish come. Aquarium developers have learned that people do not come to see "brown" fish. They want to see colorful fish from distant parts of the world that they may not actually be able to travel to themselves. What many aquarium visitors may not know is that the demand for exotic, colorful fish has fostered illegal trade in fish which often depends on a practice known as cyanide fishing. Cyanide fishing involves stunning fish with a blast of cyanide, usually issued with a plastic squeeze bottle by fishers who have few other options for employment. Stunned fish are easy to catch and sell to middlemen who then make these exotic fish available on a global black market. There is more than a single "environment" in this scenario. There is the environment of the aquarium, which is a constructed place where people expect to go and learn about "nature." Aquaria tend to foster the idea that there is a pristine environment "out there" that we can appreciate by looking at members of its ecosystem. Yet there is also the environment where fish are being stunned and sold and where people are engaging in this activity out of economic desperation. How did that environment come to be? The point is that there is no single "environment," but instead there are many environments demonstrating a complex interplay of "nature" and society.

What difference does it make if we think of ourselves – as people and as societies – as distinct or separate from our physical, "natural" environment? It is an interesting question because we might imagine that if we are separate from the environment, there is some distance between our activities and their affects on other places. If we think of ourselves as distinct from our environment, we might also think that the distance between us and the environment allows us a degree of control or an ability to manipulate ecosystems without harming our own potential for well-being. This view of humans as separate from nature has roots in Judeo-Christian thinking and is evident in many ways in Western societies today. Even before industrialization took off in Britain, for example, Francis Bacon (1561–1626) promoted his view that "science would restore [man's] dominion over nature" (Peltonen 1996, p. 19). This perspective encouraged the view that the physical, natural environment was something to be tamed and controlled for the benefit of society. We can see even in more recent times the idea that humans are separate and "in control" of the environment.

Gifford Pinchot, grandfather of the National Forest system in the US, is famous for coining the phrase "Conservation means the wise use of the earth and its resources...for the greatest good of the greatest number for the longest time" (Pinchot 1947, p. 505). His view of forestry was that "Forestry is Tree Farming. Forestry is handling trees so that one crop follows another. To grow trees as a crop is Forestry" (p. 31). Nature, clearly, was something to be managed. When Pinchot looked upon the status of forests in the USA in the late 1800s, he saw that there were no guidelines to how people were utilizing the natural resources of the country. He made it his mission to establish a theory and practice of forestry that would enable the continued production and use of natural resources for national economic benefit. After devoting over half of a century of his life to forestry, Pinchot shared his observation that "The earth and its resources belong of right to its people" and that "The first duty of the human race ... is to control the use of the earth and all that therein is" (p. 505). Clearly this view distinguishes the environment as distinct from humans and as something that should be managed and controlled by humans for the benefit of humans. This perspective persists to this day and is practiced by groups such as the US Forestry Service, which is based on a multiple use approach allowing hiking, timber harvesting, and sometimes mining in federally owned forests. Ducks Unlimited exemplifies a category of organizations that draw upon this philosophy too, as they seek to maintain habitat for ducks and other waterfowl for the benefit of recreational hunters. The very principle of conservation is that environmental resources can and should be managed for humans' economic benefit as well as for the maintenance of ecosystem services. This view necessarily distinguishes humans from "the" environment.

At about the same time as Gifford Pinchot was working to advance a conservationist philosophy in the US, Russian and then Soviet planners were promoting similar views about the physical environment. Adhering to the Marxist labor theory of value (Debardeleben and Hannigan 1995), they looked at natural resources as having little if any inherent value in and of themselves until human labor was applied to "make" something out of timber, minerals, and surging water. The driving force behind Stalin's government in the 1920s was to prepare the Soviet Union for war and expand military capacity. To do that, various inputs were required, and the economy was set on five-year plans with specific production goals. Meeting these demanding goals was required, and over-reaching the production quotas was rewarded. Economic incentives unintentionally encouraged waste by rewarding fulfilment of narrow output goals rather than cost reduction and profit maximization. The Soviet economic system not only placed a priority on expanded material output but was driven by an obsession with "gigantomania" – really large endeavors such as dams and river diversions – and scientific-technical prowess especially in heavy industrial and military industrial sectors. Granted, there were strong traditions of environmental regulation that had roots in pre-revolutionary Russia, such as the protected land system and *zapovedniki* network that valued nature on its own terms (Oldfield 2005), and the expansive Soviet system did not result in a uniform degree of environmental damage (see Figure 1.1). Nevertheless, it is instructive to note parallels in attitudes that have viewed humans as distinct from "nature" in different contexts.

Geographers have long recognized humans' capacity to alter the environment. For example, George Perkins Marsh's book, *The Earth as Modified by Human Action*, published in 1874, is still cited today as a classic text of the discipline. Recently, we have become increasingly aware of the reach and depth of changes made to the physical environment by humans: by altering entire watersheds and ecosystems with chemical fertilizers; through repeated nuclear weapons testing, use, and nuclear accidents such as Chernobyl; by

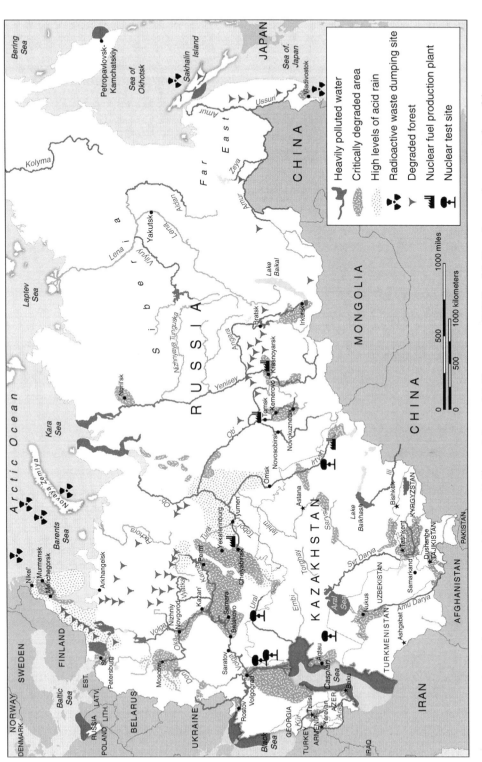

Figure 1.1 The Soviet environmental legacy. Adapted from (a) Peterson, (1993); (b) Russia: environmental problem areas (1998). In *Handbook of International Economic Statistics*. http://www.lib.utexas.edu/maps/commonwealth.html, accessed 4 December 2009; (c) UNDP, UNEP, OSCE, (2004); (d) UNEP, UNDP, OSCE, (2003).

releasing industrial volumes of chemicals such as chlorofluorocarbons and sulfur dioxide into the air sufficient to alter the atmosphere at regional and global scales; by generating and emitting long-lasting, cross-media persistent organic pollutants that have negative health effects on people and animals from the tropics to the poles; by removing a significant percentage of fish from the oceans; by increasing energy consumption; by building dams and river diversion projects – just to name a few examples. Scholars have made the case that humans have essentially brought about a new geologic era known as the Anthropocene which is characterized by irreversible, human-induced change to the globe (Crutzen and Stoermer 2000; Crutzen 2002). Simon Dalby (2007b; see also Dalby 2002) has observed that recognizing the Anthropocene opens up the opportunity to reconsider not only human–environment relationships but also the very basis of our understanding of spatial arrangements of power:

> Security threats to modernity, long the preoccupation of the discipline of international relations, have usually assumed that threats are external to states, a matter of manipulation of external environments. But in the case of environment it is clear that such formulations are seriously misleading because it is the consequences of industrial production, and the appropriation of resources and displacement of populations as a result of these appropriations, which are causing the environmental changes that are supposedly a threat in the first place.
>
> *(p. 113)*

Taking the idea of the Anthropocene seriously, Dalby argues, gives us reason to examine how our economic and political systems have contributed to the irreversible manipulation of the air, water, and ecosystems on which we depend. He challenges us to reconsider ways in which ecological issues tend to enter into political dialogue and to pay attention to spatial patterns associated with those ecological issues. Where are the "haves" and the "have nots" when it comes to resource issues, and how does our society identify and prioritize environmental "problems" and solutions? Who benefits from "our" environmental priorities, and which places or groups of people are left with few alternatives or limited options for improving their own chances for survival? How might we conceive of rearranging our systems of governance and ways in which political power and decision-making are distributed in recognition of humans' integral relationship with the environment?

A key objective of this book is to encourage the reader to think critically about how environmental issues are discussed in mainstream media and in conversations both public and scholarly. There is no overarching, singular understanding of "the environment" used throughout this book. Instead, each topic will be considered in how it represents an entanglement of environmental, spatial, economic, social, and political processes. By examining the cases included in the book, which represent but a small selection from a staggering array of current environmental concerns, the book demonstrates how two particular tools or perspectives may be applied to environmental topics even beyond the covers of this book. These two tools help us in a critical assessment of environmental issues which means that we will question assumptions made both overtly and implicitly in how these issues are discussed and presented. The two tools or perspectives that frame the inquiry in this book are spatial scale and power. The following sections elaborate on these concepts.

Scale

Thinking spatially, as geographers do, involves looking at ways in which various phenomena interact across space. A way to capture the spatial dimension of a particular process is to look at its spatial scale. What is scale? Geographers consider spatial scale one of several concepts defining the discipline alongside other core geographic concepts such as territory, space, and place. An important beginning point to understanding how scale is conceived throughout this book it that scale is not the container for human activity. Instead it is a spatial product of human activity. Human processes produce spatial scales. We might think of administrative levels (e.g., city, county, state, country, etc.) as scales, and administrative levels are one, narrowly defined type of scale, but human processes of defining territory and administrative units have created these levels of activity. Social practices or activities may coincide with administrative levels (e.g., state- or city-level activities), but scale is described in part by how these activities are related to, constrained by, or enabled by other processes. For example, a group of students enrolled in a particular university or college is beholden to the rules, regulations, and opportunities associated with that institution, yet those administrative aspects of the university do not necessarily describe the full spatial scale of student activity. That same group of students might be involved in a study abroad program in Ecuador, a national political campaign, or a service learning project through which they engage with a local community off campus. These activities constitute a spatial scale of activity that might be made possible through the students' matriculation in the university, but these activities also expand the spatial dimension of student experience that is not necessarily captured or contained by the institution's physical or administrative structure. This illustration shows why equating the student "university experience" to the scale of the university campus misses important spatial dimensions of student activity that may be part of a student's university career. Scale is more than administrative level as the following discussion aims to explain.

Across natural and social sciences, scale has multiple meanings including the spatial extent of a study area (observational scale), the resolution of data (measurement scale), the spatial extent of particular processes (operational scale), and the representation of phenomena on a map (cartographic scale) (Lam and Quattrochi 1992). In recent years, scholars have continued to discuss and debate the meaning of scale (see Howitt 1998, Marston 2000, Herod 2003, Sheppard and McMaster 2004, and Mamadouh *et al.* 2004 for more thorough reviews of the literature), but part of the difficulty in understanding what is meant by scale is that there are different and often implicit definitions, models, and understandings of scale that are frequently used without distinction (see Sheppard and McMaster 2004).

Robert Sack, a geographer, has considered how humans construct places to meet our needs and according to our values and views of reality (Sack 2001). At some point the work of constructing a place began with bare ground and parameters of the physical environment, but constructing places can also refer to how groups of people have constructed cities, farms, schools, hospitals, churches, athletic clubs, national parks, military bases, demilitarized zones, refugee camps, research centers, neighborhoods, homes, and other places that meet particular needs or objectives of a society. People are constantly engaged in changing or maintaining places, and that means changing or maintaining rules about whom or what a particular place includes or excludes. Places are necessary for spatial interactions such as the flow of ideas, practices, and physical materials.

If we are interested in how a place and processes unfolding in a place are connected to other places, then we are interested in scale. Scale can be understood as a relationship among specific processes and places. We can think of scale as having three elements: place, actors, and a relational dimension that links places and actors (O'Lear and Diehl 2007). Place refers not only to a physical location but also rules, values, and meanings associated with a place. How is a place maintained, monitored, controlled, valued, described, and justified? Actors can include states, individuals, corporations, scientists, journalists, organizations, consumers, producers – in short, any type of agent that plays a role in a particular phenomenon. Places and actors are linked in different kinds of relationships of exchange that might be social, economic, political, or physical. The spatial scale of any particular process can be described by relationships among actors and places and includes systems of rules or values that emerge to shape these relationships. Scale can continually change. As noted earlier, scale is not the container for human activity, but instead it is a way to understand spatial dimensions of human activity and relationships. Administrative scales (cities, institutions, states, etc.) capture certain types of human activity, but human activity generates other spaces and networks beyond administrative levels.

When scale serves as a starting point or container for research, most often involving an assumption of a pre-existing scale (e.g., the state), our understanding of the spatial dimension associated with the research question is crystallized. That is, if we start with a question about particular processes within a country, we can easily find ourselves limited to conceptualizing human activity only within the country. We might overlook how that activity transcends or flows across the border and how the activity might be influenced by or have an impact on other places. For example, to understand why Wangari Maathai, the Assistant Minister of Environment and Natural Resources in Kenya won a Nobel Peace Prize, we have to understand more than just her work in Kenya. Ms. Maathai won the Noble Peace Prize for her work planting trees in Kenya to support local communities. She had observed how the process of colonization in Africa had significantly changed the livelihoods and well-being of people who lived there (Maathai 2005). Mt. Kenya, for example, had been revered by all communities that could see it as sacred and as something to be respected. Colonizers brought Christianity and shifted the idea of the sacred heavenward. She notes that "Once it was no longer revered, the mountain was no longer protected" (p. 19). Colonists also introduced commercial crops that were not native to the land and that required the destruction of forests to grow. Large areas that had been farmed traditionally or used for grazing were cleared of vegetation to grow crops for export such as wheat and exotic species of trees for the international timber industry. Wheat, for example, could only be harvested from the land one time, and then other locations were cleared for subsequent harvests. Once harvested, exotic timber species were rarely replaced with seedlings, exotic or otherwise. Deforestation led to soil runoff and the degradation of water supplies. Scarce water in rural areas motivated men to seek jobs in cities, abandoning their families and the hardships of living off the land. Communities and family networks unraveled. All of these changes – physical, economic, religious, political, and social – altered the "places" of Kenyan communities.

Between 1950 and 2000, 90% of Kenya's forests were lost (Maathai 2008). Ms. Maathai founded the Green Belt Movement, which focused on supporting rural women to teach them how to plant and care for trees (Figure 1.2). This approach aimed to overcome an attitude that solutions to problems

Figure 1.2 Wangari Maathai's Green Belt Center. The center is home to Green Belt Movement and serves as a meeting place for many groups active on environmental issues. Photo courtesy of Karyn D. Ellis.

would come from "outside." By creating healthier environments that can sustain communities, the Green Belt Movement is also helping to create spaces in which people who are affected by environmental degradation may have a voice in the negotiation of sharing and managing resources. By this process, the Green Belt Movement is also strengthening local cultures and economies and giving them an alternative to the past negative influence of colonization and world commodity prices.

Ms. Maathai's work has more than local implications and is significant beyond Kenya. The scale of her work with the Green Belt Movement involves not only rural women, but also the influence of past colonization and changes in land use practices, physical environments recaptured by tree-planting efforts, and a reconnection with belief systems that reinvigorate an identity with traditional culture. The fact that an international body such as the Nobel Peace Prize committee recognized the value of Ms. Maathai's work demonstrates that her work reaches beyond Kenya as a demonstration of positive change that could be implemented in other places as well. In short, the scale of Ms. Maathai's Green Belt Movement concentrates on small communities in Kenya, but it is not "just" local or "just" a phenomenon within Kenya's borders. We can see that the spatial extent of her work involves particular villages, a civil institution network (the Green Belt Movement), the support of the Kenyan government (particularly in her role as the Assistant Minister of

Environment and Natural Resources), and recognition from the international community in the form of her Nobel Peace Prize. That international recognition publicizes her work and opens doors for the work to continue both in Kenya and beyond. The spatial scale of her work is immediately local yet is enabled and empowered through international recognition. Once we understand the richness and complexity of Ms. Maathai's work, we can see more clearly how it addresses human connections with place.

Another example where it is useful to understand spatial scale on its own terms is the example of commodity chains. You might have purchased your cup of coffee at your favorite coffee shop this morning, but where did your coffee really come from (Durning and Ayres 1994)? If the scale of a cup of coffee involves the places and processes that contributed to its production, we would want to know where the beans originated, where they were roasted, how they were transported and in what packaging, not to mention where the transportation fuel and packaging materials originated. What about the paper or Styrofoam cup – where did that come from? Was the coffee brewed with local tap or bottled water? Was a paper filter or a metal filter used? Additionally, to really capture the commodity chain of the cup of coffee, we would want to know how the cup was disposed of and where, unless the cup was reusable. We can also think about commodity chains associated with blue jeans, diamonds, pencils, and computers and about waste streams involved with these and other products. We can also think about the impact that these commodities have in different places. Do they motivate workers' unions promoting employee health and safety standards? Do they inspire new laws or policies on water treatment, offshore banking, agricultural subsidies, or trade restrictions? It does not take long to realize that any one everyday commodity – from chocolate bars to iPods – might easily connect many places and represent a particular scale unique to that commodity and which goes well beyond "the country of origin." Commodity chains allow us to trace a particular item back to its origin and all of the places that played a role in its production. Again, rather than thinking of your coffee as being from Ethiopia, Colombia, or even Starbucks, once we understand how the process of producing coffee connects several places and shapes human activities in different places, then we can more clearly appreciate the spatial scale of coffee production.

Since this book is centrally concerned with environmental issues, we also need to recognize spatial scales related to the physical environment and ecosystems. The previous section has considered ways that social activities (e.g., social activism, consumption of commodities, etc.) describe spatial connections, but ecological processes also describe particular spaces. We can, for example, map discrete areas where a particular type of soil may be found, where a specific type of tree is a dominant climax species, or patterns of species migration and seasonal ocean currents. Spaces described by these processes may shift and change over time, but we can see that the physical environment constitutes spatial scales, too. Returning to the idea of the Anthropocene, however, it becomes interesting to think about human–environment interactions and the generation of new or different spatial scales. For example, where and how exotic plant and animal species have diffused and with what kinds of impacts, changes in biogeochemical cycles that result in, for example, an overabundance of nitrogen and eutrophication in some water systems, intensified trends of drought emerging in places where agriculture systems overdraw on water supplies, and so forth, all reflect human–environment interactions. Human–environment interactions also refer to systems or institutions that societies establish to deal with the allocation and management of natural resources. For example, common pool resources are managed with a variety of institutions ranging from government ownership to privatization and deal with the flow, appropriation, maintenance, and provision of a variety of resources. Yet the legal and management systems set up to manage, allocate, and control the use of natural resources do not necessarily match the spatial scales of the specific phenomena they are intended to address (Ostrom *et al.* 1999).

Consider that the watershed for the Mississippi River extends from the Canadian side of Montana's border through Wyoming, Colorado, New Mexico and Texas on the west side and as far east as New York, Pennsylvania, West Virginia, Virginia, North Carolina, Tennessee, Mississippi, and Alabama and includes nearly all of the Midwest states in between. Water from small streams and larger rivers in these areas feed into the Mississippi River and travels southward to the Gulf of Mexico. Agricultural and other activities in all of these states release phosphates and forms of nitrogen into the Mississippi watershed all of which contributes to the eutrophication of the Gulf of Mexico (Figure 1.3). That is, the nitrogen feeds algae blooms that lead to a precipitous drop in oxygen levels in the water making it difficult if not impossible for a range of plants and aquatic species to survive. Along the coastline of the Gulf of Mexico is a dead zone where oxygen levels are so low at certain times of the year that very few species are able to survive. What kind of governance system could be established to limit the use and release of phosphates in the Mississippi basin to bring the dead zone back to life? A national level monitoring system would include all of the states in the watershed but also many others that do not contribute to the problem, but a state-level system might not be able to coordinate with other states in the watershed. Nitrogen levels are not uniform

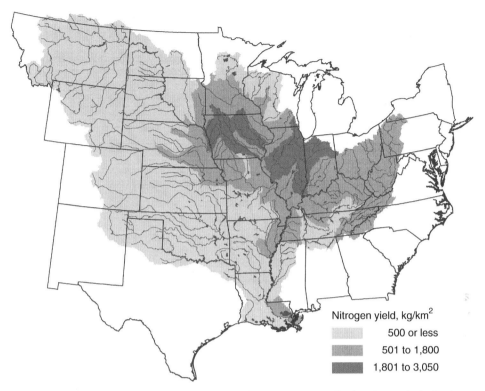

Figure 1.3 Multiple spatial scales of Nitrogen loads in the Mississippi watershed. Adapted from Goolsby and Battaglin (2000).

throughout the entire watershed but are higher in predominantly agricultural areas, so perhaps a national level system could be established to set and enforce limits of phosphates use in agriculture. Yet setting limits on agricultural inputs such as the fertilizers that contain phosphates might alter agricultural productivity and have ramifications for food supply and international trade agreements. Besides, agriculture is not the only contributor of phosphates. Other industrial activities contribute to the nitrogen load, and any individual household that regularly does laundry using most brand name detergents also contributes phosphates to the water system. Since part of the Mississippi watershed extends into Canada, any system to address the dead zone in the Gulf of Mexico should realistically include Canadian representation as well.

Through this brief assessment of the phosphate-generated dead zone in the Gulf of Mexico, we quickly run up against the problem that our administrative units (i.e., countries and states) do not fit the scale of ecosystemic processes. More than that, though, we realize that what initially seems to be a simple issue of too much phosphate leads to other complicated issues of agricultural and international trade policies and possibly to the regulation of consumer activity as well. Perhaps not surprisingly, research suggests that regulatory regimes for ecological systems are most effective when they are sensitive to the scale of the ecosystem in question (Wilson *et al.* 1999; Dietz *et al.* 2003). The challenge, then, is not only to identify the appropriate spatial scale of the ecological system in question, but also to identify how political, economic, and social dimensions of human systems can or should be constructed in a particular regulatory regime. Following that, there are also questions of how best to prioritize goals, identify stakeholders, incorporate scientific knowledge, and respond to monitoring and feedback of the regulatory system.

Where does spatial scale stop? The analogies of commodity chains and ways that humans have impacts on a single ecosystem suggest that one could carry out the identification of scale to infinitesimal degrees. Consider Benoit Mandelbrot's reconsideration of Euclidean geometry. Thinking about the essence of complexity, Mandelbrot raised the question "How long is the coast of Britain?" (Gleick 1988, p. 94). His answer is that any coastline is infinitely long depending on the length of the ruler used to measure it. Using a yardstick to measure a coastline will miss turns and curves smaller than one yard. If the same stretch of coastline is then measured with a one foot ruler, more of the detail will be included in the measurement, but not as much detail as when the coastline is measured using a four inch ruler, and so forth. Mandelbrot argued that the measured length of a coastline becomes longer as the unit for measuring becomes smaller and more able to capture detail. How long is the coastline? It depends on how it is measured. The objective of this book is to take a closer look at a selection of environment-related phenomena – e.g., climate change, resource conflicts, food security, etc. – to understand spatial and power dimensions beyond how they are usually discussed or understood. In so doing, we will reconsider the scale of these phenomena. The exploration here, as is true with most explorations, cannot be absolute and exhaustive.

When we look at an environmental issue, are we limiting our view to a single dimension (such as cutting carbon in response to climate change) rather than examining the building blocks of spatial processes and patterns contributing to that issue? The aim in this book is to assess the spatial scale of environmental issues more clearly by investigating how a particular issue represents a complex and incomplete set of physical, political, social, and economic relationships among different processes and places. These examples illustrate the value of approaching spatial dimensions of human activity not with predetermined parameters but with flexibility so that we may more clearly see how human activities generate new kinds of spaces. They also highlight why it is useful to problematize scale – rather than take scale as a given – and to explore the agency involved in developing or challenging a particular scale or spatial arrangement. Indeed, scale "explains nothing in and of itself, but its perspective may influence the discovery of pattern and process" (Easterling and Polsky 2004, p. 66). The geographic literature reflects a growing recognition that scale is continually produced "through everyday habits, routines, practices, negotiations, experiments, conflicts and struggles" (Brenner 2001, p. 606). These activities are carried out in particular places, so scale is, in essence, about relationships among different processes and places.

Politics and power

The title of this book, *Environmental Politics*, warrants clarification. The title is not *Environmental Policy* which might suggest a focus on established laws, protocols, and penalties dealing with pollution limits, water quality stand-ards, or land use guidelines. Instead, the focus here is environmental politics which suggests a concern with processes of defining human relationships with the environment – property rights, acceptability of genetically modified foods, recognition of toxic substances, for example – and ways in which these relationships become established, widely accepted, or challenged. Often our views towards the environment and our understanding of how we interact with the environment become so commonplace that we forget that our way of looking at the world was likely established through competition with other views or perspectives. An analogy can be made to keyboard technology. In the early days of typewriters, lettered keys were arranged alphabetically. Typists were able to learn the logical arrangement of keys easily and could type so quickly that the typebars of each letter would frequently become stuck together when several were in motion near the platen or roller. To address this inconvenience, the lettered keys were rearranged in a more random order to slow down typing speed and keep the typebars from clumping together. Today, typewriters are a rarity, and most people use electronic keyboards with no physical typebars. Yet we still use the QWERTY arrangement of letters, named for the top left line of letter keys, because it is familiar to most people around the world through the diffusion of technology. Technology and our ways of viewing particular issues can get stuck in a familiar pattern. When our views or conditions are accepted as inevitable, they tend to be de-linked from politics as the struggle for power. If we do not question how current systems and perspectives about the environment became dominant, the power embedded in establishing those norms becomes crystallized. In this way we can speak of our understanding of the environment as becoming depoliticized.

Environmental politics, then, inquires into commonly accepted views of the environment and considers dimensions of power embedded in these views – who benefits, who loses, and what are other ways to think about a particular issue? We can refine the discussion further by considering the difference between politics and the political. The political arena of society is usually understood as involving elections, systems of governmental representation, and governmental institutions aimed at maintaining state power. Jenny Edkins (1999) offers a different view that

> ... the political represents the moment of openness or undecidability, when a new social order is on the point of establishment, when its limits are being contested. Politics, in contrast, is what takes place once the new order is institutionalized. It is the debate that occurs *within* the limits set by that order. In an important sense, then, the political could be described as a moment that depoliticizes: The most intensely political moment, the moment of decision, itself brings about the forgetting of the political that instills politics.

> *(p. 126)*

Following this view, the title of this book suggests that attention will be paid to discussions, debates, and struggles within established systems of government and environmental management. That is part of what this book aims to address. However, this book also concerns itself with the political – the moments or opportunities of reconsidering the spatial scope and power dimensions of environmental issues. A focus on politics involves examining power dynamics and competing conceptualizations of nature, and the generation, interpretation, and incorporation of scientific knowledge into political practice (Lipschutz 2004). Essential to this project is intellectual critique or criticism. Criticism, in the scholarly context, is the questioning of taken for granted categories and priorities as well as the evaluation of our own understandings and assumptions (after Dalby 2007a). Thinking critically about environmental politics and about political processes associated with human–environment interactions will aid in a more clear understanding of factors that have shaped thinking about environmental issues and help us to identify alternative ways of understanding these issues.

The concept of scale has already been introduced, but the concept of power also requires discussion. There are many definitions and forms of power, but this book will draw primarily on the work of Michael Mann who has applied his conceptualization of power across a broad sweep of history. Two of his

Table 1.1. *Mann's forms of organizational reach*

	Authoritative	Diffused
Intensive	Army command structure	A general, labor strike
Extensive	Militaristic empire	Market exchange

Source: Mann, M. (1986). *The Sources of Social Power Volume 1: A history of power from the beginning to A.D. 1760.* Cambridge: Cambridge University Press, p. 9.

books in particular, *The Sources of Social Power Vol. 1: A history of power from the beginning to A.D. 1760* (Mann 1986) and *The Sources of Social Power Vol. 2: The Rise of Classes and Nation States, 1760–1914* (Mann 1993), demonstrate that his approach to power is not constrained to a limited timeframe but is applicable across a range of spatial and temporal contexts. His work is widely cited by political geographers (e.g., Allen 2003; Ó Tuathail *et al.* 2006) in part because his definition of power, although deeply relevant to sovereign states, can also be considered at spatial scales other than the territorial state. Mostly, his view of sociospatial dimensions of power will be helpful in disentangling different elements that contribute to current thinking about the environment.

Mann's work emerged in part as a response to sociological theories of society that tend to simplify social relations in order to single out a "core, ultimately determining element of society" (Mann 1986, p. 5). Mann recognizes, instead, that "societies are much messier than our theories of them" (Mann 1986, p. 4). He argues that "Power is the ability to pursue and attain goals through mastery of one's environment" (Mann 1986, p. 6). Fundamental to power, then, is the ability to organize, coordinate, and cooperate. Mann outlines four types of organization and reach: authoritative, diffuse, intensive, and extensive (see Table 1.1). Authoritative power takes the form of commands or rules issued from centralized institutions, whereas diffuse power takes the form of "self-evident common interest" and diffuses through a population spontaneously. Extensive power reflects an ability to organize many people in some form of cooperation over a large spatial area. Intensive power reflects an ability to "organize tightly and command a high level of mobilization or commitment from the participants, whether the area and numbers covered are great or small" (Mann 1986, p. 7).

Organizational control in any of these forms is more powerful when it is institutionalized in the norms and laws of a given society. On the other side of the coin, however, Mann observes that the masses tend not to revolt because "they lack collective organization . . . They are organizationally outflanked" (Mann 1986, p. 7).

In addition to these types of organizational reach, Mann frames his work with four ideal types of social power each of which offers a different means of organization and social control: ideological, economic, military, and political. He acknowledges that these networks of social interaction overlap but that each represents a different source of power.

Ideological power is associated with the meaning imposed on our direct perceptions and experiences. The meaning that we apply to our experience, the understandings we share about societal norms or appropriate behavior, and the ritual practices, religious or secular, that we value are examples of ideological power that can be shaped to influence social organization and objectives. Mann explains that the knowledge and meaning promoted through ideological power "cannot be totally tested by experience," and "Powerful ideologies are at least highly plausible in the conditions of the time, and they are genuinely adhered to." (p. 23). Examples of ideologies that can intensify the cohesion of group identity and power are religious beliefs, theories such as Marxism, and national identity. Ideological power tends to be diffuse and may be intensive or extensive depending on its form. Controlling dominant belief systems in society is one major source of ideological power.

Economic power can be seen in groups of people or organizations that control the processing and transport of raw materials into consumable goods that meet basic needs. "Those able to monopolize control over production, distribution, exchange, and consumption" (Mann 1986, p. 24) become a dominant class in society. Economic power tends to be diffuse. It may be intensive in terms of control over local production or extensive in terms of networks of exchange.

Military power organizes around the need for physical defense and for possible aggression. It can be both intensive in terms of its impacts on individual lives and extensive in terms of territories controlled. Military power is usually centrally controlled, but "militaristic forms of social control" (p. 26) may be employed in peacetime to establish behavioral norms with which populations are likely to comply.

Political power is exercised by the "central polity, including the state apparatus and (where they exist) political parties" (p. 11). Political power is defined by Mann as coinciding with state power because this form of power reflects territorially bounded regulation and control. Mann makes the important observation that "political power heightens boundaries, whereas the other power sources may transcend them" (p. 27). As with other work on the notion of state sovereignty (e.g., Litfin 1997a), Mann recognizes that state power must be exercised both internally in domestic affairs and externally in the arena of international geopolitics and diplomacy. He also notes that there is no technique of power unique to the state that has not also been employed by civil society for developing infrastructures of power (Mann 2003, p. 57).

To illustrate how these sources of power interact in a particular instance, we can look at the story of Greenfreeze and hydrocarbon-based refrigeration technology (Ayers and French 1996). The story begins with The Montreal Protocol on Substances That Deplete the Ozone Layer, known colloquially as simply the Montreal Protocol, which aimed to ban ozone-depleting chloro-fluorocarbons (CFCs). This agreement was opened for signature in 1987, originally signed by 26 countries, and was eventually ratified by 150 countries due in part to the support of major chemical manufacturing companies that anticipated making significant profits from developing and patenting substi-tutes for CFCs. CFCs were widely used as coolants and in aerosols and were favored due to their low toxicity. The chemical industry supported the development of hydrofluorocarbons (HFCs) to be used as coolants and hydrochlorofluorocarbons (HCFCs) for insulating foam. HCFCs are also ozone-depleting, but less so than CFCs, and both HCFCs and HFCs are extremely potent greenhouse gases thought to contribute to climate change: "Over a 20-year span, for example, a molecule of HFC-134a, a substitute coolant now being produced for refrigerator compressors, will produce 3,400 times as much global warming effect as a molecule of carbon dioxide; over 100 years, it will have 1,300 times the effect" (Ayers and French 1996, p. 17). The HCFCs in particular, because they are ozone-depleting chemicals, were viewed as a transitional substitute and were planned to be phased out of usage. HFCs, however, being ozone-benign, were not regarded as transitional and were not viewed as temporary. There is no planned, legal phase-out of HFCs. The chemical industry is not only concerned about impacts of refrigeration technology on its productivity and profits, but it is also concerned about the possibility of converting air conditioning to new tech-nologies. Air conditioning requires greater amounts of energy than does refrigeration and therefore holds significant potential for future business.

Here we see dimensions of economic power in action. The chemical indus-try, wielding its far-reaching economic power to influence research and development, to shape markets by promoting certain chemical technologies over others, and to advance certain international policies that will, in turn, boost the industry's strength by favoring patentable technologies, demon-strates a form of economic power. On the one hand, this form of power is placeless because the chemical industry includes many corporations with headquarters and operations around the world, yet in a very real sense this industry has specific impacts in particular places which supply its raw materials, house its operations, transport its products, store its waste, where people consume its products, and which succeed or struggle economically or environmentally depending on individual siting, conservation, waste disposal, transport, and other decisions. By favoring and promoting one technology over others, the chemical industry is able to influence economic conditions in a variety of places not just at the scale of international policy but also in many locations where the demands and requirements of international policy have tangible effects.

Meanwhile, the story of Greenfreeze continues. Two medical doctors in Germany developed a refrigerant that used a combination of propane and butane – rather than chlorine gas like most refrigerants – in quantities small enough not to be a fire hazard. This new technology was a form of hydrocarbon-based refrigerant. This refrigerant posed no ozone depletion problem and was only a minor greenhouse gas. Since it was a mixture of two common gases, it could not be patented. That meant that this refrigerant could be made available cheaply without large, corporate profit. The propane and butane technology caught the attention of a Greenpeace activist, Wolfgang Lohbeck, who persuaded a nearly defunct, small refrigerator manufacturer to design and develop refrigerators that used the propane and butane refrigerant technology. This effort was aptly labeled "Greenfreeze" since it promoted a technology thought to be healthier for the environment. Despite the efforts of the German government to shut down the factory and stifle a press conference about the new technology, news of the new refrigerant got out to the press. Greenpeace, as an established environmental group well-skilled in activist strategies, was key in keeping the small factory open and in getting the news of the propane/butane refrigerant out to the public.

Here we see a form of ideological power playing into the story. Greenpeace, as an environmental activist organization, was operating on its view of the world that promoting environmental well-being is not only important, but it requires activism beyond the established political channels. Greenpeace has a reputation of challenging powerful entities through thoughtful, risk-taking, citizen activism. In the past, Greenpeace has challenged commercial whaling, nuclear testing, and the destruction of ancient forest ecosystems, to name a few of its projects. In this case, Greenpeace challenged the chemical industry as well as public thinking about refrigerators. Using a range of strategies that are flexible and adaptable and that adhere to Greenpeace principles centered on saving the environmental health of the planet, Greenpeace demonstrates a form of ideological power. Similar to the chemical industry's spatial influence that has had far-reaching effects, Greenpeace has global reach in its international campaigns, but it also has place-specific impacts that have emerged from careful strategizing and activism.

Major refrigerator manufacturers, with the support of the chemical industry, responded to the unforeseen emergence of hydrocarbon refrigeration technology as a threat to the dominance of HCFCs and HFCs and the patents and profits associated with those chemicals. These actors launched a campaign claiming that the propane and butane refrigerators were likely to burn or explode and were a risk to consumer safety. Orders for the new refrigerators, however, multiplied. New manufacturers incorporated the propane and butane technology, and within a few years 90% of the refrigerators in Germany were hydrocarbon-based. The technology was also diffusing to other parts of the world. In economically developing countries, old, CFC-based refrigerators are still in use. There is the possibility that given appropriate policies and incentives, people in places such as China and India could "leapfrog" to hydrocarbon-based refrigerators and skip HFC and HCFC technologies altogether. Whether or not international aid agencies support hydrocarbon-based technologies will greatly influence the extent and speed of adaptation of these new technologies. In the US, however, the propane/butane refrigeration technology did not catch on initially. Despite the fact that a hydrocarbon refrigerator has an amount of fuel equivalent to two and a half cigarette lighters, and despite the fact that there was no record of one of these refrigerators catching fire or exploding, US manufacturers claim to be concerned about the safety and liability risk of these appliances. The litigiousness of US society, in comparison to the relatively low level of lawsuits filed by consumers in Europe, motivates extra precaution on the part of manufacturers of products for use in the US.

The role of aid agencies, state-level policies, and the legal system of the USA all reflect aspects of political power. As noted above, political power is associated with states that have control over regulations within sovereign territories. Most aid agencies rely on state contributions to make their work possible, but they are also subject to donor state preferences. States that make significant donations to international aid agencies can often shape the kinds of projects and values that aid agencies promote. As states make decisions about what kinds of technologies or activities are permitted in their territory, they are demonstrating political power. Similarly, established legal systems dictate the rules for interactions among actors within a state or between a state and its population. Each of these examples – international aid, state policy, and state legal systems – are elements of political power that have effects at different spatial scales but that are tied to state-level priorities.

As HFCs become more widely recognized as a hazard for global warming, major corporations such as McDonald's and Coca-Cola are trying to phase out these chemical refrigerants as quickly as they brought them into use

(Ball 2005). The refrigerant that many of them favor is carbon dioxide, but now these companies face a significant perception problem since carbon dioxide is known to be a greenhouse gas, too (Deutsch 2007). Unilever PLC, on the other hand, is promoting propane refrigeration technology and has been the first major company to do so in the USA (Environment News Service 2008). Ben & Jerry's ice cream, a Unilever brand, is rolling out the new freezers in stores in Boston and DC area stores as Unilever seeks approval from the Environmental Protection Agency for widespread use of this technology. DuPont, one of the major players in supporting the Montreal Protocol, supports the phase-out of HCFCs since it claims to have developed safer alternatives (Sissell 2007). Once again, it seems that corporate interests are driving refrigeration technology and shaping the direction of environmental policy – another demonstration of economic power.

A military power dimension is not directly evident in the story of Greenfreeze. However, if decisions about HCFC, HFC, or hydrocarbon technologies had implications for military interests, we could see how these interests could become interwoven with other forms of power. It could also happen that a technology that is either banned or promoted by international policy would be of great interest to military initiatives. Disrupted supplies of particular commodities could also pose a threat to the maintenance of military strength. For example, the US military is dependent on other countries to supply key strategic minerals such as cobalt, platinum, manganese, and chromium metal groups (Butts 1993). These minerals are critical for the development of high-tech weapons systems, and the US must purchase the bulk of its supplies of these metals from various states in Africa. Economic and political instability in the countries where these minerals are concentrated could threaten US military preparedness, and there are no substitutes for these metals. The availability of these minerals, then, has implications not only for military power and a state's ability to execute organized aggression or defense, but it also shows how economic and state dimensions of power may be tightly integrated with military power. The Greenfreeze story about international policy and refrigeration technology and the example of strategic minerals illustrate economic, ideological, political, and military sources of power. These sources of power are not neatly distinct from one another. In fact, they overlap. Understanding these sources of power allows us to examine events and discussions around particular environmental issues so that we may more clearly understand how these environmental situations are rooted in particular places, how they transcend, are limited by, or redefine borders, how they diffuse across space or otherwise generate unique spatial scales.

Another important element to consider when looking at sources of power is the issue of information. How decisions are made and by whom, in response to what kinds of public sentiment, and with what kinds of spatial implications are all issues pertaining to the flow of information. Where do we get our information about environmental issues? It is a critical question, because where we get our information and the quality of that information can influence how we vote, how we consume, what we talk about, what we teach, and what we believe to be worthy of research. It is worth noting that in this era, at least in some sectors of Western society, of rapid access to a wealth of information beyond our capacity to absorb it, the mass media are actually controlled by a handful of companies. Television, magazines, mainstream books, films, billboards, and much of the advertising to which we are exposed is engineered and controlled by a small number of interests that can shape the images and ideas that fill much of our time and thoughts. Just as those corporations have economic and political priorities, we can expect that those priorities will be evident in the media issued by those organizations. A clear political or economic agenda amidst the flow of information might not be obvious, however, since the best public relations is the kind that goes unnoticed but that still gets its message across.

Outline of the book

Following this introductory chapter, each chapter of the book considers spatial and power dimensions of a selection of topics. We begin with climate change. How is climate change usually discussed and presented? Chapter 2 begins by considering Mark Hulme's (2008a, 2008b) recent work on climate change in which he argues that the dominant discourse about climate change, exemplified by the Intergovernmental Panel on Climate Change (IPCC) report, is limited in its globe-encompassing, quantitative model approach to understanding and addressing changing climate patterns. He discusses how this widely accepted approach to climate change overlooks cultural meanings of climate change and does little to mobilize societies to generate local responses and adaptations. Chapter 2 looks at ways in which states tend to be prioritized as actors in climate change discussions and how focusing on the state scale can limit our understanding of climate change. The chapter also looks at the "scaling down" of climate change to discuss how substate actors, groups and individuals have initiated adaptive responses to "global" climate change.

Chapter 3 considers oil and energy. Are we really running out of oil? This chapter begins by providing a summary of what is currently known or estimated about remaining reserves and the rate at which the world is consuming oil. The chapter then looks at the phenomenon of "extreme oil." That is, much of the remaining oil (and gas) reserves are in places or forms that are technologically challenging or politically tedious to access. Oil now has, more than ever, the potential to be used for geopolitical leverage. Witness Russia's display of clout in the winter of 2006 as it cut gas supplies to Ukraine and Georgia and increased fuel costs to other states on its periphery. US involvement in Iraq and the US projection of power into Central Asia are often discussed as strategies in the interest of stabilizing global oil flows. In response to what appears to be a growing challenge to meet the world's oil demand, the "solution" of promoting ethanol and other alternative energies has become increasingly popular. This chapter will consider ethanol in particular, the power dynamics underlying its promotion especially in agriculturally productive areas, and ways in which ethanol is not a feasible solution, for example, due to the huge water inputs required for its production and the impacts that its production is having on food supplies in many places. This chapter considers ways in which the dominant conversation about oil and fuel substitutes favors certain power arrangements and avoids particular scales of action and types of power such as individual and commercial conservation efforts.

Linked to the issue of alternative energy sources is the topic of food security, the subject of Chapter 4. Food prices are increasing. Should we be concerned? Food tends to be overlooked as an environmental issue for people who do not grow their own food and have become distanced from their food supplies. In many countries, governments are issuing fixed prices for food – a fact that provides an interesting window to the power dynamics behind ensuring a stable food supply. This chapter examines the evolving notion of food security. Food security has, it turns out, much to do with other forms of human security. Although it is does not have the cachet in the donor world that HIV/AIDS has, malnutrition is a more significant threat to more people in more places. The US Farm Bill is examined in this chapter. Not only does the Farm Bill do much to dictate what kinds of crops are grown and how (with implications, therefore, for other environmental issues such as the use of pesticides, herbicides, and water), but we can also see that the scale of the US Farm Bill reaches to other countries where relatively poor farmers cannot compete with subsidized crops from the US. Patterns and processes underlying food security – and insecurity – are shown to reflect spatial dimensions of power arrangements.

Chapter 5 considers garbage and waste. When we throw something away, where is "away"? The fact that the Fresh Kills garbage landfill in New York is larger than either the Great Wall of China or the Great Pyramids as far as human-made structures go should give us pause for thought. Additionally, when people in Western societies "donate" used computer hardware to less privileged people in, say, Africa, are they aware that much of this unusable hardware is burned in the open releasing toxic fumes in the proximity of people going about their daily lives? What are some of the underlying factors of the geography of garbage? What kinds of waste products are generated where, and what contributes to uneven and unjust practices of waste disposal? The very phenomenon of trash pickers in less economically developed places suggests a valuation of garbage that devalues the health and education of certain groups of citizens. The theme of garbage is interwoven in the story of human history, but how can we understand the implications of our waste in this era of the Anthropocene? An examination of garbage and waste contributes to our understanding of power dynamics at play in how societies value and consume resources and how garbage is dealt with – or not – and where.

A fact of daily life is the exposure to chemical toxins, the topic of Chapter 6. For example, DDT, produced in the US but banned for use there, is used in tropical areas for mosquito and malaria control as well as to enhance the production of bananas for export to richer countries. More recently, the dangers of Bisphenol-A in plastic #7 have been widely publicized. Although they may be regulated by particular states, chemical toxins are an environmental issue at the scale of the body. In richer parts of the world, the public may trust that government policies keep them safe from harmful chemical toxins. Indeed, the US Toxic Substances Control Act restricts the domestic use of many harmful toxins, but it also grandfathers in many chemical toxins that were in use prior to 1972. The Environmental Protection Agency is overwhelmed, understaffed, and underfunded when it comes to chemical substances that have yet to be thoroughly tested for their safety level. People are often left on their own to research and control their exposure to chemical toxins such as parabens – a staple ingredient of the cosmetics industry and which are thought to be endocrine disruptors that wreak havoc with hormonal functions. Chemical toxins focus our attention on risk assessment as we consider how safety is determined, by whom, for whom, and where. These are questions pertaining both to the spatial scale and politics underlying the production and management of chemical toxins. This chapter expands consideration of the spatial scale of chemical toxins beyond state level regulation to look at health implications of toxins.

Finally, Chapter 7 aims to complicate an oversimplified discourse that tends to correlate the location of a resource with the location of armed conflict. Here, the concepts of spatial scale and power are applied to contribute to a more nuanced understanding of power dimensions of natural resource use. From diamonds to oil, the topic of resource conflicts has captured considerable public attention. The vast scholarly literature on resource conflicts tends to make one of two main arguments about how natural resources are linked to conflict. The first, neo-Malthusian argument argues that resource scarcity drives conflict. Michael Klare's popular books, such as *Blood and Oil* (Klare 2004), embrace this perspective. The second type of argument often found in the literature is that resource abundance drives conflict. In this view, economically developing countries that rely heavily on natural resource exports have a tendency to substitute resource rents for statecraft (Karl 1997). That is, rather than take the necessary and possibly painful steps to build democratic institutions that would grant the government legitimacy, it has been observed that leadership in resource-dependent states may instead opt to buy public approval (or silence dissent).

This chapter, however, considers geographic dimensions of not only natural resources, but also the scale of their control and use. Scholars such as Philippe LeBillon (2001, 2008) and Richard Auty (Auty 2001a; Auty and De Soysa 2006) have examined why the type of resource – diamonds, oil, timber, water, drugs, etc. – is critical for understanding how the resource is controlled and at what scale conflict involving that resource might emerge. Additionally, it is also important to understand the "scale" of the resource itself (O'Lear and Diehl 2007): What is its value and to whom? Where is it located? Where is it consumed? What kind of transportation or processing does it require? What kind of power struggle or conflict might it involve? What is more, it has also been argued (Barnett 2000; Dalby 2007b) that the entire focus on resource conflict is little more than an attempt by powers in the global North to set (or continue) an agenda that justifies militarization of relationships with countries in the global South which again returns our attention to scale – how the spatial parameters of resource conflicts are understood – and power in terms of how and why resource conflict, and discourses about resource conflict, persist.

In actuality, all of the topics addressed in this book are intertwined. Dividing the book into chapters helps us to focus on individual topics, but in reality it is difficult to isolate discrete environmental issues from a broad spectrum of human–environmental relationships and overlapping political, social, economic, and physical dynamics.

2

Climate change

Number of saplings that [Brad] Pitt paid to have planted in Bhutan last year to counteract his personal CO_2 production: 1,700
— Harper's *Index, January 2005*

Estimated number of cars that it takes to produce as much CO_2 as a single large cargo ship: 10,000
— Harper's *Index, August 2009*

Introduction

We often hear of "global" climate change, and we also hear about local impacts. A perusal through *The Atlas of Climate Change: Mapping the World's Greatest Challenge* (Dow and Downing 2007) provides an illustration of current understanding of causes and anticipated impacts of climate change. Causes include the link between fossil fuels and greenhouse gases that blanket the earth, the role of other gases such as methane and hydrofluorocarbons in warming the atmosphere, and the impact that changing land use patterns have on the carbon cycle and, consequently, on climate change. This atlas also considers consequences that we can expect from climate change including the disruption (and possibly degradation) of ecosystems, heightened water scarcity, food security concerns resulting from changing temperature patterns and crop yields, threats to human health, rising sea levels and risks posed to coastal cities and cultural, historical, and archaelogical sites. Tim Flannery's book, *The Weather Makers: How Man Is Changing the Climate and What It Means for Life on Earth* (Flannery 2005) provides a more conversational survey of the history of humans' understanding of the atmosphere, how we study climate change, and signals of climate change held in ice sheets, coral reefs, and amphibian populations. Many of the actual and anticipated impacts of climate change described in these two books are familiar and relatively undisputed. It is also generally accepted, at least by most scientists, that climate change is occurring due to human activity rather than natural oscillations in the earth's climate. So which is the appropriate spatial scale for understanding climate change? As Wilbanks and Kates (1999) have noted:

Where global change is concerned, it can be argued that a focus on a single geographic scale tends to emphasize processes operating at that scale, information collected at that scale, and parties influential at that scale – raising the possibility of misunderstanding cause and effect by missing the relevance of processes that operate at a different scale. Focusing exclusively at a local scale can lead to explanations in terms of local causes when some important determinants lie in processes at larger regional and global scales. Focusing exclusively on a larger scale can lead to ready generalizations that are just that – much too general.

(p. 608)

Although climate change discussions were framed early on by quantitative, global scale measures, social sciences and humanities insights can help us to identify other variables and spatial scales that are important and worth understanding (Hulme 2007). It is useful to consider how power and knowledge interact in current discussions and debates about climate change and to ask "Who has power and for what purposes?" and "What is knowledge, how is it defined and created?" (Pettenger 2007).

The public may still not be convinced about climate change – either as a reality on the horizon or as the effect of human actions. Who can blame them? Despite the fact that media coverage of climate change has been increasing and despite the fact it recognizes the potential harm of global climate change, much of that coverage imparts messages that are either mixed, unclear, or that suggest the global climate change is not necessarily harmful (Liu *et al.* 2008). Media coverage of climate change tends to focus on the uncertainty of the science behind climate change research without pointing out that uncertainty is precisely what drives scientific endeavors – a nuance that might not be too surprising considering that few journalists have substantial training in the sciences (Boykoff 2007, 2008). However, it was big news in 2007 when former US Presidential candidate Al Gore was awarded a Nobel Prize jointly with the Intergovernmental Panel on Climate Change (IPCC). This recognition of the IPCC brought into public awareness this organization that is widely recognized as the voice of climate change science. What exactly is the IPCC?

Established in 1988 by the World Meteorological Organization (WMO) and by the United Nations Environment Programme (UNEP), the Intergovernmental Panel on Climate Change:

... was established to provide the decision-makers and others interested in climate change with an objective source of information about climate change. The IPCC does not conduct any research nor does it monitor climate related data or parameters. Its role is to assess on a comprehensive, objective, open and transparent basis the latest scientific, technical and socio-economic literature produced worldwide relevant to the understanding of the risk of human-induced climate change, its observed and projected impacts and options for adaptation and mitigation. IPCC reports should be neutral with respect to policy, although they need to deal objectively with policy relevant scientific, technical and socio-economic factors. They should be of high scientific and technical standards, and aim to reflect a range of views, expertise and wide geographical coverage.

(IPCC website, http://www.ipcc.ch/about/ index.htm, accessed 24 November 2008)

The IPCC is widely regarded by most governments as the authoritative source of information and analysis on climate change. Only work that has been published in peer-reviewed, scholarly journals is included in the IPCC reports, and hundreds of scientists have contributed to the reports. Despite, or perhaps because of its dominance in climate change discussions, the IPCC reports and protocols have been critiqued as producing an understanding of climate change at the "global" level as calculated through quantitative data analysis and computer modeling and as described by "Western" scientists in elite institutional settings (see Hulme 2007). These critiques merit further exploration, but it is worth mentioning that the IPCC reports are not limited to physical science alone. The report from Working Group 2 (IPCC 2007), "Impacts, Adaptation and Vulnerability," discusses human vulnerability to climate change not only in terms of changing conditions in the physical environment but also as influenced by stresses caused by "poverty, unequal access to resources, food insecurity, trends in economic globalization, conflict, and incidences of diseases such as HIV/AIDS" (IPCC 2007, p. 19) as well as issues of governance and population distribution. Chapter 7 of this report (Wilbanks *et al.* 2007) focuses on industry, settlement, and society which are very broad themes to consider in terms of how climate change might affect their operation. The authors acknowledge the chapter "emphasizes that climate-change impacts, adaptation potentials, and vulnerabilities are context-specific, related to the characteristics and development pathways of the location or sector involved" (p. 361). They recognize the importance of scale:

Scale matters in at least three ways in assessing the impacts of climate change on industry, settlement and society. First, climate change is one of a set of multiple stresses operating at diverse scales in space and through time. Second, both the exposure to climate change and the distribution of climate-sensitive settlements and industrial sectors vary greatly across geographic scale. The primary social and economic conditions that influence adaptive capacity also differ with scale, such as access to financial resources. One could say, for instance, that at a national scale industrialized countries such as the UK and Norway can cope with most kinds of gradual climate change, but focusing on more localized differences can show considerable variability in stresses and capacities to adapt ... Third, temporal scale is a critical determinant of the capacity of human systems to adapt to climate change; for instance, rapid changes are usually more difficult to absorb without painful costs than gradual change.

(Wilbanks et al. *2007, p. 360)*

These are important dimensions and interactions to consider when projecting the influence of development pathways from this point into the future and for improving strategies to increase adaptive capacity. Despite the value of recognizing that exposure to climate change, sensitivities, and coping capacities differ from place to place thereby diluting the usefulness of broad generalizations in specific places (Wilbanks 2003), a critique of the IPCC approach to climate change is that it generates a particular meaning of climate change. Central to the IPCC conception of climate change are global climate models (GCMs) which allow scientists to experiment, virtually, with different levels of greenhouse gases in the atmosphere and observe cascading effects on heat transferring ocean systems, moisture transferring atmospheric systems, ice sheets, and ecosystems. These global climate models, or GCMs, carry intriguing implications for spatial scale and power.

Global climate models, the state, and "the local"

Global climate models (GCMs) tend to isolate attention to levels of individual greenhouse gases such as CO_2, methane, and hydrofluorocarbons, but they do not address the complex political economy of greenhouse gas production. That is, global scale modeling reduces an assessment of climate change to a partial inquiry that does not question who is benefitting from greenhouse gas production or whether or not or how we should calculate "luxury" emissions such as those from the burning of fossil fuels from "survival" emissions emanating from rice fields and livestock (Agarwal and Narain 1991, 1998). The focus on GCMs shapes scientific findings which are used by policy-makers such as government officials who use the IPCC reports to formulate their responses to climate change. In addition to this downstream flow of information, there is also an upstream political influence on the parameters of science. Global climate models, along with other post-World War II scientific developments in the US, originated from military concerns and expertise. Civilian uses of nuclear power (Farber and Weeks 2001) and the Internet's roots in ARPAnet (see O'Lear 1996) share similar storylines. By the 1970s, public awareness of air pollution and nascent, widespread recognition of atmospheric change further motivated the advancement of climate modeling. At that time, the concern was about global cooling and the possibility of a nuclear winter (see, for example, Ponte 1976). Global climate models are mathematically reductionist to enable a quantified simulation of earth system elements, and this is the dominant method for climate assessment. These models are not the exclusive means of studying climate change. Other approaches to studying climate change such as earth observation satellite analysis and paleoclimatology are also funded by governments in North America and Europe, but they tend to serve the data input and validation needs of global climate models thereby reinforcing this global, quantitative view of climate change. Since these models do not necessarily engage with questions about the uneven economic, political, and social patterns of greenhouse gases, they may be said to "conceal, normalize, and thereby reproduce those unequal social relations" (Demeritt 2001, p. 316). These models also tend to look at changes in levels of atmospheric gases in isolation from possible changes to social and economic processes, again, thereby normalizing existing economic and political relationships and limiting the range of possible solutions to the climate change problem as interpreted by global climate models (Cohen *et al.* 1998). We can take this argument a step further and say that climate models mask social and political dimensions of anthropogenic (human-induced) climate change by operating on the assumption that climate change is both global in scale and purely physical as opposed to emerging from uneven geographies of economic and political imbalances (Demeritt 2001).

The GCM approach relies, out of technical necessity, on the assumption that climate change is appropriately analyzed as having objective properties with universal meanings that may be interpreted and understood by experts. Among practitioners, it is often assumed that more complex models are better for policy applications. Impact assessment scientists use simulations generated by global climate models to construct scenarios of future impacts of climate change for the benefit of policy- and decision-making often at regional scales, but how accurately may global scale models be applied to regional scales? As Demeritt (2001) has phrased it:

Arguably, the application of complex GCMs to the generation of regional climate change scenarios for impact assessment is tantamount to using a laser guided missile to swat a fly: a fly swatter might do just as well without suggesting a degree of precision unwarranted by unknown levels of modeling uncertainty and future indeterminacy.

(pp. 319–320)

In other words, the general acceptance of global climate models as the best way to understand climate change is mismatched to the needs of practitioners at spatial scales smaller than the globe. Whereas the scientists programming the climate models may have uncertainty about the details of their models because they have the expertise to understand inherent complexities of the models, other users of these models may trust these models because they are so widely accepted and, quite simply, because they have no choice but to trust scientific expertise. When they put their faith in the perceived certainty of science, policy-makers reinforce a view of climate change that is limited to the physical parameters of greenhouse gases and thereby do not have to make difficult decisions about inequitable systems generating these gases. Science is important and valuable, but societies might be better served by thinking about effective uses of science with the understanding that it is not absolute and comprehensive but rather that it is "the best that we can do for the moment" (Demeritt 2001, p. 329).

Power dimensions of global climate models are illuminated more clearly when we consider a critique of earth observation satellites. Karen Litfin (1997b) has explored cultural assumptions embedded in how society under-stands the use of "global" technologies. Taking a feminist perspective, she aims to demonstrate how seemingly "neutral" science and technology are not necessarily neutral at all but in fact reinforce certain dynamics of power. She examines the case of earth observation satellites, but her arguments might be applied to GCMs as well. She notes that monitoring the earth from space is conducive to the idea that such a vantage point enhances "global security" since large-scale environmental trends and patterns may be identified and studied. What, though, does "global security" mean in a world where economic disparity has become the norm? Furthermore, the view of earth from space, while useful for observing some phenomena, renders invisible "humans as agents and as victims of environmental destruction" (p. 38). Litfin questions the assumption that science leads to rational action and that the decision-making process is linear (see Chapter 5 and the model for rational decision-making). She points out that such a view ignores the reality that science is often drawn into the policy process selectively or framed within pre-existing understandings or value systems rather than being interpreted as objective information. Science does not necessarily increase our certainty. In order for the scientific process to move forward, science must overlook significant uncertainties which then render these uncertainties invisible. "Para-doxically," Litfin points out "incorporating more detailed information into models of stochastic [random] systems may generate more uncertainties in the conclusions" (p. 36). She notes the irony in looking to science and technology to solve problems that have, in many ways, been exacerbated by science and technology. She encourages us to think critically about assumptions that are implicitly built into our science and technology systems:

The ultimate goal of [earth remote sensing] is to *predict*, which, as Francis Bacon recognized over four hundred years ago, is exactly how knowledge becomes power. Earth system science aims to uncover nature's secrets in order to enable policymakers to 'manage the earth'. The celebratory discourse surrounding the undertaking reflects just such an uncritical acceptance of this ambition.

(p. 37)

A similar critique might be made of GCMs in the sense that they, too, must simplify variables of the earth system in order to generate a global scale, predictive model of specific features of the atmosphere, landmasses, and oceans. The institutional support networks created for and required by both earth observation systems and global climate models have a particular geography defined in large part by education and research facilities in richer, more powerful countries. As Litfin (1997b) notes "Global problems are amenable to large data banks, to Big Science, to grand managerial schemes" (p. 38) which, the more they demonstrate a contribution to society's understanding of environmental problems and the more society is convinced of their value, the more powerful they become. Although, as mentioned above, the global view is indeed valuable in some pursuits, it is not necessarily the best scale for understanding multiple dimensions of climate change.

Although we might look to the "grand science" behind global climate models to reduce our uncertainty about climate change, it is useful to see how science can serve, instead, to complicate our understanding and policy processes around environmental issues (Sarewitz 2004). There is a wide variety of available facts that may be used to construct competing stories of current conditions and future scenarios. Rather than being objective, the starting point for scientific construction, that is, the values or scope defining the problem to begin with, shape the outcome. For example, plant geneticists and molecular biologists working on genetically modified organisms are more likely to pay attention to cause-and-effect relations exhibited during controlled experiments while ecologists are more likely to focus on unintended consequences resulting from widespread use of genetically modified organisms. Each of these groups frames their investigation of genetically modified organisms at a different spatial scale (e.g., the gene or an entire ecosystem) and arrives at different conclusions about advantages and disadvantages of genetically modified organisms. Both views may, in fact, be scientifically legitimate, but their conclusions do not necessarily reduce uncertainty about whether or not genetically modified organisms should be widely used. Both sets of science may help to characterize uncertainty, but that is different from reducing uncertainty. Additional research may reveal previously unknown information about natural systems, and it may also highlight an appreciation of what remains unknown. Daniel Sarewitz has discussed how these features of science rarely have combined to illuminate a path of action defined by scientific certainty. In his words:

... we have few good examples of science providing sufficient clarification to point the way through politically charged, open-ended controversies, yet innumerable examples of decisive political action in all realms of society taken despite controversy and uncertainty, and with science playing little or no formal role in the debate.

(2004, p. 397)

Some political controversies become scientized, or complicated by an abundance of competing scientific information, and others do not. In political arenas such as partisan campaigns or debates, value preferences are explicit. Significant decisions are made under conditions of uncertainty but are supported by commitment to stated values or objectives. In contrast, there persists the idea that scientific facts are supported by objective methods and are devoid of value preferences. Political controversies become scientized as different political actors draw upon scientific research that supports their political agenda and stated value preferences, but the science itself is unlikely to bring different political views into alignment. As Sarewitz has pointed out "Even if science brings such a controversy into focus (for example, by documenting a rise in atmospheric greenhouse gases), the controversy itself exists only because conflict over values and interest also exists" (2004, p. 399). More science does not mean greater certainty despite the suggestion of the cartoon in Figure 2.1. In fact, it may result in just the opposite. What is more, the complexity of science may be used to justify inaction in the face of a politically difficult decision.

   Another view of global climate models has questioned the way these models prioritize state-level data collection and decision-making. Paterson and Stripple (2007) have argued that the spatiality of the dominant discourse of climate change is defined by state-centric territorialization. That is, the way that climate change tends to be discussed and understood is that it is a problem that states must deal with. This view legitimizes current climate politics and limits possible responses to climate change to the level of state governments. Climate change is often discussed as posing both danger and opportunity to states. Danger takes the form of possible threats to the state's ability to secure sufficient resources such as water and food, and there is the

Figure 2.1 Uncertainty. Image courtesy of xkcd.com, used with permission.

risk of sea level rise and a surge of environmental refugees either from national coastlines or from across borders. In this way, climate change is securitized. It is discussed in terms of a concern for state-level security with the assumption that state authorities are the most appropriate and best-suited agencies for assuring the safety and well-being of people living within state borders. Danger also takes the form of economic threats posed to states by proposals to limit greenhouse gas emissions. President George W. Bush pulled the US out of the Kyoto Protocol due in large part to the perceived negative economic impacts that compliance would entail for US companies, workers, and consumers. However, proponents of ecological modernization argue that "environmental regulation can stimulate innovation and improve competitiveness in a global(izing) economy" (Paterson and Stripple 2007, p. 154). Whether climate change regulations and mandates are viewed as a danger or an opportunity, the spatial focus is centered on the state and defines actions and options at the level of the state. Yet states themselves are not permanent. The world political map is in constant flux, and there was a time before territorial states, defined by recognized boundaries, even existed. The present-day, commonly accepted sovereign state is a social construct generated by human societies to control access to physical resources and to define inclusion in particular identities (Sack 1986). By glossing over the fact that states are themselves generated and maintained for political advantage by some groups over others, the discussion of climate change as a state-level concern normalizes this type of power. As Paterson and Stripple (2007) have phrased it "Since the territorial configurations of political space are made to appear as natural, certain political and economic solutions to the climate issue becomes [*sic*] legitimized" (p. 150).

We can see an example of how solutions to climate change tend to be defined at the state level by looking at the way in which greenhouse gas emissions are calculated as discussed by Paterson and Stripple (2007). It is generally accepted that global climate change is caused by increased concentrations of various greenhouse gases, most notably carbon dioxide. The United Nations Framework Convention on Climate Change aims to reduce these emissions. The convention considers that contributions of greenhouse gases are not uniform across the globe. Negotiations have aimed to distribute the limitations of greenhouse gas emissions equitably and fairly, and thus created the idea of Annex 1 and Annex 2 states to recognize that states contribute differently to greenhouse gas emissions and have different capacities for reducing emissions. Agarwal and Narain (1991, 1998) challenge this strictly state-centric approach based on calculations and methods generated from the global "North" or economically developed countries. They propose that greenhouse gas emissions should be calculated by relating a country's percentage of the world's population to the world's total carbon sink capacity. The result, they argue, would be a more equitable distribution of obligation to reductions in greenhouse gas emissions. Either way, state by state obligations or per capita calculations, justice in climate change is defined by one's membership in a territorial, sovereign state hence territorializing rather than individualizing people (Paterson and Stripple 2007).

These critiques challenge the way in which climate change discussions and policies prioritize the state and warn us against what John Agnew has called the "territorial trap" (Agnew 1994). We fall into the territorial trap when we assume that the best spatial scale for understanding problems and solutions is the state level. Agnew demonstrates that state-centered views are limiting because they tend to ignore processes flowing across borders (e.g., migration of people, the transfer of ideas, technologies, financial resources, traded commodities, pollution, etc.). They tend to assume homogeneity within state borders (i.e., a uniform national identity instead of a varied texture of differentiated cultural groups, economic classes, and spatially diverse patterns of access, mobility, and interests). Also, state-centric views tend to disregard the interplay of states and global processes (e.g., what *is* a national economy given that corporations are not necessarily state-owned and may have stockholders, manufacturing activities, suppliers, and investments across the globe?). In short, when we look at the world as a set of state-level containers, we limit the ways in which we might understand complex relationships and spatial flows. Additionally, when we assume that states are equal actors in a world system, we dismiss the importance of imbalances of power and unequal distribution of resources. States certainly play a significant role in decision-making, and the forms of political, ideological, economic, and even military power that they bring to bear should not be dismissed. However, if we assume that states are the only source of meaningful action, then our understanding of how things might change (or why they persist) can only be partial at best.

Other critiques of mainstream understanding of climate change highlight contrasts between the "global" view and "local" views. Heather Smith (2007) has pointed out several ways in which the emphasis on "global" dimensions of climate change blurs or discourages an understanding of "local" aspects of climate change and carries implications for power, too. "Global" implies a recognition of shared problems and vulnerabilities, but in reality the issue of global climate change is promoted by a certain set of actors, it is not necessarily a global idea, and it does not reflect homogeneous insecurities. These arguments echo those made by Karen Litfin, discussed above. The idea of global climate change has a tendency to adopt an "eye in the sky" perspective that externalizes and subordinates nature to human security concerns. It reinforces a divide between humans and nature rather than recognizing our dependent relationship on the "natural" physical environment. This view discourages a consideration of place-specific contributions to environmental change and enables unchanged consumption patterns. The global view also shifts attention away from historic trends in the sources of emissions. The focus on global emissions or concentrations of greenhouse gases enables the avoidance of reductions "here" in favor of promoting offsets somewhere else. The global view blurs and distances the local from the center of our focus. Smith considers eight declarations that groups of indigenous people in Russia, Mexico, Kenya, New Zealand, the USA, Canada, Guatemala, Colombia, Nepal, Thailand, and Panama have made regarding climate change. These declarations challenge the "global" view of climate change. First, most every declaration recognizes that the planet is in crisis, but the crisis is the result of an economic order that commodifies nature and is driven by unsustainable industrial production and consumption practices. She also points to concerns about racism embedded in the historical roots and destructiveness of colonialism that has contributed to current patterns of inequality. From the indigenous perspective, "inequality is masked by arguing that climate change is global. There is no 'common future'" (p. 208). Second, the declarations made by indigenous groups focus on local attachment rather than detached disregard for local activities and decisions. "The global gaze is flipped as the indigenous vision is not one of dominance *over* nature, but rather a spiritual and cultural connection *to* nature. It positions Mother Earth to be respected and revered, not dominated and controlled" (p. 208).

Figure 2.2 Protesting carbon offset forests. During the United Nations Framework Convention on Climate Change Negotiation held in Nusa Dua Bali, Indonesia in 2007, the World Bank was met by outrage when it announced the Bank's Forest Carbon Partnership Facility. Photo: Anne Petermann, Global Justice Ecology Project – Global Forest Coalition.

Another clash of global and local scales may be seen in the Clean Development Mechanism of the 1997 Kyoto Protocol which aimed to fund tree-planting projects predominantly in economically developing areas of the world. Newly planted trees would serve as carbon sinks to offset carbon emissions in other parts of the world (more on offsets later in this chapter). From the perspective of economists, scientists, and policy makers in economically developed parts of the world, the equation of carbon sinks and carbon emissions calculated at the global scale made sense, but from the view of indigenous communities in areas targeted for tree-planting projects, these projects were seen to undermine the rights and interests of local communities (Fogel 2004). The dominant framework through which tree-planting schemes were promoted viewed carbon trading as a technical matter relevant at a global scale. Local perspectives, however, saw this agenda as excluding and marginalizing their interests as depicted in Figure 2.2. By this view, not only did the tree-planting schemes erase local spaces of traditional knowledge and interaction with the environment, but it also constructed empty spaces available for the "global good." Indigenous communities that resisted these schemes argued that they had played minimal if any role in the production of carbon emissions. They saw these schemes as yet one more way economically developed elites were colonizing their resources and constructing the idea and identity of the "noble ecological savage" (Fogel 2004, p. 117).

Social scales of climate change

So far, we have considered aspects of climate change at global, state, and local scales, but this approach might suggest that spatial scales are like distinct, nested containers that fit nicely inside one another. Administrative scales (e.g., city, county, state) might fit that description, but as outlined in the introduction, this book takes the view that human activity produces spatial scale. In a similar vein, Rachel Slocum (2004) has considered ways in which different campaigns localize climate change and bring the scientific models and measurements of global climate change home to citizens and policy makers. In choosing how to focus public attention and encourage people to care about and act on climate change, such campaigns highlight certain relationships or linkages but conceal others. Identifying an issue as active at one scale may obscure important linkages to other scales, and it can also serve to over-generalize an issue and thereby blur an understanding of place-specific charac-teristics. Slocum examines how the fate of polar bears serves to focus attention on climate change in a particular way. The polar bear is an example of charis-matic megafauna that conjures up public concern in the same way that other appealing, at-risk animals do (e.g., we care about dolphins and look for dolphin-free tuna, but we are not too concerned about the tuna!). Through various advertising and informational campaigns, the North American public has become well aware of the perilous fate of this unique animal as we view footage of polar bears adrift on small bits of ice. As global temperatures increase, the Arctic ice is melting. The snowy white ice has a high albedo which means it reflects much of the incoming solar radiation. As the ice melts, more dark sea surface is exposed which absorbs solar radiation and leads to more ice melting. Polar bears are struggling to survive in this rapidly changing environment.

We have seen polar bears in zoos, and we care about them in the face of realities of global climate change. Polar bears are also a national icon for Inuit, Cree, and other indigenous communities of North America. Realizing that our grandchildren may never see a live polar bear, the wonders of captive breeding programs notwithstanding, motivates us to do something (Avoid extra trips in the car! Turn off the lights when we leave a room! Donate money!). Slocum observes that polar bears, in this scenario, become the victims of climate change that we, most likely, have caused. This perspective draws a clear line between polar bears who are suffering from global climate change and us. An identity of humans as separate from nature is reinforced. Our fate and that of the polar bear, a wild animal, are not intimately intertwined. They live in such an extreme climate, but we are still safe for some time. The scale of global climate change, in this instance, is bordered by an invisible line that distinguishes human society from the wild environment including polar bears. Yet polar bears are easier to comprehend than invisible greenhouse gases, so we might become intrigued, concerned, or motivated by scientific claims of global climate change. As Slocum notes "Localizing climate change means to transform it into problems that are materially and culturally relevant to citizens and also *to change what is relevant*" (p. 433, emphasis in original).

The question of what is relevant about climate change depends greatly on who is setting the parameters of discussion and what climate means for different people. An anthropological study of people's experience of weather might consider how individuals and groups talk and feel about weather and climate, what they describe, and how they respond to weather and climate on various time-frames. There are different ways of communicating about weather, climate, seasons, and significant weather events that might be captured in myths, rituals, and practices (Strauss and Orlove 2003). If you ask a waterman on Maryland's Chesapeake Bay, he might tell you how daily weather observations are critical to each day's work fishing for crabs, but no one really knows – or can regulate – what the weather patterns will be from year to year. In fact, this element of unpredictability, or call it God's plan, is key to the crabs' survival and the continuation of the crab fishing industry (Paolisso 2003). Farmers in Burkina Faso observe the landscape and draw upon the spiritual world to formulate predictions about precipitation and adjust their planting accordingly (Roncoli *et al.* 2003). Their interpretation and use of external scientific forecasts is determined by how farmers think about rainfall and what they are interested in knowing, suggesting that "scientific and technical knowledge is not a 'product' that can be prepackaged and delivered to 'users'" (p. 197) without first being filtered through particular cultural meanings and values. Research in the Pio-Tura region of Papua New Guinea demonstrates multiple ways of understanding changes in weather and climate patterns over time (Ellis 2003). During a dry season associated with an El Niño event in 1997, the relatively small number of people living in this forested region implemented social and subsistence practices and drew upon historical myths and religious beliefs to survive the unusual conditions. That self-reliance turns out to have been a good thing since it was only after the rains returned that aircraft delivering food aid appeared. A greater sensitivity to realities of social life might have aligned humanitarian efforts more efficiently with actual need.

Clearly, climate change is relevant at several scales simultaneously. Global climate models capture and quantify current understandings of global scale and process-specific dimensions of the earth's physical systems allowing a view of trends and possible future scenarios aggregated at global and regional scales. States are important actors in funding research and formulating and implementing policies to vulnerability- reducing and capacity-building efforts. Local interpretations of climate change are also critical for understanding cultural meanings of climate. Indeed:

As a social construction, climate change is no one thing. Instead it is an ensemble of constitutive processes, yielding an ever changing panoply of agents and institutions, fixed in place and meaning only for the moment.

(Onuf 2007, p. xv)

Climate change is constructed, or conceived and understood, in different ways by various actors at multiple scales. How climate change is defined shapes the way in which actors (e.g., international organizations, corporations, research institutions, states, policy makers, city governments, farmers, individual consumers, etc.) proceed with plans for adaptation, mitigation, or business as usual. There is no one scale at which we can have a comprehensive appreciation of climate change. A better question to ask is what can we learn about climate change at different scales? We can, and should, also ask what kinds of power are evident in the ways that climate is interpreted at different scales, and what kinds of knowledge or values move between scales and what kinds of knowledge or values are limited to certain scales. Recall from the introduction that scale is understood here not as a pre-existing, spatial container but as the spatial extent and pattern of a particular process or phenomenon. Global climate models, utilizing particular types of data and generating projections for different regions of the globe, demonstrate a very different scale of climate change than do daily crab fishing practices in the Chesapeake Bay area. These multiple interpretations of climate are useful for different purposes, and neither one can replace the other. How, though, do interpretations of and responses to climate change align scale and power? In what ways do human responses to climate change exhibit power at the same spatial extent as an understanding of climate change? Below are two examples. In the first example of city responses to climate change, we can see that the application of power may be said to be in line with the spatial scale of how effects of climate change are interpreted. In the second example, a close examination of the strategy of carbon offsets illustrates how power dynamics may promote the notion that the climate change "problem" is being addressed while not necessarily doing much to reduce greenhouse gas emissions.

That is, power is being used to define a scale of climate change, but there is debate about whether or not the strategy being pursued can actually address the problem as defined.

Cities responding to climate change

In an article titled "Zen and the art of climate maintenance," Steve Rayner and Elizabeth Malone (1997) note that "sustainability is about being nimble, not being right" (p. 334). Rather than rely on rigid targets and timetables, they suggest different strategies for coping with the unpredictability of climate change. Local-level activities, for example, can have significant effects on energy use and pollution generation while at the same time being sensitive to local values, economy, and geographic situation. They point to the International Council for Local Environmental Initiatives and its campaign, the Cities for Climate Protection program, as a means to such local action. The International Council for Local Environmental Initiatives was established in 1990 and is now known as "ICLEI-Local Governments for Sustainability." It was originally established at a meeting, the World Congress of Local Governments for a Sustainable Future, which included 200 local governments from 43 countries. ICLEI is an international network of local, national, and regional government organizations committed to sustainable development. Membership now includes over one thousand local governments and their associations across 68 countries. According to the organization's website:

Through its international campaigns and programs, ICLEI works with local governments to generate political awareness of key issues; establish plans of action towards defined, concrete, measurable targets; work towards meeting these targets through the implementation of projects; and evaluate local and cumulative progress towards sustainable development.

   Our campaigns, programs, and projects promote Local Agenda 21 as a participatory, long-term, strategic planning process that addresses local sustainability while protecting global common goods. Linking local action to internationally agreed upon goals and targets such as Agenda 21, the Rio Conventions, the Habitat Agenda, the Millennium Development Goals and the Johannesburg Plan of Implementation is an essential component.

                   (*"Our Campaigns and Programs," http://www.iclei.org/ index.php?id=640,*
                                          accessed 5 January 2009)

The Cities for Climate Protection campaign that the ICLEI supports comprises five milestones that may be achieved by local governments committed to reducing greenhouse gas emissions generated by local government operations and by their communities. These milestones include:

Milestone 1. Conduct a baseline emissions inventory and forecast. Based on energy consumption and waste generation, the city calculates greenhouse gas emissions for a base year (e.g. 2000) and for a forecast year (e.g. 2015). The inventory and forecast provide a benchmark against which the city can measure progress.

Milestone 2. Adopt an emissions reduction target for the forecast year. The city establishes an emission reduction target for the city. The target both fosters political will and creates a framework to guide the planning and implementation of measures.

Milestone 3. Develop a Local Action Plan. Through a multi-stakeholder process, the city develops a Local Action Plan that describes the policies and measures that the local government will take to reduce greenhouse gas emissions and achieve its emissions reduction target. Most plans include a timeline, a description of financing mechanisms, and an assignment of responsibility to departments and staff. In addition to direct greenhouse gas reduction measures, most plans also incorporate public awareness and education efforts.

Milestone 4. Implement policies and measures. The city implements the policies and measures contained in their Local Action Plan. Typical policies and measures implemented by CCP participants include energy efficiency improvements to municipal buildings and water treatment facilities, streetlight retrofits, public transit improvements, installation of renewable power applications, and methane recovery from waste management.

Milestone 5. Monitor and verify results. Monitoring and verifying progress on the implementation of measures to reduce or avoid greenhouse gas emissions is an ongoing process. Monitoring begins once measures are implemented and continues for the life of the measures, providing important feedback that can be used to improve the measures over time.

(From "How CCP Works," http://www.iclei.org/index.php?id=810,
accessed 5 January 2009)

How these milestones are achieved in any given locality will depend on several factors including funding, availability of data, political motivation, and public support, but the framework is intentionally flexible and applicable in urban and suburban settings throughout the world.

Why is it important that cities, as opposed to national governments or even individual consumers, get involved in efforts to reduce greenhouse gas emissions and promote sustainability? As Simon Dalby (2007a) has argued, current global migration patterns tend to center on metropoles of economic activity, not rural spaces. He offers the term "glurbanization" to capture the growing economic and environmental roles, demands, and impacts of cities on a global scale. In their book, *Cities and Climate Change*, Harriet Bulkeley and Michele Betsill (2003) summarize several factors that make cities an ideal venue for addressing greenhouse gas emissions. First, cities tend to be places where consumption levels and waste generation levels are high. City governments can exert considerable influence over both energy and resource consumption and various forms of waste generation through energy and transportation supply, land use planning and architectural requirements, waste management, and by supporting local efforts in, for example, composting, recycling and rain garden construction. Local authorities are in a unique position to encourage action at the national scale (through lobbying appropriate representatives for funding or other forms of support), the local scale (through various economic incentive plans and political or social campaigns), and at international scales through their involvement in global networks of activism such as the Cities for Climate Protection program and ICLEI. Bulkeley and Betsill challenge the notion that environmental policies are either "top-down," dictated by higher levels of government towards local administrations or "bottom-up," initiated by grass-roots, local action, and pushed up the administrative ladder. Instead, they suggest that networks such as the Cities for Climate Protection program exemplify a different form of governance that works across several administrative scales and involves multiple levels and forms of authority simultaneously. That is, local governance of climate change in the Cities for Climate Protection program is not restricted to local values, knowledge, and politics. Rather, it integrates the power and influence of transnational, state, subnational, local, and non-governmental actors to build communities of interest around certain issues and to promote policy learning as local authorities integrate climate change mitigation into their decision-making processes.

In this example, we see that power is aligned with spatial scale towards a specific objective. The spatial scale of interest is the city. Returning to Mann's (1986) conception of power as the ability to organize and coordinate, we see that power, in this instance, is the influence that local authorities and elected officials have to adjust various city-level services and resource use patterns in the interest of reducing greenhouse gas emissions to meet city-scale milestones. However, this power and locally implemented strategies are informed by the city government's involvement in a broader network of knowledge and experience. Participation in a larger network of governance, which includes many different kinds of actors, encourages a sense of being part of something bigger than "just" one city. Members in the Cities for Climate Protection program are not making isolated efforts to promote sustainability, but are connected to a larger movement with tangible results. We might say, then, that the spatial scale is primarily member cities, but it is, at the same time, the multilevel interaction that drives climate mitigation action across the Cities for Climate Protection network. Similarly, the power to influence and organize action in discrete cities is not limited to local forms of power but draws upon the ideological power of others' experience and economic power that may result from successful lobbying of state or national governments to increase funding for local projects. Dimensions of political power are also evident here since local authorities may leverage contacts and knowledge from other places and agencies to bring about real change in local settings. Being part of a transnational network gives local authorities more options on how to organize and coordinate their city's efforts towards climate change mitigation.

Carbon offsets: making the most of infidelity, sin, and celebrities

Since the sixties, concentrations of heartbreak in the atmosphere have risen dramatically. CheatNeutral.com offers a unique market-based solution to this essential problem of modern life. For the cost of a condom, those who have cheated on their partners can have their cheating 'offset' by a global network of fidelity.

(Bullfrog films promotional material, http://www.bullfrogfilms.com,
accessed 5 January 2009)

Alex Randall and Christian Hunt's satirical documentary, *Cheat Neutral*, depicts their efforts to promote a website that allows people who have cheated on their partners to pay a small fee to encourage others' fidelity thus offsetting their own cheating. As the film shows the filmmakers talking to various radio and television hosts about their innovation, they are repeatedly met with disbelief. Do they really think that paying a financial penalty makes up for an altogether non-financial transgression? What good would such fees actually do to solve problems caused by relationship infidelity? The filmmakers justify their approach by pointing to the precedent of carbon offsets (and, by implication, carbon trading) as a way to ameliorate the effects of greenhouse gas emissions.

What are carbon trading and carbon offsets? Carbon trading, cap-and-trade, and carbon offset schemes all follow the precedent of a number of pollution emissions trading systems that became popular in the US in the 1970s. These include the US Environmental Protection Agency Emissions Trading Program, the national Acid Rain Program for sulfur dioxide (SO_2), and other national and region-specific schemes addressing single pollutants. These pollution trading schemes aim to maintain a certain limit on specific pollutants in a defined geographic area. The geographic area for any particular trading scheme may be the whole country or a particular region, but it is commonly referred to as a "bubble." After determining an acceptable level of pollutant for a given bubble, a trading scheme is established. A successful pollution trading scheme manages to balance emissions of that pollutant within the defined bubble. Success is measured at the scale of the bubble. As utility companies and other stationary emission sources negotiate their pollution levels, it often happens that older facilities must purchase more pollution allowances in order to conform to the established requirements.

What can emerge is an uneven concentration of the pollutant in some areas within the bubble. At the scale of the bubble, this irregularity does not matter as long as the overall goal is achieved, but for people living in the "toxic hot spots" created by these concentrated pollutants, it is a very real concern (Solomon and Lee 2000).

Carbon trading programs follow a similar protocol. Industries or other major, stationary emitters of specific greenhouse gases (e.g., carbon dioxide (CO_2), methane (CH_4), nitrous oxide (N_2O), hydrofluorocarbons (HFCs), perfluorocarbons (PFCs), and sulfur hexafluoride (SF_6)) would be subject to limits, or caps, on acceptable emission levels of those gases, and the government would provide permits for emission up to the cap limit. Those emitters unable to restrict their emissions to the permitted levels would have to purchase credits or allowances that would legally enable them to emit at higher-than-acceptable levels. Only a limited number of allowances would be made available for purchase or auction as a way to encourage investment in greenhouse gas reduction technologies or practices. If an emitter is able to reduce its emissions below the acceptable level, it could sell its rights to the additional emissions that it is not producing. By this process of balancing over- and under-production of greenhouse gases, the thinking goes, an acceptable overall level of greenhouse gas emissions would be achieved. The cap would be lowered over time to bring about reduced emission levels overall.

This cap-and-trade approach is a market-based approach because it is generated by economic calculations of what carbon emissions and a right to generate them are estimated to cost. Those who can afford to purchase allowances may legally emit greenhouse gases, and innovative producers can save (or earn) money by reducing their emissions. Carbon offset plans encourage emitters of greenhouse gases (CO_2, most commonly) to invest in efforts to expand carbon sinks such as forests. Cap-and-trade and carbon offset programs are often referred to interchangeably since they both rely on economic principles either by purchasing emission "rights" much like the purchase of private property or by calculating carbon sinks to equate with greenhouse gas emissions.

In April 2007, the United States Supreme Court ruled, in *Massachusetts v. EPA* (Environmental Protection Agency), that CO_2 is an air pollutant according to the Clean Air Act. Following this ruling, a bill known as America's Climate Security Act, S-2191, was introduced in Congress in October 2007. The bill essentially outlines a cap-and-trade program to reduce CO_2 emissions in the United States and is thought to be the first piece of legislation to consider anticipated impacts of climate change seriously.

Although there is wide support for this program, there are also many opponents among both business and environmental interests (see Miller 2009, Chapter 4 for a thorough discussion of this bill).

During the 2008 United States Presidential campaign, both Barack Obama and John McCain promoted carbon trading systems on their websites as their key strategy to address global climate change (perhaps the only point on which the two candidates agreed!). However, in the heat of the campaign in October 2008, anthropologist Steve Rayner (2008) described in *Wired* magazine why a cap-and-trade approach to curbing greenhouse gases would not work. He pointed out that scientific estimates suggest that emissions should be stabilized by mid-twenty-first century. He argued that such a timeframe is not sufficient to increase carbon prices to a level that would motivate research, development, and dissemination of competitive energy technologies. He also stated that the loose monitoring and accounting systems underpinning cap-and-trade schemes are unlikely to hold emitters responsible and would enable "speculators to work the system, amassing fortunes while achieving nothing for the atmosphere" (http://www.wired.com/politics/law/magazine/16–10/sl_rayner/, accessed 5 January 2009). Rayner is not alone in his critique of market-based carbon reduction programs.

In his book, *The Carbon Neutral Myth: Offset Indulgences for your Climate Sins*, Kevin Smith (2007) draws a parallel between current carbon offset schemes and the Catholic Church's approach to alleviating sin. As mercantilism spread through Europe in the late Middle Ages, the Catholic Church devised a way to address funding problems by adopting a market ethic of supply and demand. The clergy, committing very few sins, were generating a surplus of good deeds. Sinners who had money but lacked the time to repent for themselves, were invited to purchase the effects of these good deeds, or indulgences, to offset their own transgressions. Through an exchange of goods, the imbalance between good and evil was overcome. The parallels with Cheat Neutral are clear. In both instances, commodities are generated according to belief systems. As one commentator has summarized "Offsets are an imaginary commodity created by deducting what you hope happens from what you guess would have happened" (Welch 2007). Through ideological power, people accept these systems wherein they agree to pay for something they cannot necessarily see or touch but that they believe will do them good. Smith argues that a similar process is occurring with carbon offset schemes. If consumers pay extra for a good, such as airline tickets that include an additional carbon offset fee, then there is a sense that one's consumption has been somehow balanced or neutralized. Consumption patterns need not change. Business may proceed, conveniently, as usual (see Figure 2.3). It is a moment of decision that is

Figure 2.3 The power of commodification. Courtesy of Andy Singer.

depoliticized. As market based schemes, the value of vastly different goods is quantified for calculation purposes, but this quantification simplifies complex differences. Planting trees is often environmentally friendly, and it may ease accounting to equate the atmospheric CO_2 absorbed by trees with the CO_2 emitted from the burning of fossil fuels. Yet, from an ecosystem perspective, considering that trees have a limited life span, making such general calculations is about the same as trying to add up oranges and pineapples.

Another form of power exercised in carbon offset schemes is evident in celebrity endorsements. For example, Ronnie Wood, English guitarist and bassist widely known as a member of The Rolling Stones, has invested and promoted carbon offsetting projects in Mozambique. In his autobiography, he writes:

More recently, I created the Ronnie Wood Wood, a forest in Mozambique. I teamed up with the Carbon Neutral Company to plant trees in the Gorongosa National Park, an area under serious threat. The trees we planted help to soak up carbon dioxide, and in turn protect our climate. Obviously, I can't do it alone, so I started offering fans a chance to help me. Thousands stepped up to the plate, joining the crusade and filling the Ronnie Wood Wood with trees.

(Wood 2007, p. 350)

The Hollywood blockbuster, *The Day After Tomorrow*, portrayed sudden and dramatic climate change that froze much of the Northern hemisphere in the course of a weekend. The director, Roland Emmerich paid an organization called Future Forests to plant trees to offset the carbon emissions generated by the film's production. Jake Gyllenhall, who starred in the film, reportedly spent approximately $10 000 to have trees planted in Mozambique, and he was joined in his efforts by Cameron Diaz, Leonardo DiCaprio, and Brad Pitt (Treehugger 2005). The band Coldplay also worked with Carbon Neutral to have 10 000 mango trees planted in Karnataka State in India to offset the carbon emissions produced by the release of a new album. On the band's website, fans of the band were invited to participate in the forest-building for £17.50 (about $29). In return, fans would receive a certificate documenting their investment in The Coldplay Forest (Dhillon and Harnden 2006). Many of the trees did not survive in the arid environment.

Celebrity endorsement equates a product (in this case, carbon offsets) with a popular image or personality and a desire to be like that celebrity. Although celebrity involvement and promotion of carbon offsets may attract greater public attention to climate change concerns, it is not clear that it motivates thoughtful analysis of the causes and contributors to climate change (K. Smith 2007). In a society that reveres actors and athletes, celebrity endorsement is another example of ideological power. The public, in general terms, values celebrities and, by extension, what they say and what they do. Media promotion of actors and athletes as role models, and the public's willingness to believe that celebrities speak with authority, combine in a form of power that helps to organize and coordinate public acceptance of, if not demand for, celebrity-endorsed goods such as carbon offsets. Again, though, this approach to "solving" climate change restricts the range of potential responses by presenting individualistic commodity choices as the only available course of action. It ignores complexities of uneven resource distribution and global inequity and obscures the fact that fossil-fuel consumption has enabled capitalistic economic expansion in ways that are not necessarily sustainable. Simplifying climate change to a matter of individual or corporate purchase of offsets delays a discussion of the potential of social change as a means towards addressing climate change at multiple levels. Celebrities might instead use their high profile to demonstrate active involvement in "confrontational direct action or resistance or to take prominent roles in community organising for climate-friendly societal changes like more bike lanes, affordable and improved public transport or community-based renewable energy projects" (K. Smith 2007, pp. 47–48). In that case, celebrities and the media could still use ideological power but direct it more effectively towards political engagement and public involvement to bring about social change at individual, corporate, and multiple government levels.

One observer has summarized limitations of carbon trading as follows:

Numerical emissions targets, no matter how ambitious, are no substitute for historically-informed political programmes to set industrialized societies on pathways towards the required structural social and technological changes. Whether emissions reductions have anything to do with addressing global warming depends on how those reductions are made. This is precisely the question that cap and trade (and its variants such as cap and auction) are designed to ignore: cap and trade ignores the fact that cutting a hundred million tonnes of emissions through routine efficiency improvements that leave everything else as it was will have long-term emissions consequences very different from cutting a hundred million tonnes through investment in new renewable technologies or ways of organizing social life.

(Lohman, forthcoming, p. 5 citing Lohman 2006: 101–121)

Regardless of how well-implemented a cap-and-trade or carbon offset scheme may be, it is not a suitable instrument to incentivize an overhaul of the industrial practices thought to have contributed to accelerated climate change in the first place. Part of the problem is that cap-and-trade systems tend to neglect both how carbon emissions are cut as well as where emission cuts are made (Lohman, forthcoming). Ignoring the spatial distribution of carbon emissions contributes to environmental injustice. This point echoes the work of Cathleen Fogel (2004) and Heather Smith (2007), described earlier in this chapter, which highlights concerns of indigenous peoples and marginalized groups whose day-to-day lifestyles are particularly threatened by climate change "solutions" identified by powerful interests at larger scales. True, CO_2 and other greenhouse gases are uniformly mixing pollutants. That means that their radiative forcing properties are, in the long run, expected to have global effects rather than cause discrete pockets of warming at their sources. If we begin by defining the problem as one of reducing greenhouse gas emissions, we have effectively determined that appropriate solutions are best calculated at the global scale as well. However, effects of carbon trading and carbon offsets, in the shorter term, have the potential to exert greater, negative impacts on particular places, ecosystems, and lifestyles (e.g., manipulation of forests, substituting greenhouse gases with other, toxic chemicals, erasure of traditional knowledge, marginalization of "local" interests for the "global" good, etc.). It is not clear that these strategies do much more than shift the spatial location of negative, environmental impacts of consumption (Layzer and Moomaw 2007).

Carbon trading, cap-and-trade, and carbon offset schemes tend to emerge by means of political, economic, and ideological power as governments, transnational businesses, popular media, and celebrities promote these solutions, arguably, to ameliorate the effects of increased levels of greenhouses gases in the atmosphere thereby reinforcing their own claim to power. So much energy and effort is devoted to these schemes that their shortcomings are often overlooked. One counter example, however, comes from the Union of Concerned Scientists. This organization is a science-based, non-profit body aimed at fostering citizen action, generating positive change in government policy and business practices, and implementing practical solutions out of concern for the future of the planet and the people who live here. Their official stance on cap-and-trade programs to reduce greenhouse gas emissions is twofold: (1) A well-designed emissions scheme is a responsible means towards managing our use of environmental resources; and (2) cap-and-trade schemes are not sufficient to address climate change:

> The government must implement parallel policies alongside a cap-and-trade regime to ensure development and deployment of the full range of clean technologies. These policies include requiring utilities to generate a higher percentage of their electricity from renewable energy sources, requiring automakers to increase vehicle fuel economy standards, stronger energy efficiency policies, incentive for investments in low-carbon technologies, and policies encouraging smart growth. Studies have shown that a comprehensive approach including these parallel policies would lower the price for allowances, cut emissions, and save consumers money by lowering their electric and gasoline bills.
>
> *(Cleetus, cited in Miller 2009, p. 153)*

This more comprehensive approach to climate change mitigation shifts concern away from a focal point of reducing greenhouse gas emissions by including a range of other approaches. Even though these suggestions center on government policies, the activism of the Union of Concerned Scientists on this point is an effort to repoliticize thinking and action in regards to climate change. Through citizen action and by utilizing its members' scientific credentials, the Union of Concerned Scientists is applying ideological power to open the dominant narrative about climate change mitigation to investigation, analysis, and critique. It is attempting to expand the scale of action to include an array of potential policy actions that involve multiple facets of government authority and corporate behavior. By addressing the interests of individual consumers, this strategy also aims to motivate public enthusiasm for these proposed policies. The Union of Concerned Scientists illustrates an approach to meaningful change in its efforts to expand the scope of power and redefine the scale of potential action in regards to climate change.

Conclusion

Science tells us that the problem of greenhouse gases and climate change is global, so solutions that seek to balance greenhouse gas emissions through global scale calculations often go unchallenged. Never mind that only five countries produce 56% of greenhouse gas emissions – USA 22%, China 18%, Russia 6%, India 5%, and Japan 5% (Rayner 2008) – with the other 44% coming from over 200 other countries, combined. Clearly, the contributing factors to greenhouse gas levels in the atmosphere are not evenly distributed geographically. Even state-level emission reduction schemes overlook the fact that they may generate negative, immediate impacts or externalities either within the "bubble" of their own territory or in other, distant places. Focusing on quantified interpretations of climate change misses the qualitative and place-specific meanings of weather and climate which shape human activity.

Stepping back from the complex science of climate change, Sarewitz and Pielke (2000) offer two sobering observations:

1. Regardless of proposals and plans to reduce CO_2 emissions, such as the Kyoto Protocol which is currently being implemented, atmospheric CO_2 levels will continue to increase.
2. Even if it were possible to reduce greenhouse gas emissions back to pre-industrial levels, climate change would continue to exert impacts on human populations and on the environment.

The earth's human population was approximately 1.6 billion at the beginning of the twentieth century, and it has grown to today's estimate of 6 billion people. Effects of climate change will be felt by more people. Additionally, the global economy has integrated many parts of the world and has rendered a greater number of people dependent on distant resources and reduced, in many cases, local self-sufficiency. Effects of climate change will likely affect more places. More people and more vulnerable environments suggest that

"The implicit moral imperative is not to prevent human disruption of the environment but to ameliorate the social and political conditions that lead people to behave in environmentally disruptive ways" (Sarewitz and Pielke 2000, p. 63). People in desperate circumstances (or with few alternatives) often take options that are not environmentally sound. This point holds true not only for farmers who cut down ecosystemically valuable trees to maximize arable land, but also for the person who drives her car across town rather than make use of an inconvenient (or non-existent) public transportation system. Unsustainable resource use is often caused by poverty, but it can also be caused by government policies. The same may be said for society's vulnerability to weather. Extreme weather events such as drought, storms, or unusually high or low temperatures are experienced by more people today, and how well people can cope with weather events is often determined not only by poverty levels, but also by infrastructural integrity, availability of insurance or other economic safety nets, flexibility of economic activity, and the assurance and provision of security and public safety. There are many sound reasons to reduce greenhouse gas emissions, but anchoring climate change discussions on CO_2 and other greenhouse gases distracts from practical actions that could be taken to fortify society's resilience to weather. Reframing the climate change problem as reducing vulnerability to weather offers:

A clear, uncontroversial story rooted in concrete human experience, observable in the present, and definable in terms of unambiguous and widely shared human values, such as the fundamental rights to a secure shelter, a safe community, and a sustainable environment.

(Sarewitz and Pielke 2000, p. 64)

This shift in focus is inherently sensitive to place and to people's lived experiences in places. Reducing vulnerability to weather events, especially in places where people are already vulnerable either due to poverty or to their physical setting (e.g., low-lying coastal areas), means to improve adaptability.

Increasing a system's adaptive capacity to climate change may be achieved in three key ways: by reducing the system's sensitivity to anticipated climate change effects, by adjusting the system's exposure to these effects, and by increasing the system's resilience in the face of change (Adger *et al.* 2005). The system might be an ecosystem or a social system. All of these forms of adaptation may be implemented at multiple spatial scales including the individual, the home, the community, the city, the state, the region, the corporation, the economic sector, and other spatial systems created by human activity such as transportation and food distribution systems. Increasing the adaptability of a system at one spatial scale may actually contribute to negative effects at other scales or in other places. For example, fortifying river embankments to prevent flooding in one place may increase the likelihood of flooding downstream. Therefore, it is useful to gauge the effectiveness of adaptation by examining the "robustness to uncertainty and flexibility" of a given adaptation action (Adger *et al.* 2005, p. 81). In other words, does the action increase the likelihood that a system can adjust in response to change? The debate about greenhouse gas emissions and what to do about them will probably rage on for years to come. Paying attention to systemic adaptability and resilience at multiple spatial scales is a different effort altogether. It acknowledges that "the" answer is not captured at any single scale of human activity. Careful consideration of ways that government policies, citizen action, community organization, and corporate behavior can be encouraged to foster flexibility across the realm of human activity and environmental systems has the potential to bring about meaningful change even without the risk of climate change. Different forms of power could be mobilized towards practical and immediate strategies to reduce human vulnerability by making adjustments to human systems and human–environment interactions at multiple scales. If climate change unfolds in ways that we might (or might not) anticipate, then so much the better to have improved our ability to cope with it.

3

Oil and energy

Estimated revenue from ethanol that a quarter acre of Iowa farmland can earn per year: $300

Amount it could earn each year with a wind turbine on it: $10,000
> – Harper's *Index, August 2008*

Introduction

Imagine the following news story from the future:

News release: Algae-to-oil discovery devastates Russian oil market[1]

Dateline: Zurich, Switzerland, 15 January 2016

The resource curse is not a myth. This was a lesson post-Soviet leaders lived first-hand and worked assiduously to avoid. Throughout the '00s, the Russian leader, joined by co-leaders-for-life in Astana, Ashgabat, and Baku jealously guarded and carefully managed the flow of hydrocarbons – oil and natural gas – to Europe. But while they could control the pipelines, they could not control Craig Venter. No one controlled Venter. And though his colleagues dubbed him "Darth Venter, an idiot and an egomaniac," *Time Magazine* got it right: Venter's "incandescent idea" of unlocking the genome freed Europe and the West from mercurial and autocratic oil producers.

Tired of his peers' constant derision and the prying eyes of the US President's Advisory Board for Biosecurity, Venter welcomed the European Union's invitation to participate in its €100 billion Genome Initiative. In 2010 Venter shuttered his Rockville and La Jolla labs, crossed the Atlantic and set up shop in Cambridge. While his cash-starved colleagues in the US waited for Washington and the President to move beyond the distracting stem cell debate, Venter's startup, Synthetic Genomics, achieved the holy grail of the biofuel industry: direct organism to oil production. Through metabolic engineering, Venter's team coaxed microalgae to secrete oil directly through cell membranes, thereby eliminating the costly processing steps that plagued other biofuels like corn, switch grass and rapeseed. The European Union Patent Office ultimately agreed with its US counterpart: Venter could not play God and patent genomes, even synthetic genomes in single-celled algae.

There would be no "Microbesoft" in genomic engineering. Venter was not bothered; "Dr. Green" as he is now hailed could afford to be generous. A Nobel was better than a patent and the scientist was already wealthy beyond belief.

Not everyone was uncorking the champagne. While Stockholm feted Venter in December 2014, leaders in Moscow, Astana, Ashgabat and Baku huddled behind closed doors. A few weeks earlier the German Chancellor and Polish President met in Schwedt, on the German–Polish border, and ceremoniously shut the valve on Russia's Druzhba oil pipeline. The transition to green energy was swift and, for everyone but the old energy exporters, painless. There was no need for massive capital investments in wind and solar, for new transmission lines to link these alternative energy sources to the grid, or for hydrogen stations to fuel a new generation of cars. The only visible changes, other than lower prices at the pump, were the suddenly unclogged maritime shipping lanes. Algae-oil farms located next to coastal refineries, taking advantage of the existing hydrocarbon infrastructure. In short, it was business as usual, except that the old oil producers were out of business.

Imagine that an inexpensive alternative to oil has been found. It is easy to generate, it can use transport and refining infrastructure already in place, and there is no patent, so no corporations have an advantage nor does any particular country or region control a greater share of this resource. What kinds of political, economic, and social (or other relationships) would likely be affected by this discovery? We can imagine how disruptive such an open-access resource would be to oil companies and their degree of economic control and political influence throughout the world. The hierarchy of their power would also be shaken since "Mom & Pop" upstarts could feasibly get into the game of providing fuel. What would happen to US interests in the Middle East if that region was no longer a key supplier of critical energy resources? Would there still be a drive to influence power arrangements within and among countries there if the region was no longer a critical supplier of energy resources? What would happen to the governments around the world that have secured and maintained power through tight control of oil and gas earnings? Many governments long ago nationalized their oil industries and use the leverage of oil wealth to remain in power: Russia (nationalized in 1920), Mexico (1938), Iraq (1972), Saudi Arabia (1976), Venezeula (1976), and Nigeria (1978) (Falola and Genova 2005, p. 49) not to mention newer states such as Azerbaijan, Kazakhstan, and Turkmenistan. What would happen in these places if those countries' key export commodity plummeted in value? If an oil substitute made cheap gas (petrol) widely available, would there still be widespread concern about global climate change? How might definitions of "power" and "security" be adjusted with a discovery of a substitute for oil?

This chapter considers current scholarly thinking about fossil fuel energy as well as possible scenarios for transitioning to the next fuel source, whatever that may be. The discussion focuses on oil and gas pipelines as a particularly important lens through which to analyze power relationships pertaining to these energy sources. Pipelines, more so than an analysis of the geographic distribution of fossil fuel resources, are indicators of current and projected power dynamics surrounding energy, and they can be used to advance our understanding of complexities underlying energy both at global, regional, state, and substate scales. The chapter then turns to consider ethanol. In recent years ethanol was enthusiastically promoted as the new fuel that could alleviate the world's dependence on fossil fuels, but just as quickly, the idea of ethanol attracted criticism as being inefficient and generating too many spin-off problems. Its popularity persists in some circles, and we will look at how the official promotion of ethanol, particularly in the US, maintains and generates power dynamics beyond US borders.

Dominant narratives of "the problem" of oil

There has been an explosion of scholarly and mainstream literature on oil and energy in recent years. Many of these books are widely read by the public due in part to the enthusiasm with which they deliver grim or optimistic views of the future energy situation in the West. One of the more well-known among these books is Michael Klare's *Blood for Oil: The Dangers and Consequences of America's Growing Dependency on Imported Petroleum* (Klare 2004). Recognizing the central role of fossil fuels in the American way of life (as well as the importance of fossil fuels in the sustenance of US military activity and instalments around the world), Klare provides a history of the role that energy has played in US military policy with a particular focus on the Middle East. He emphasizes the significance of the Carter Doctrine of 1980 which identified "the secure flow of Persian Gulf oil as a 'vital interest' of the United States (Klare 2004, p. 4)." That designation justified any means necessary, including military action, to maintain the uninterrupted flow of oil from that region. Klare describes how the US military has been reconfigured in recent years in large part to increase its agility and technological prowess so that it can more effectively engage in unstable, energy-rich areas at relatively short notice. Recall the "Shock and awe" strategy in Iraq that showcased a smaller but technologically savvy military invasion (Figure 3.1). He argues that the uninterrupted flow of oil through the world economy will continue to exact a loss of US military blood and is unlikely to be sustainable in the long term. In his more recent book, Klare (2008) analyzes what he refers to as "the New International Energy Order" in which the contours of power reflect a division between countries with an energy surplus and those with an energy deficit.

Figure 3.1 Commentary on US involvement in Iraq. Courtesy of Carl J. Winowiecki II.

Clashes over energy and the hardening of military alliances in energy-rich parts of the world, he argues, may lead to a new Cold War in which states' increasing focus on energy security contributes to a deficit in democracy and an increase in economic plight for many people already living in hardship.

The easy to reach oil and gas has mostly been exhausted. We are in an era of "extreme oil" that means higher risk in extracting reserves, in ensuring the safe transport of oil and gas, and in the environmental impacts resulting from these activities especially for already marginalized groups of people. The discovery of and reliance on oil in economically developing or transitional countries is not necessarily positive for people living in those countries. Indeed, negative impacts of extreme oil may be exacerbated in contexts of economically developing countries given the limited attention to environmental impacts, a general lack of social services, and obstacles to the expression of public opinion (Falola and Genova 2005). We turn to the question: Are we really running out of oil?

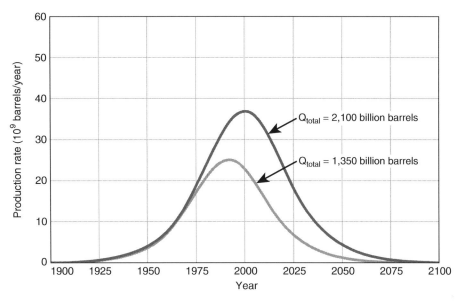

Figure 3.2 Hubbert's Peak. Adapted from Hubbert (1969), p. 196.

"Hubbert's Peak" is a phrase used widely in recent publications to capture the idea that global oil production is destined to decline. M. King Hubbert introduced this concept in a paper published in 1969. His eponymous and now famous graphic is a bell curve of oil production (see Figure 3.2). The graph shows world crude oil production increasing slowly in the mid-1900s and increasing to a peak around 2000 followed by a sharp decline to nearly zero production by 2075. Kenneth Deffeyes (2005) offers the perspective of a geologist in *Beyond Oil: The View From Hubbert's Peak*. He explains M. King Hubbert's (1969) methodology of estimating when global oil production would peak and then decline, and then he considers the prospects of other fossil fuels, uranium, and hydrogen in the face of declining oil output. Another popular book on the topic is Richard Heinberg's *The Party's Over: Oil, War and the Fate of Industrial Societies* (Heinberg 2005). Taking a social science perspective, Richard Heinberg traces the importance of fossil fuels since the Industrial Revolution through to the current day. He discusses estimates of oil production in decline and projections of global population on the rise to conclude that society as we know it will likely collapse. In particular, China and India are expected to become especially competitive in the growing struggle for oil since their populations continue to increase in number just as global oil production is predicted to decline (Hiro 2007).

Vaclav Smil (2003), a geographer who analyzes energy, offers a more critical assessment of the future of fossil fuels. He distinguishes between fossil fuel *resources* as the total presence of a particular mineral naturally present in the earth's crust and *reserves* which are the well-explored portion of these resources that are available through human action. Smil describes the bumpy history of accounting for earth's fossil fuels. Part of the complication of assessing oil reserves is that no international standards have been established. Despite that fact, even the most widely cited surveys of oil reserves, *Oil & Gas Journal* and *World Oil*, list reserves with seeming accuracy to the third decimal value. He also notes that the largest annual increase in reported world oil reserves resulted from a change in accounting practices by OPEC members in 1987 and not from the discovery of new oil extraction potential. The history of failed oil forecasts to date has repeated two mistakes: "underestimating the amount of the ultimately recoverable oil, and overestimating the role of oil in future energy supply" (p. 199). Even though Hubbert's curve of oil production has generated a wealth of follow-up studies, there is no consensus on production totals, dates of the peak and subsequent decline, or the rate of declined production. Smil argues that the history of energy forecasts gives us reason to question today's predictions. He challenges the limited focus that common narratives of oil tend to take by introducing a well-known theory of abiotic hydrocarbons. This theory rejects the accepted understanding of petroleum as a biogenic resource in which high energy oil and gas molecules result from the compression and heating of low energy organic matter. Instead, this alternative view, put forward by Russian and Ukrainian scientists, is that hydrocarbons may in fact be the result of high pressure exerted in the Earth's mantle (see also Falola and Genova 2005, pp. 171–172). By this reasoning, we should be looking for oilfields in "such nonsedimentary regions as crystalline basements, volcanic and impact structures and rifts, as well as in strata deep below the already producing reservoirs" (Smil 2003, p. 202). The popularity of this idea has not spread beyond Russia and Ukraine. Smil's point, however, is not to advocate this view but to remind us that other theories such as plate tectonics, which were not initially accepted, have led to paradigm shifts in the way we understand particular physical phenomena. Our understanding of energy systems is most likely incomplete.

In *Addicted to Oil: America's Relentless Drive for Energy Security*, Ian Rutledge (2005) looks at the unique characteristics of oil as a fuel that has made it particularly convenient: it is relatively lightweight, energy dense, and transportable. Infrastructure and the combustion engine emerged in tandem with oil use bringing us to our current "locked in" status. Demand in residential, commercial, and industrial sectors has remained relatively stable since the 1980s, but demand for transportation has skyrocketed. US dependence on imported oil, especially from the Middle East, makes the US vulnerable to energy shortages and shocks. Rutledge traces former US President George W. Bush's career as a Texas oil man, Condolezza Rice, his National Security Advisor, and her previous position as Director of Chevron [Oil] Corporation, and Richard Cheney, Bush's Vice President, in his role as the President of Halliburton, a premier oil industry service company. Rutledge discusses the importance of links to oil industry colleagues that each of these three brought to bear in their top roles in the Bush Administration. National security was understood and operationalized as "unimpeded motorization" (p. 78): increased vehicle use, expansion of the motor transport system, and increased consumption of gasoline per capita. To ensure this form of national security, the Bush Administration vigorously pursued three key energy strategies with support from oil industry interests: increase domestic production of oil, promote open markets to enhance "energy integration" within the Western hemisphere (and in particular with Canada, Mexico, and Venezuela), and shift imports away from the Middle East by developing ties with, for example, oil-producing countries in the Caspian Sea region.

However, the Caspian Sea region and other areas of potential oil expansion (such as Alaska's Arctic National Wildlife Refuge or ANWR) proved to be less productive and more difficult to exploit than the Bush Administration had envisioned. This fact returns us to two points of central concern to the Bush Administration: (1) the US is dependent on oil and, barring a drastic change in policy, is likely to remain dependent on oil for the foreseeable future; and (2) the most obvious source of this oil remains the Middle East. The US would fare poorly in the event of an oil shock emanating from the Middle East, but Saudi Arabia and Kuwait have tended to resist opening their oil supplies to foreign investment. The events of September 11 2001, in combination with the Bush Doctrine, which radically moved away from a policy of containment to justify preventive wars in the interest of preserving US security, served to catalyze a proactive effort to gain control of oil supplies in the Middle East. From this assessment of current events, Rutledge draws the conclusion that oil prices are likely to remain high, and an oil shock from the Middle East is likely to happen within the next 10 years unless the US can drastically reduce oil consumption and its reliance on inefficient motor vehicles.

Garry Leech takes a similar line in his book, *Crude Interventions: The United States, Oil, and the New World (Dis)order* (Leech 2006). He discusses consequences of the Bush Administration's foreign policy priority of forcibly opening up economies of oil-rich, economically developing states. In his book, he describes US national energy policy as driving harmful foreign policies and as being environmentally unsustainable. One of his main concerns is how US (and Western) intervention in economically developing countries tends to support corrupt elites rather than supporting democracy and economic sovereignty – a result which is at odds with US rhetoric. Oil, among the many valuable and highly traded resource commodities, has increasingly been linked to global power politics (Yergin 1992) and to the maintenance of dictatorships that often degrade the environment and contribute to conflict (Bacher 2000, Friedman 2008). Beyond these concerns, though, much of the discussion about oil centered on US oil consumption tends to miss a significant point: US oil imports are not the fundamental problem since most of the world is dependent on oil (Sandalow 2008).

So far, we see how different elements of power are intertwined in the current energy system as described by recent mainstream literature: military power is implicated in securing oil and gas reserves and pipelines through the organization of military initiatives, economic power is reflected in the control of circuits of energy flow and exchange, political power is demonstrated in state-level priorities, strategies, and policies implemented within and beyond state borders. Ideological power is also present in the meaning and value that we have come to place on oil as the driver of the world economy. Ideological power is also reflected in the norms or shared understandings that we have come to have that serve to justify patterns of energy control and consumption. For example, Smil (2008, p. 356) has observed:

By 2005 nobody could deny that if the U.S. objective were gaining access to Iraqi oil, it would have been much cheaper (and casualty free) to give Saddam Hussein interest-free loans to boost Iraq's production capacity rather than to occupy the country in 2003.

So why did the US or some collective of states or international actors not simply make such an offer? Iraq was part of the "Axis of Evil," along with Iran and North Korea, which US President George Bush named in January 2002 as promoting terrorism and seeking weapons of mass destruction. Placing Iraq in this unenviable category meant both to the Bush Administration and to an American (and perhaps world) public still reeling from the events of September 11 that Iraq did not deserve to be treated as an equal player in the global community. Making loan offers to Iraq at that point in time would have run against growing perception of Iraq as a rogue state to be dealt with firmly and with a degree of suspicion.

Other observers have looked beyond US energy and foreign policy to the role of non-state actors in the dynamics of global oil. Oil companies, for example, exercise economic power and political leverage. As far back as 1890, The Sherman Antitrust Act targeted Standard Oil which had become a ruthless monopoly. Several bills were introduced in Congress in the 1970s to break up large oil companies which had once again become incredibly powerful and influential. Today, there are calls to go further in deflating the power of Big Oil (Juhasz 2008). Strategies proposed to restrict the influence of Big Oil in politics have included cutting subsidies to oil companies, enforcing new tax requirements, requiring investments in public transportation and alternative energy, encouraging a reduction in the country's oil consumption, and a widespread demand that the US military retreat from oil-protection initiatives. Another form of economic power involved with oil may be seen in OPEC. The Organization of the Petroleum Exporting Countries, commonly known as OPEC, was formed in 1960 and represents several state governments acting in unison in regards to oil production and pricing. Participating states were willing to sacrifice a degree of independent sovereignty in order to gain the strength of negotiating as a group. Here we see the value of considering power beyond the state level, yet at the same time it is important to understand that benefits of OPEC varied within and among each of the member states, for example, accruing predominantly with an elite in each country. Founding members were Iran, Iraq, Kuwait, Saudi Arabia, and Venezuela, and other members have included Algeria, Ecuador (until 1992), Gabon (until 1994), Indonesia, Libya, Nigeria, Qatar, and United Arab Emirates.

The organization gained momentum in the early 1970s in response to power wielded over national oil supplies by international oil companies (Falola and Genova 2005). OPEC formed a united front against the major oil companies which were active in those countries, and for several years these groups negotiated over tax rates and profit sharing. Eventually, these negotiations led to an overall increase in the price of oil. Tensions over Western support of Israel sparked the 1973 oil embargo which involved a shut down in oil shipments from Middle Eastern countries to the US. The embargo resulted in panic in the US and vows to become energy independent by the 1980s through the exploitation of domestic oil and nuclear power. That vision did not materialize; nor did the vision of crippling the US through an oil embargo:

This was because the embargo lasted less than one year and because the oil industry is so complex that it is virtually impossible for a producing country to control where its oil actually goes once it is pumped out of the ground.

(Falola and Genova 2005, p. 78)

Location of oil reserves, then, is not the most important feature for understanding power relationships that come into play with fossil fuel energy. This is a lesson that the US has faced with its Strategic Petroleum Reserve which is but one piece of the world's massive infrastructure for managing the flow and control of oil and gas resources.

Energy infrastructure: spatial networks and power

The US responded to the oil embargo by establishing the Strategic Petroleum Reserve. The idea was to provide "the President with a powerful response option should a disruption in commercial oil supplies threaten the US economy" (US Department of Energy 2009). The Strategic Petroleum Reserve is a system of salt caverns and pipelines located in four sites along the Gulf Coast. It was designed to hold 700 million barrels of oil as an emergency supply. The capacity was increased to 1 billion barrels in The Energy Policy Act of 2005. Now that world oil prices are no longer tightly controlled, the location of oil reserves is not as important as previously. Additionally, it is not clear that the Strategic Petroleum Reserve (SPR) could adequately substitute for regular oil imports in a time of crisis:

Together, all the SPR sites are capable of pumping out only 4.4 million barrels a day when they're running at full tilt. That's about a third of the quantity of oil that the U.S. imports daily (assuming that there's even that much room in the pipelines to carry it). Adding potential oil imports from Canada and Mexico to the SPR, you still end up with a 4.3 million barrel shortfall – nearly 20 percent of the oil the United States consumes daily. That's three times the size of the 7 percent cut that triggered a crisis and economic restructuring in the 1970s. Even if the SPR works perfectly, it still doesn't protect the economy.

(Margonelli 2007, pp. 114–115)

These observations suggest that today the purpose of the Strategic Petroleum Reserve is less about emergency supply and more about market manipulation. Using the oil in the Strategic Petroleum Reserve appears to be all but forbidden, and there seems to be no clear plan for how to use it. The original purpose of the Strategic Petroleum Reserve was to develop infrastructure to ease potential economic turmoil, yet the domestic politics surrounding this backup system suggest that it has actually served to complicate the politics of oil in the US.

Other infrastructure concerns have influenced political decisions – and economic impacts – surrounding oil. The Bush Administration adamantly denied that the 2003 invasion of Iraq had anything to do with that country's oil supplies. However, Deputy Secretary of Defense Paul Wolfowitz contradicted that narrative. In a response to a question about why the US was treating Iraq so aggressively when it was widely known that North Korea was developing weapons of mass destruction, Wolfowitz reportedly stated "Let's look at it simply. The most important difference between North Korea and Iraq is that economically, we just had no choice in Iraq. The country swims on a sea of oil" (Tirman 2006, p. 22). The more interesting comparison, perhaps, is why the US pursued different policies in Iraq and Venezuela, another oil-producing country. In late 2002, President Bush faced increasing tension on two fronts: relations with Venezuela's President Hugo Chavez and the unfolding situation in Iraq (Rutledge 2005). A key point of US energy strategy, as already noted, was to shift imports away from the Middle East, and another point was to integrate more closely the energy markets of the Americas. Hugo Chavez, outspoken in his anti-American rhetoric, was seized by military agents and briefly overthrown from power. Pedro Carmona, the newly appointed leader, intended to relax oil production quotas and create favorable conditions for foreign investors. The US acknowledged Carmona's "transitional civilian government," but Chavez was quickly reinstated to power with widespread support. President Bush was encouraged to support anti-Chavez factions that might lead to better conditions for US oil imports from Venezuela. Simultaneously, war in Iraq was imminent, and there were concerns about possible increases in oil prices.

It would seem to have been an ideal time to act forcibly in Venezuela even if oil supplies from there might be temporarily disrupted. Yet observers noted two important aspects of Venezuelan oil. First, shipments of oil to the US from Venezuela take approximately 5 days as opposed to 5 weeks for shipments from Iraq. Venezuelan oil is, therefore, considered "short haul" oil as opposed to "long haul" oil. Energy security favors long haul oil because there is a greater supply in the commodity chain at any given time which allows more time to deal with unexpected events. A shock in short haul oil supply, however, would be felt almost immediately. Second, US refineries on the Gulf coast are designed to process heavy crude which is imported from Mexico and Venezuela. Lighter crude, such as the type of oil imported from Middle Eastern countries, cannot be processed at these refineries. These two points explain why upsetting the oil supply from Venezuela was viewed by the Bush administration as an option to avoid since it would lead to supply problems almost instantly. This situation highlights nuances of the geopolitics of oil that are often overlooked. That is, oil itself does not drive or ameliorate conflict, but many other political and geographic factors come into play. We can understand power dynamics of oil and gas better by examining energy infrastructure. In particular, the rest of this section focuses on transport pipelines.

General understandings about oil and gas often focus on places of supply, and attention to the distribution of reserves is certainly important. However, the spatial and political significance of transport pipelines is often overlooked. That may be because oil and gas pipelines are taken for granted as "just" infrastructure, or maybe because the politics surrounding pipelines can be complicated. Pipelines involve several factors. There are questions about the physics of fuel transport (e.g., coordinating production at the well-head, available capacity to transport fuel, the location and level of consumer demand and safety concerns depending on the type of fuel being transmitted). There are also realities of shifting global demand away from oil towards liquefied natural gas and the epochal change since World War II in the geopolitics of Europe and Asia (Kandiyoti 2008). These factors make it particularly worthwhile to consider how pipelines are tied up in power relationships. Pipelines, also, are an example of scales as networks. They enable exchange among certain places and with limited directionality: they serve as a conduit of power.

A recent book titled *B-Zone: Becoming Europe and Beyond* (Franke 2006) compiles a variety of written and artistic projects tracing the transformation of social and political geographies along major transnational infrastructure pathways in former Soviet-dominated states. An idea explicit throughout the book is that infrastructure, such as a pipeline project, changes places:

> If there is a rhetoric of political language, there is a rhetoric of political space ... [look at] infrastructure as powerful gestures that extend time into space, regulating movement, duration, expansion, and relationality, while telling stories of what has become increasingly apparent: that, as much as highways, media networks, and pipelines may connect, they also divide; as much as they integrate, they also disintegrate; and as they compress time and value in space for some (the new mobile class), they devaluate it for those who have to remain immobile.
>
> *(Franke 2006, p. 8)*

Pipelines are more than physical infrastructure. They connect places and they divide places. They reflect arrangements of power as they direct the flow of benefits to some places and signify relationships between places. Bouzarovski and Konieczny (forthcoming) have considered the proposed Nord Stream Pipeline from Russia under the Baltic Sea to Europe. They demonstrate that pipelines have a unique geography that includes not just the area spanned by a pipeline network but also the borders – political, economic, and social – created or overcome by these projects. Differential impacts of such infrastructure projects may exacerbate existing tensions at some scales while easing tensions at other scales. Pipelines motivate or challenge economic and political relations between and among states, because these projects bring benefits and costs to participating states. Impacts of oil and gas pipelines, however, are not spatially homogeneous within those states. Short-term construction impacts and longer term economic and environmental impacts of pipeline systems create new landscapes, opportunities, and costs for people living near these projects. Just as oil and gas pipelines have impacts at different spatial scales, they also imply or demonstrate power at different spatial scales.

Below, three examples of pipelines illustrate how power associated with oil and gas pipelines plays out in three different contexts. First, the Chad–Cameroon pipeline in Africa and the Caño Limón-Coveñas Oil Pipeline in South America are briefly assessed for their local impacts and power dynamics. Next, the more complex and far-reaching case of Russia's energy export system to Europe is explored in more depth to emphasize how energy reflects different forms of power and the construction of spatial scales at which the power is manifested.

Chad–Cameroon oil pipeline

The Chad–Cameroon oil pipeline in Africa connects the inland oilfields of Chad to the coast of Cameroon. In the developmental stages of the pipeline, the project was applauded for its innovative plans to integrate an HIV/AIDS-prevention campaign along the pipeline route (Kigotho 1997). Intervention programs would be, according to the plans, targeted at construction workers drawn to the region for work and truck drivers who would be driving along the pipeline route through an area known to have a high incidence of HIV/AIDS among prostitutes. The intention was for the pipeline to have tangible, positive impacts at the local level.

Chad is a landlocked country with limited economic potential outside of the oilfields discovered in the 1970s. The proposed 1100 km pipeline, the Chad–Cameroon Petroleum Development and Pipeline project, would allow the export of Chad's oil from Cameroon's Atlantic coast. Although Cameroon has experienced alternating stages of economic boom and bust since the 1960s, Chad had endured civil war and had some of the world's lowest socioeconomic indicators. It was anticipated that royalties from oil exports for Chad, transit fees for Cameroon, and tax revenues for both countries would allow Chad and Cameroon to improve poor economic and social conditions, provide a source of employment and training opportunities, and allow for infrastructural improvements (Ndumbe 2002). The World Bank viewed the project as having significant potential for enhancing economic development in both countries. Not only did the World Bank lend financial support to the project, it also assisted Chad's government in planning how to use revenues to alleviate poverty, promote transparency in how revenues were used, increase ways that parliament, citizens, and the private sector could have input in decisions about revenue management, and execute an extensive educational campaign to inform people about the project (ibid). The World Bank's involvement was also intended to enforce high environmental standards and risk management for the project and to ensure public input into the development of the construction plans. Again, positive, local impacts were at the forefront of the planning process.

Despite these admirable intentions, criticisms of the project pointed to poor democratic track records in both Chad and Cameroon as obstacles to including any meaningful public input and questioned the overall sustainability of the project since both countries were starting from a limited or non-existent baseline of basic infrastructure (Ndumbe 2002). The World Bank's approach to the Chad–Cameroon Pipeline reflected the thinking that the resource curse (see Chapter 7) could be avoided with the implementation of sound economic policies and the application of good governance, but the failure of policy interventions on the part of Chad and Cameroon suggests that international organizations would have to be radically more involved and the institutional overhauls would have to be far more significant for this approach to succeed (Pegg 2005). The reality is that health initiatives and HIV/AIDS issues remain untouched by the project, and surveys of village residents along the pipeline capture an overall disappointment with the pipeline's local impact (Schwartz 2005). In the village of Djertou, for example, residents report no identifiable, positive change in access to electricity or health care or improved economic opportunities, and in the village of Bélel, opinion is starkly divided between those who see only positive aspects of the pipeline and those who refuse to recognize any benefits of the pipeline (ibid). Either way, one outstanding concern about the pipeline is that it has already attracted several acts of sabotage since it was completed in 2004, and this point raises security concerns for people living along the pipeline.

In other work on the development of energy infrastructure in Africa, Michael Watts has considered different, overlapping social, economic, and political spaces that have emerged in response to the expansion of the international oil industry footprint in Nigeria. He has noted that oil has unique qualities in the public imagination in Nigeria (Watts 1994) and points out that oil "harbours fetishistic qualities; it is the bearer of meanings, of hopes, of expectation of unimaginable powers: unprecedented wealth, avarice and power" (2003, p. 17). In the Nigerian case, and in other instances as well, oil has enabled the centralization of state power since the government acts as gatekeeper to international oil contracts, yet it has also compromised the idea and practice of the modern, sovereign nation state since oil wealth can engender a false sense of economic development (Watts 2003). This contradictory position of the state in regards to oil allows for the creation of spaces that may be seen to undermine or otherwise challenge the operation of a coherent state in the modern, Western conceptualization of a state (ibid). Rather than enhance territorial statehood, Watts argues, oil wealth can diminish a sense of national community by creating tensions between "imperial oil" and community (2004). He quotes Polish journalist Kapuściński (1985) who identified a similar tension in pre-revolutionary Iran:

> Oil creates the illusion of a completely changed life, life without work, life for free ... The concept of oil expresses perfectly the eternal human dream of wealth achieved through lucky accident ... In this sense oil is a fairy tale and like every fairy tale a bit of a lie.
>
> *(Kapuściński 1985, p. 35; cited by Watts 2004, p. 213)*

Years before the recent upwelling of academic work on resource conflict, Olson (1963) noted that rapid economic growth based on natural resource exports can generate a "revolution of rising expectations" (p. 541) which would appear to be reflected in this fantasy of public expectations about oil. For people living in proximity to oil extraction or pipeline projects, these expectations may be particularly pronounced since they live with tangible evidence of oil export every day. In the case of communities along the Chad–Cameroon pipeline, the lack of actual benefits may in fact serve to heighten expectations about pipeline-associated benefits in the future. In that case, the pipeline project, involving state governments, the World Bank, and oil companies, was successfully executed so far as those interests were concerned, but there is little evidence of improved quality of life in communities along the route. Economic and political power were consolidated at the scale of the project drivers, but local communities remain unenriched and unempowered.

Caño Limón-Coveñas oil pipeline, Colombia

"Oil is vehemently and simultaneously local, regional, national, and global" (Dunning and Wirpsa 2004). Oil is found in specific locations, and it is a commodity in global demand. Export pipelines enable a continued supply from source to client, but the seemingly smooth journey of oil from local source to global markets belies complex political and social institutions at multiple scales. In the mid 1980s, the Mannesmann construction company and multinational Occidental oil corporation were responsible for oil production in the Arauca region of Colombia. In the face of weak, national institutions, these companies contracted with the National Liberation Army (ELN) guerillas to provide security for the new oil pipeline to the coast. In so doing, they contributed to a decline of local socioeconomic structures which in turn generated additional militia activity. In an in-depth study of the oil-rich Casanare region in Colombia, Jenny Pearce argues that when assessing oil and local conflict, it is important to look beyond armed actors and to consider the sociopolitical conditions within which oil exploitation takes place (Pearce 2007). In Colombia, policy failures at the national level and a lack of sustainable institutions at the regional level led to predation by armed forces and "contributed to decomposition rather than articulation of social forces around a governance project" (ibid, p. 260).

Yet even a small community can make a difference. As British Petroleum (BP) conducted exploratory work on a small oilfield called La Floreña, relations with the approximately 1500 residents in nearby El Morro community became tense. Although some infrastructural developments were made by BP in concession to the community (e.g., paving of a main road), education levels remained low and child labor levels remained high: "The hopes of this community that oil could offer a way out of this poverty trap, its frustrations as such hopes failed to materialize and its sense of powerlessness in the face of large-scale and poorly understood transformations around them were behind the civic strike that took place in January 1994" (Pearce 2007, p. 241). That civic strike escalated tensions which drew the attention of international non-governmental organizations and led to a qualitative shift in the local conflict and in the strengths and strategies of local paramilitary groups. In other places, too, the region's oil wealth has not translated into human development. Pearce tellingly quotes women that she interviewed as saying "There is no development, only infrastructure" (p. 243).

In this case, the Mannesmann construction company, Occidental Oil Corporation, British Petroleum, the National Liberation Army, and the Colombian government enabled the construction and security of the pipeline. Reponses from local communities (either in acquiescing to the power wielded by armed guerrillas or in resisting BP's explorations near El Morro) and from the international NGO community illustrate the complex and multiple-scaled web of relations surrounding pipeline projects. The involvement of guerrilla forces in the face of an inadequate state military and the involvement of international corporations demonstrate different dimensions of power involved in exercising control over territory and access to resources. The actions of an active and resistant local community illustrate a response to this territoriality as people refused to have their living space altered solely for the benefit of others elsewhere. In comparison to the Chad–Cameroon pipeline, this case illustrates that the same kind of infrastructure project, namely, an oil export pipeline enabled and promoted by and for state and international corporate interests, can have different impacts depending on local perceptions and actions. However, these two cases share elements of overlooked local-scale needs or preferences in favor of larger scale objectives both in terms of resource use, economic benefit, and political control of space.

Russia, Europe, and energy security

Ukraine inherited a major portion of Soviet-era pipelines that connected Russia's gas supplies to Europe when the Soviet Union dissolved in 1991. Almost 20 years later, Ukrainian pipelines still transfer approximately 80% of Russia's gas exports towards Europe giving Ukraine a monopoly on Russia's Westward gas transit. Russia, in turn, has a monopoly on the gas supplies that fill the pipelines. This "dual monopoly" locks both sides into an interdependent, structural stalemate that is implicated in recent tensions between the two countries and beyond (Torbakov 2009). In 2005 and 2006, Russia shut down its gas supplies to Europe via transit pipelines in Ukraine and Belarus (the only other direct transit route for gas from Russia to Western Europe), respectively. Russia justified these actions by pointing to payment concerns and technical difficulties. Domestic consumers in European countries that normally rely on Russian gas were left with drastically reduced energy supplies during the winter. However, when Russia shut down its gas supplies to Ukrainian transit routes in January 2009, the situation escalated into a gas blockade affecting much of Europe. Gas supplies were held up for 18 days. Finally, on 19 January Russia and Ukraine agreed to put into effect a "Memorandum of Agreement" that had been signed in October 2008 to address commercial disagreements between the Russian gas company, Gazprom, and Ukraine's Naftohaz Ukrainy (Kupchinsky 2009). Had this agreement been implemented earlier, the gas "war" could have been avoided.

Other factors may have motivated Russia's actions. Russian–Ukrainian relations have been particularly strained since Russia made overt attempts to intervene in Ukraine's 2004 Presidential election but failed to bring the pro-Russian party to power. As with other post-Soviet republics, Russia is interested in supporting Russians who continue to live in now independent republics and who face restrictions on the use of Russian language as well as other infringements on their Russian identity. Russia has continued to issue passports and citizen rights to residents of Ukraine who adhere to a Russian identity – an act which challenges Ukrainian identity and sovereignty. By shutting off gas to Ukraine, Russia may have been hoping to incite public dissent in eastern Ukraine against the Western-leaning leadership of Ukraine (Kuzio 2009). Russia's government may also have wanted to punish Ukraine for selling weapons to Georgia (Baev 2009), a particular point of contention since the Russian–Georgian armed conflict in August 2008. Russia's leaders may have been hoping to demonstrate Russia's critical role in European energy security. In particular, Russia's leaders may have been aiming to persuade European countries of the need to build new pipelines that would increase European access to Russia's gas supplies. Russia is already facing a shortfall in its gas production, and its ageing energy infrastructure is in need of significant investment, preferably from its European customers. Russia's President Medvedev underscored the importance of constructing the proposed Nord Stream pipeline on the Baltic Sea bed to provide direct gas links to Germany and the South Stream pipeline that would bypass Ukraine by carrying Russian gas exports over the Black Sea bed to the Balkans and Central Europe. Additionally, Russia's Prime Minister Putin has also promoted Yamal Two (a proposed pipeline westward through Belarus and Poland), and the expansion of Blue Stream (by way of the Black Sea from Russia to Turkey), as well as a proposed gas pipeline eastward to China that would parallel a planned oil pipeline. Without European investment, these improvements to Russia's export capacity are unlikely to come about, but there is also question about whether or not Russia actually has the gas resources to fill those pipelines (Socor 2009b).

Russia's leadership has made it clear that energy sources are a centerpiece of its international policy. Russia continues to negotiate with former Soviet republics in the Caspian Sea basin and Central Asia for their oil and gas supplies. On the heels of the Russian–Ukrainian gas blockade, Russia and Uzbekistan came to an agreement that Russia's Gazprom would increase the rate it pays Uzbekistan for its gas, and Uzbekistan, in exchange, would allow Russia a monopoly of the existing and projected gas exports crossing the Uzbek border into Kazakhstan (Socor 2009d). There, a Soviet-era pipeline system carries gas from Uzbekistan and Turkmenistan through Kazakhstan into Russia for consumption or resale to Europe. Russian and Uzbek leaders have agreed to improve this pipeline infrastructure which currently operates below capacity. Uzbekistan may still sell gas to its neighbors, Kyrgyzstan, Tajikistan, and Kazakhstan, but Gazprom will get the most significant portion. Russia's policies also prioritize accessing energy resources in other parts of the world such as the Middle East, the Barents Sea, and the Arctic Region. There has been growing interest in the world's seabed as a possible source of minerals and energy, and there is speculation that there may be significant energy resources under the Arctic Sea. As the Arctic ice sheet retreats (due to global climate change, many scientists would point out), those energy resources would become more accessible with the possibility of new, ice-free shipping routes. In a nearly made-for-Hollywood moment in August 2007, Russian explorers traveled in two mini-submarines to plant a rust-proof, titanium flag on the Arctic seabed 14 000 feet (4200 m) below the North Pole to stake a claim for Russia (see Figure 3.3). Sergei Balyasnikov of the Russian Arctic and Antarctic Institute was quoted by BBC News as saying "It's a very important move for Russia to demonstrate its potential

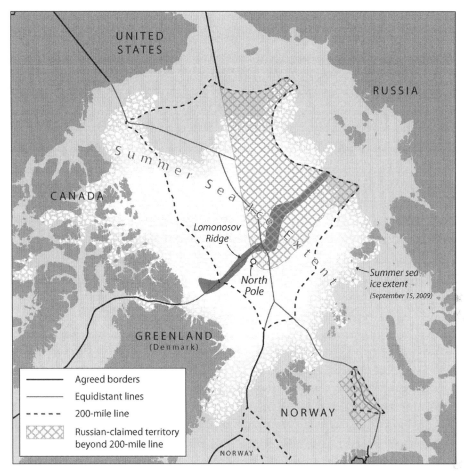

Figure 3.3 Russia's territorial claim of the North Pole. International Boundaries Research Unit (2008). Ice extent data from National Oceanic and Atmospheric Administration (NOAA).

in the Arctic ... It's like putting a flag on the Moon" (BBC News 2007). Russia's territorial claim is based on maritime territory associated with the underwater Lomonosov Ridge. Russia argued that the ridge is an extension of Russian continental territory, but this point has been disputed by much of the international community and in particular by the US, Canada, and Denmark – countries which have also made claims in the Arctic region.

The gas "war" between Russia and Ukraine has caused several European countries to question the reliability of Russia as an energy supplier. Germany, for instance, has a particular dilemma in terms of its energy security since it relies on Russia's gas more than any other European country. In Germany, 40% of the gas consumed and 40% of the crude oil is imported from Russia, and those levels are increasing (Socor 2009a). Germany has not developed significant alternative energy infrastructure such as Liquified Natural Gas terminals and remains particularly dependent on Russia's gas supplies. This is a key reason why Germany supports Russia's initiative to build the Nord Stream pipeline which would serve as an additional link to Russia's gas supply. Other European countries have pursued different energy strategies. France, for example, has developed its nuclear power system and was relatively unaffected when Russia shut off the gas. Several Eastern European countries have taken the opportunity provided by the gas blockade to promote the development of a Southern Corridor ensemble of pipelines. These pipelines would carry gas from the Caspian Basin to Europe and bypass Russia altogether. The main pipeline among these is the Nabucco pipeline which would initially carry gas from Azerbaijan and eventually from Turkmenistan along a route through Georgia, Turkey, Bulgaria, Romania, Hungary, and Austria to connect with other infrastructure in Germany. Recent, promising audits of gas deposits in Turkmenistan suggest that this pipeline plan would be well worth the investment required from European states to construct this pipeline. Other proposed and planned pipelines in the Southern Corridor include the Turkey–Greece–Italy Interconnector, the Trans-Caspian pipeline, and the White Stream pipeline which would carry gas from Azerbaijan to Georgia, the Black Sea, Romania, and on into Western Europe (Socor 2009c). Meanwhile, Russia has been negotiating with its Caspian neighbors to purchase their oil and gas at or near world market prices. This situation raises the question if any newly constructed pipelines could even be economically competitive.

The 18-day gas blockade against Ukraine left Russia to reflect on its concerns about power. Russia's former President-turned-Prime Minister Putin focused on three, interrelated themes during his presidency: Russia's pursuit (or reclaiming) of greatness, control of energy resources, and positioning its military forces to underscore state power. Yet as Pavel Baev (2008) has observed, Russian military forces can remain strong only with a substantial injection of investment, most likely from energy wealth. Russia's energy wealth can only be sustained with new investment, mostly likely from clients in Western Europe and with steep Russian investment in its energy-rich, former Soviet neighbors in the Caucasus and Central Asia. Given these contradictory demands on limited resources, Russia has not demonstrated agility in shaping its energy-related endeavors into effective political or military power. In speculating about scenarios for post-Putin Russia, Baev goes on to suggest that a "more of the same" approach to state-building after Putin will likely face the reality that shortages in domestic energy supply and distribution may lead to internal political instability among the leadership and/or among the populace. If Russia pursues a "hard power" approach and opts to flex its military muscle to assert its claims to greatness, Baev continues, it is unlikely to be able to substitute energy wealth for a decaying industrial economy that is scattered geographically like an archipelago across Russia's vast and thinly populated territory (Dienes 2002). Baev also notes that past Russian aggression often stemmed more from desperation than from boldness. He quotes Dominique Lieven (2002):

> ...what seemed like aggression and expansion to foreigners might in fact be born of a sense of weakness and vulnerability. Indeed, looking at Russian foreign policy over the centuries, vulnerability and weakness were often at least as powerful a factor as an instinct for territorial expansion.
>
> *(Lieven 2002, pp. 266–267, quoted by Baev 2008, p. 160)*

Russia's sense of a loss of empire and a desire to recapture international prestige and regional clout (Trenin 2002, 2007) may have contributed to the decision to shut off gas supplies to Ukraine. The objective may have been to demonstrate the importance of Russia as an energy supplier, but instead the result is that European countries realize the importance of developing alternative energy infrastructure to reduce their dependence on Russian energy. Energy resources might motivate Russia to use military force as well, for example, as a pretence for Russia to move into Georgia again to influence control of the Baku–Tblisi–Ceyhan pipeline (Felgenhauer 2009). This pipeline already represents a low-level conflict between the US, which supported its construction, operation, and security, and Russia which views the pipeline as an unnecessary invasion of its "backyard" (Kandiyoti 2008). Clearly, oil and gas pipelines are laden with power dynamics. They reveal a great deal about the spatial reach or scale of multiple forms of power in different places.

Breaking the oil addiction

It is generally accepted that the US is taking the lead in an addiction to oil. How do we break the addiction? Liquified natural gas (LNG) comes to the fore as a particularly promising "bridge" fuel that may ease the transition to a post-oil way of life. Production and use of LNG is already on the rise, and supplies are relatively abundant. LNG is versatile, can be refined for multiple uses (including pure hydrogen which might fuel power cells), emits less pollution and CO_2 than either coal or oil, and it is also another commodity for big oil companies to sell in the face of increasing difficulty to replace every barrel of oil sold with a newly discovered barrel of oil (Roberts 2004; see also Smil 2003, ch. 4). For a long time, gas was considered a waste product of oil drilling. As a gas, it is more complicated and expensive to package and transport with minimal leakage. Gas reserves in remote parts of Siberia, for example, are "stranded" since it is too expensive to get a sufficient amount to consumers. The process of liquefying natural gas eased these difficulties since it allowed gas to be transported by tanker. LNG could advance progress in a transitional energy economy, for example, to fuel gas-fired turbines. Since these turbines can be built in a range of sizes, they are a form of distributed power system that could serve to get individual companies and entire communities off the centralized power grid system (Roberts 2004). However, society would still find itself vulnerable to pipeline security risks (just like oil), and most societies would still need to find an external source to supply this energy (just like oil).

Wind and solar power offer other options for alternative energy. Technology advances in wind power have increased the output capacity per turbine, project size has been increasing, and both of these points have led to increased investment in this sector in the US (Bolinger 2008). As wind turbine efficiency has increased linearly, wind farm energy output has been increasing exponentially (Vick 2007). Wind power is currently the least expensive energy resource following natural gas and coal. The most significant obstacles to the expansion of wind power include the limited availability of transmission and siting and permitting conflicts (Bolinger 2008). With governmental assistance in the form of state tax and financial incentives, new or expanded installations could offer wind power as a competitive resource option, particularly in regions with strong wind resources (Bird *et al.* 2003). The electric grid in the US will need continued investment to serve continuing load growth regardless of the source of energy, so proponents of wind power point out that the relatively incremental transmission required to connect wind energy to the electric power system would be well worth the investment (US Department of Energy 2008).

Most of the recent research related to solar energy has to do with technical limitations, improvements, limitations, and theoretical limits. Some believe the technology is in its infancy and will require increases in efficiency and decreases in cost if solar technologies are ever to be competitive in supplying world energy needs (Service 2005). Proponents of solar energy focus on the development of technologies more than the implementation of large-scale projects (such as wind turbine farms). The US Department of Energy's stance on solar energy, for example, emphasizes research and development in photovoltaic technologies that will enable solar power to achieve "grid parity" or competitiveness with other energies. The Department of Energy also aims to address regulatory, technical, and economic barriers that hinder the integration of solar power into existing energy systems and to find ways to encourage adoption of solar technologies (Solar Energies Technologies

Program 2008). Solar energy seems to have fewer obstacles to its advancement than do other renewable energy sources:

Biomass, geothermal, and energy from ocean waves also have potential. But biomass's potential is limited by the need to use arable land to grow food; geothermal energy's potential is limited by high drilling costs; and ocean power has been stalled in part by high construction costs.

(Service 2005, p. 549)

Both wind and solar are promising, but they require new infrastructure – not as familiar or parallel to the current petroleum-based energy network. Wind and solar are unlikely to be as useful as fossil fuels for transportion unless or until plug-in hybrid cars become a widespread reality. Before biofuels can meet a significant portion of the transportation energy demand, several steps would need to be taken to ensure stability in such an energy system: the market would have to be expanded, policies would need to be in place that facilitate the transition to next-generation technologies, sustainability principles would need to guide the protection of soil and water resources and ecosystem services, and international trade in biofuels should aim to distribute the benefits of biofuels equitably among stakeholders (Worldwatch Institute 2007).

Regardless, in February 2009, President Obama declared that the US would double its supply of renewable energy over the next three years. If hydropower is excluded from this definition of renewable energies, the task is doable but arguably will make only a marginal difference:

The conversion of electricity into oil terms is straightforward: one barrel of oil contains the energy equivalent of 1.64 megawatt-hours of electricity. Thus, 45 493 000 megawatt-hours divided by 1.64 megawatt-hours per barrel of oil equals 27.7 million barrels of oil equivalent from solar and wind for all of 2008.

Now divide that 27.7 million barrels by 365 days and you find that solar and wind sources are providing the equivalent of 76 000 barrels of oil per day. America's total primary energy use is about 47.4 million barrels of oil equivalent per day.

Of that 47.4 million barrels of oil equivalent, oil itself has the biggest share – we consume about 19 million barrels per day. Natural gas is the second-biggest contributor, supplying the equivalent of 11.9 million barrels of oil, while coal provides the equivalent of 11.5 million barrels of oil per day. The balance comes from nuclear power (about 3.8 million barrels per day), and hydropower (about 1.1 million barrels), with smaller contributions coming from wind, solar, geothermal, wood waste, and other sources.

(Bryce 2009)

Even doubling wind and solar power – and doubling it again – will not dramatically reduce US dependence on fossil fuels.

Suggestions abound for how to reduce dependence on oil, especially in the US, and deal with an impending radical shift in energy availability. Governments (the US government in particular) should transition to more appropriate vehicles first by improving efficiency of combustion engines (Roberts 2004; Deffeyes 2005) and by promoting electric cars and affordable plug-in hybrid vehicles (Sandalow 2008). Making natural gas and LNG more widely available and usable will be an important step in our energy transition. Another obvious solution is energy conservation through improved efficiency of appliances, light bulbs, electricity systems, architecture and in lower consumption levels of material commodities that require high energy inputs and transportation. We are reminded to think systematically: "Regulations requiring improved energy efficiency look attractive on paper ... However, it is not something for nothing. Requiring better automobile highway mileage has to consider the entire system, including petroleum refining" (Deffeyes 2005, p. 181). Initiating and implementing these practices would rely on sound public policy. On this point, Smil has observed:

Examination of historical trends shows that many critical transitions took place even in spite of deliberate policies, or that planning and assorted ways of government intervention have not played critical roles in the diffusion of new conversions or new consumption patterns. On the other hand, many energy-related developments would not have taken place without such interventions. These are the challenges of public policy that never go away.

(Smil 2003, p. 367)

This observation returns us to points made by Sarewitz (2004) in Chapter 2 about how some political issues become "scientized" and overwhelmed by an abundance of scientific input. Scientific information does not necessarily provide a clear guide to decision-making particularly in value-laden situations where a variety of stakeholders have competing interests in a particular outcome. In the same vein, advances in technology do not necessarily lead to changes in policy, nor does the establishment of policy necessarily lead to changes in behavior. The very non-linearity of actions pertaining to environmental issues, like many other issues, can serve to highlight dimensions of power that drive, hinder, promote, or obfuscate opinions and information for a host of interests.

The controversy around ethanol as an alternative fuel source is an excellent example to highlight disjuncture among policy initiatives, as a form of organized power at the state level, economic power reflected in networks of exchange, and ideological power reflected in the value and meaning that society attaches to scientific understanding. Here again, we see that not only are different forms of power involved in shaping the emergence of ethanol, but we also see that interactions of these forms of power create spatial scales at which power is either reinforced or depleted.

Last call for ethanol?

In December 2007, the US Congress passed the Energy Independence and Security Act of 2007. The bill aims to increase fuel efficiency standards for vehicles, improve energy savings by improving efficiency standards for lighting and building, increase energy savings in government and public institutions, accelerate research and development of alternative energies, and advance carbon sequestration strategies. One section of the bill is titled "Energy Security Through Increased Production of Biofuels," and it sets guidelines for levels and types of biofuels production. The bill recognizes different types of ethanol including that made from corn starch, cellulose, sugar, and waste materials including crop residue and animal waste among other types of biofuels. The optimism for ethanol is reflected in the anticipated production increase from 4 billion gallons in 2006 to 36 billion gallons in 2022 – 16 billion of which is to be derived from corn. Additionally, The Food and Energy Security Act of 2007 (also known as The Farm Bill of 2007) also gives a significant boost to ethanol in the US. It provides a tax credit for cellulosic biofuels production from agricultural waste, wood chips, perennial energy crops, and other non-food feedstocks through 2012. Funds are to be allocated as follows:

... $320 million for new loan guarantee program for the development and construction of commercial-scale biorefineries; provides $300 million in the Bioenergy Program to provide assistance to biofuel production plants for the purchase of feedstocks; provides $118 million for biomass research and development efforts; reauthorizes and provides $250 million for grants and loan guarantees for renewable energy and energy efficiency projects; and authorizes a new program, the Biomass Crop Assistance Program to help producers transition to new energy crops for biofuel production.

(Zimmerman 2008)

Both of these bills pave the way for the expansion of biofuels production in the US by simultaneously promoting the supply of biofuels materials and the construction of refineries that will turn these materials into usable biofuel.

Proponents of ethanol argue that this biofuel provides an alternative to dependence on potentially unreliable or politically risky international supplies (see, for example, Figure 3.4), it supports domestic agricultural productivity, and it may help to reduce greenhouse gas emissions as a substitute for fossil fuel. Two other advantages of ethanol are its portability (in contrast to

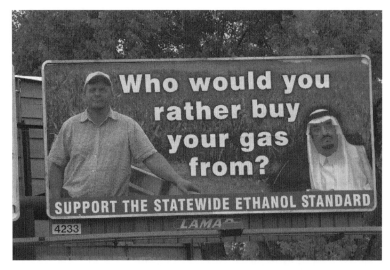

Figure 3.4 Ideological power of ethanol. In 2006, this image, featuring an unlabeled picture of the former king of Saudi Arabia, appeared on billboards throughout Missouri. The billboards were paid for by the Missouri Corn Growers' Association which promoted a bill that would have joined Missouri with Hawaii, Minnesota, Montana and Washington in mandating the use of ethanol in gas. Available at http://www.newstribune.com/articles/2006/04/26/news_state/249news05.txt, accessed 4 December 2009. Photographer: Stephen Brooks/News Tribune photo; used with permission.

some other forms of alternative energy such as wind and solar power) and the fact that ethanol is a relatively high quality fuel for combustion engines that requires fewer additives than regular gasoline (Smil 2003). However, ethanol made from corn, either despite or because of its promotion in the Energy Independence and Security Act of 2007, has attracted particular critique as having more drawbacks than advantages. First, it may not be realistic to expect that growing corn for ethanol can really serve as a substitute for fossil fuel imports. Dedicating all of the US corn production to ethanol would only meet 12% of American gasoline demand (Hill *et al.* 2006). Put another way by Smil (2003), "if the US vehicles were to run solely on corn-derived ethanol ... the country would have to plant corn on an area 20% larger than its total of currently cultivated cropland!" (p. 264). Second, expanding corn cultivation for ethanol would mean reduced production of other food crops and of wood for paper and timber, and in many countries, arable land is already limited or under pressure. Third, corn is already one of the most input-intensive crops in terms of pesticides and herbicides, and corn production contributes more than most crops to soil erosion and water and air pollution. Fourth, corn production also requires considerable amounts of fossil fuels in the use of machinery for cultivation and inorganic fertilizers. Hybrid strains of corn – the standard in the US – require even higher levels of energy inputs (Pimentel 2003). One gallon of corn ethanol requires nearly 30% more energy to create than it has to offer (Pimentel 2003), so the overall energy balance of corn-based ethanol is negative. Other forms of biofuels do not have such a long list of detractors. Biodiesel from soybeans, for example, provides over 90% more energy than is spent in its production, and it generates lower levels of greenhouse gases than corn-based ethanol since soybeans require fewer inputs than corn and less energy to process into fuel (Hill *et al*. 2006). Fifth, there are concerns about greenhouse gas emissions associated with ethanol. Scientific studies of ethanol have found that technologies to derive ethanol from corn require less petroleum than the production of gasoline, but the total amount of greenhouse gas emissions of ethanol production are the same as those for gasoline (Farrell 2006). If farmers wish to produce more crops to offset crops diverted to biofuel use, they most likely will convert forest and grassland to arable land that can be farmed. This land use change generates additional greenhouse gas emissions since the forest or grassland vegetation is no longer there to sequester or hold CO_2. Researchers have found that when this land use change is accounted for in global level models, corn-based ethanol almost doubles greenhouse gas emissions over a 30-year period (Searchinger *et al*. 2008).

The federal mandate to increase ethanol production is already evident on the landscape. The number of ethanol factories in the US swelled from 50 in 2000 to nearly 140, and almost 60 more are under construction. Yet in some areas there is a backlash against ethanol of all kinds for one simple reason: water. A factory that produces 50 million gallons of biofuel a year consumes nearly 500 gallons of water *per minute* for boiling, cooling, and to compensate for loss of water through evaporation and discharge. As reported in *The Economist*:

Residents went to court in Missouri to halt a $165m facility being built by Gulfstream Bioflex Energy LLC which was projected to draw 1.3m gallons of water every day from the Ozark aquifer. Projects are being challenged in Minnesota, Iowa, Nebraska, Kansas and in central Illinois, where eight ethanol facilities are situated over the Mahomet aquifer. Demand for corn is such that more land is also being ploughed up in drier regions of the Great Plains states to the west of the corn belt, where irrigation is required, increasing water demand further.

(The Economist 2008a)

Even though newer ethanol plants use much less water than older designs, the issue of water demand for ethanol production adds to the list of disadvantages.

A final disadvantage of corn-based ethanol involves ripple effects in the global food supply. Corn-based ethanol has come under particularly sharp critique since corn is a food crop, and food prices have been on the rise in recent years. The Mexican tortilla riots demonstrate a link between ethanol promotion and food supply. Tortillas are a basic staple for much of Mexico's population. In early 2007, the price of tortillas more than doubled leading to massive public riots (*The Economist* 2007). Tortillas in Mexico are made from domestically grown white corn (maize). Industrial uses of corn, such as the production of animal feed and syrup, have tended to use the yellow corn which is more common in the US. As demand for yellow corn for ethanol production increased in the US, so did the price of yellow corn. Mexico's industrial users of corn shifted to using white corn which rapidly became more scarce and expensive beyond the reach of many citizens.

The case of ethanol illustrates interactions among different dimensions of power. The Energy Independence and Security Act of 2007 represents organized ideological power and a form of political power. Ideological power captures knowledge that "cannot be totally tested by experience, and therein lies its distinctive power to persuade and dominate" (Mann 1986, p. 23). That bill is a form of ideological power in its promotion of a particular set of values and meanings: dependence on foreign oil is "bad," domestic energy supplies are "good," technological advances will preclude any need to alter consumption, etc. As a legal document, the bill does not cite scientific literature to support or question these values, but instead takes these understandings about energy as a given. The bill also represents political power in that it is establishing the interests of the state in terms of energy security and mandating how energy security is to be achieved. Economic power is also implied since promoting ethanol production and use elevates a particular set of interests that will have increased influence over networks of production, distribution, and consumption. For example, several powerful business organizations that could benefit from the promotion of a national ethanol program contributed financial support to the passing of The Energy Independence and Security Act of 2007 and The Food and Energy Security Act of 2007:

"...Archer Daniels Midland Co. spent $440,000 in the first six months of 2007 to lobby on the farm bill, the energy bill, renewable energy issues, and other regulatory and general trade issues. The Renewable Fuels Association spent $310,000 in lobbying on the farm bill, energy bill and a number of other measures of interest to the renewable fuels industry. The American Coalition for Ethanol reportedly spent $20,000 on lobbyists, and the National Ethanol Vehicle Coalition spent $30,000."

(Schill 2007)

These organizations were able to organize their efforts and political skill to bring about results that will serve to enhance their power yet further. Additionally, ethanol factories, which are likely to be controlled by larger energy-related interests and certain government agencies such as the US Department of Agriculture are empowered by this bill. Corn farmers, on the other hand, are unlikely to receive significant profits and may in fact have difficult decisions to make between subsidies for biofuel production and conservation practices.

As landscapes, particularly those in rural areas, change in response to the political promotion of ethanol, we can learn a great deal about the power dynamics driving these changes by considering who is establishing the environmental values inscribed on these landscapes (Marsden *et al*. 1996). Extractive spaces, such as agricultural areas intended for the production of biofuel crops, are constructed by simultaneously erasing the unique histories of these places while establishing a new idea of these places as sites of commodity supply (Bridge 2001). Paying attention to power dynamics in areas of resource management helps us to understand who or what is benefitting from the valuation, distribution, and usage of natural resources (Bridge and Jonas 2002). Dominant understandings of how a society values and uses natural resources are reinforced and carried out by particular governance structures, regulations, corporations, and transnational groups. The involvement of both government and business actors raises questions about how values are assigned to natural resources and environmental services (and whether or not prices should be determined for these items) as well as who should be involved in making environmental decisions (Liverman 2004). Economic decisions, especially pertaining to environmental issues, are not distinct from political decisions. Economic notions that are generally accepted, such as the prioritization of markets as a natural means to regulate exchange, the importance of private property rights, and the commodification of everything (the idea that everything has a price tag) – all core principles of neoliberal economic processes (Heynen and Robbins 2005) – are protected and enabled by the state. Therefore, economic decisions and environmental politics work together to bring about environmental change (McCarthy and Prudham 2004). That change, however, is unevenly distributed. What is more, institutional decisions about the meaning and value of natural resources may seem appropriate at one scale (e.g., the narrative of ethanol as a sound means of reducing global greenhouse gas emissions), but undercut alternative ways of valuing environmental resources at other levels (e.g., access to white corn for food in Mexico).

Establishing the meaning and value of ethanol at the state level empowers certain interests while depleting others' ability to organize or respond effectively. The ethanol boom is not limited to the US. Many EU countries, China, Russia, and economically developing countries in sub-Saharan Africa and Asia are also caught up in the ethanol frenzy. This state-level political support of biofuels enables the expansion of economic power as it pertains to the production, distribution, and consumption of biofuels. State-level support for biofuels promotes economic activities such as agricultural production of crops used for biofuels, the development of biofuel production facilities, transportation networks, and legal codification of rules that guide these economic interactions. Simultaneously, the increasing transboundary flow of biofuel materials, the standardization of biofuel products, and the predictability of these exchanges is merging with established patterns of global fossil fuel networks (Mol 2007). This globalization and expansion of biofuel production and use is leading to increased environmental vulnerability in places under pressure to expand agricultural production of biofuel materials. In addition to the environmental impacts of increased corn production for ethanol, expanded biofuels production has raised concerns about deforestation, decreased biodiversity, monocropping and decreased ecosystem resilience, land and soil degradation, and water pollution. Although there are alternatives such as growing low-input crops, such as jatropha, on marginal lands and favoring local processing and income, these are not the dominant form of biofuels production. When we consider that Archer Daniels Midland produced about 25% of the ethanol in the US in 2005 and was the second largest biodiesel producer in Europe (Hunt *et al.* 2006, p. 72), we begin to see the power wielded by corporate interests and enabled by political decisions to support and promote biofuels. Meanwhile, other groups are rendered less powerful. Small farmers, farming cooperatives, and non-governmental organizations cannot compete with large, influential actors like Archer Daniels Midland that can organize beyond the state, and those smaller actors face disempowerment.

Conclusion

This chapter began with a fictitious story about a new algae-to-oil conversion technology. That scenario seems wildly dramatic and unlikely, but it may be worth considering. One researcher discovered that an alga, *Chlamydomonas reinhardtii*, has promising hydrogen-producing potential (Roberts 2004, pp. 188–190). This development of a single-organism, two-stage photobiological hydrogen gas production process does not generate any harmful or polluting by-products (Melis *et al.* 2000; Melis and Happe 2001) but appears to accomplish sustained hydrogen gas production. Also, at least one website that focuses on alternative fuel and transportation recently offered a story with the headline "Fungi Discovered in Patagonia Rainforest Could Be Used to Make Biodiesel" (Williams 2008). These stories help us think about current arrangements of power enabled by the control of (or lack of access to) reserves and flows of oil and, to a similar extent, natural gas and other energy sources. If such a new energy source were discovered and widely available, what kinds of established power might be threatened, and how would the adoption of a new energy source alter spatial scales at which energy-related political, economic, ideological, and military power operates?

This chapter has considered several dimensions and spatial scales of power in relation to oil and energy issues. The geography of oil is more nuanced than a mere cataloguing of which countries have oil and sufficient military strength to defend those reserves. Oil-exporting states, such as OPEC members and Russia, use political and economic power to leverage their position in the international community. We also see substate forms of military power such as the National Liberation Army in Colombia increasing their ability to organize and exercise power. Other localized groups of people, such as populations along pipeline routes, tend to be unempowered by the expansion of energy networks despite the fact they live close to negative environmental impacts of energy transport. Physical infrastructure such as pipelines and refineries play important roles not only in the distribution of energy, its benefits and negative environmental impacts, but these features also influence political and economic decisions. Examining ethanol as an example of an arguably alternative fuel, we see how the political promotion of a particular form of energy has implications for what kinds of actors are able to organize and exercise power with a particular spatial reach. Despite the problematic reality of shifting to ethanol as a fuel, political promotion of ethanol rests on the power of ideological meaning of ethanol as a useful supplement or replacement for fossil fuels and as a solution to greenhouse gas emissions. This political support for ethanol enables certain actors to organize and exercise economic power over the production, distribution, and consumption of biofuels materials and products. Organization of power at transnational levels brings to bear economic influence with which more localized groups are unable to compete. Political support for biofuels, moreover, dictates a particular value on places where biofuels commodities are produced. Rather than maintaining locally defined meaning and value, these places are reinscribed as sites of commodity production and are subsumed into regional and global networks of energy provision. In these ways, organized political and economic power lead to place-specific environmental, social, and economic change.

Predictions about our energy future vary wildly. So how should we proceed? Smil (2003) is skeptical of forecasting since, in his view "Typical forecasts offer little else but more or less linear extensions of business as usual" (p. 178). Instead, he argues that a practical strategy would be to generate normative scenarios that concentrate on what *should* happen rather than what *might* happen. This kind of approach requires us to make value judgments up front. Normative scenarios are, ideally, flexible rather than rigid and "feature no-regret prescriptions" (p. 180). He offers this suggestion:

When facing so many uncertainties and when unable to foresee not just inevitable surprises but also the course of many key trends, we should pursue any effective means that bring us closer to those goals. That means adopting the ying-yang approach to reality: acting as complexifying minimalists rather than as simplifying maximalists, being determined but flexible, eclectic but discriminating.

(Smil 2003, p. 367)

In other words, we are encouraged to pursue a variety of options, to recognize the value of using minimal inputs to achieve usable outcomes, and not to exclude any particular option (e.g., nuclear energy) categorically. To that end, Smil advocates a radical change in society's attitudes about consumption and humans' place within the biosphere. He champions an approach that moderates demand rather than increasing supply. Such adjustments to consumption and energy use in the rich world are, at heart, moral issues rather than issues of economy or technology. Smil's conclusions about the future of energy use remind us of the underlying and often unrecognized role of ideological power that shapes expectations and assumptions about energy consumption among affluent societies. This power may not be insurmountable, but only a stronger ideology, perhaps one infused with economic undertones, would be necessary to change dominant consumption patterns.

Endnote

1 Thanks to Eric McGlinchey at George Mason University for this scenario.

4

Food security

Gallons of freshwater consumed in the production of a gallon of milk and beer, respectively: 1,000, 300

– Harper's *Index, May 2009*

Square miles of African farmland acquired by Chinese investors since 2006: 10,851

– Harper's *Index, August 2009*

Introduction

When we think of security, we might think first of international relations and conflict, military concerns, or systems that monitor borders, personal movements, and computer networks. We might not initially think of farming, food processing, or access to food. This chapter considers food security at multiple spatial scales and ways in which food supply is connected to power. Three key themes are relevant to a consideration of food security: stability, access, and quality. Beginning at the global scale, this chapter examines climate change and implications for the world food supply. Yet food is not evenly distributed around the globe, so we must then consider issues of access to food. We will look at how food became an international policy issue, how the definition of food security has changed over time and how it has also been challenged. Examining issues pertaining to access to food draws our attention to the question "Who controls the food supply?" and leads us to investigate aspects of food quality and content. Asking the question "What are we eating?" brings the discussion full circle back to the overarching themes of the book, namely, power and spatial scale.

Climate change and food supply

If the earth's atmosphere, precipitation, and temperature patterns are changing, what kind of effects might there be on global food supply? (Lal *et al.* 2005). Projections of climate change imply impacts on soil quality, water resources, temperature patterns, duration of growing seasons, and net primary productivity in different places. Changing concentrations of soil carbon and atmospheric CO_2 could influence agricultural productivity in specific places while the global demand for food increases or shifts. Carbon trading schemes could further influence agricultural practices and patterns of food production, for example, if arable land is shifted from supporting food production to supporting carbon sink forests. These physical and social processes are likely to result in new patterns of food production and concerns for food security. Climate change will affect agriculture positively in some places and negatively in others depending in part on latitude. Climate change can exacerbate processes that degrade soil quality such as hydrolysis (the leaching of silica), cheluviation (the removal of aluminum and iron), ferrolysis (oxidation of clay), dissolution of minerals by increased acids, and reverse weathering altering clay formation (Lal 2005). The decline in soil quality resulting from such processes is likely to be steeper in the tropics where soils tend to have low productivity and do not respond well to inputs such as fertilizers.

Current trends show that population growth is greatest in several economically developing countries. Not only is malnutrition already a significant issue in many of these places, but many of them also include significant tropical areas which may be more negatively affected by climate change processes (Parry *et al.* 2004; Rosenzweig and Hillel 2005). Alternatively, increased levels of atmospheric CO_2 and an associated increase in nitrogen fixation could help to increase biomass productivity and contribute to a higher rate of new soil formation (Lal 2005). Climate change processes are likely to generate changes in water supply and demand. Arid and semi-arid regions may be particularly susceptible to drought that follows the plow as warmer temperatures, water evaporation, and land use techniques combine (Glantz 1994). Increased rates of urbanization and uneven population increase may exacerbate water stress in some places. Likewise, warmer temperatures are likely to contribute to thriving pest populations and a negative impact on agricultural productivity (Rosenzweig and Hillel 2005, ch. 10).

There is uncertainty in how global climate models can aid an understanding of climate change impacts on smaller scale agricultural systems (Mearns 2003). Spatial variations in agricultural productivity resulting from global climate change, such as the expansion of food production in places like Canada and Russia and possible decline in food production in places like Indonesia and

Bangladesh (which might become inundated with rising sea levels), could balance out leading to the conclusion that "global warming does not threaten global food availability in the 21st century" (Tweeten 2005, p. 658).

Global availability of food, even if it remains relatively stable, is only part of a much larger question about food security. The availability of food at one spatial scale does not necessarily mean that everyone has equal or reliable access to food. The following section considers how the definition of food security has changed over time and why the widely accepted definition raises concerns about health and justice.

Food security: definition and policy approaches

The roots of the concept of food security may be traced back to US President Franklin D. Roosevelt's 1941 State of the Union address. In that speech, later known as the Four Freedoms Speech, he promoted the idea of "freedom from want," an idea which helped to bring about the 1948 Universal Declaration of Human Rights and its recognition of the right to food (Rae *et al.* 2007). The International Covenant on Economic, Social and Cultural Rights (ICESCR), which was ratified by 156 states and entered into force in 1976, went beyond recognizing the right to food as a human right. It referred to "freedom from hunger" with the understanding that states would protect people's right to life by acting to keep people from starving. Other conventions, such as the 1979 Convention on the Elimination of all Forms of Discrimination against Women (CEDAW) and The Convention on the Rights of the Child (CRC) of 1989 also integrated concerns about access to proper nutrition. The 1998 Rome Statute of the International Criminal Court identifies the intentional starvation of civilians as a war crime. Other international conventions have also recognized and reaffirmed a universal right to food.

By 1999, the Committee on Economic, Social, and Cultural Rights, under the Economic and Social Council of the United Nations, had refined the idea of the right to adequate food: "the availability of food in quantity and quality sufficient to satisfy the dietary needs of individuals, free from adverse substances, and acceptable within a given culture" and "the accessibility of such food in ways that are sustainable and that do not interfere with the enjoyment of other human rights" (paragraph 8). Currently, the most widely used definition of food security comes from a 1996 Food and Agricultural Organization statement: "food security exists when all people at all times, have physical and economic access to sufficient, safe and nutritious food to meet their dietary needs and food preferences for an active and healthy life" (FAO 1996). This is the current standard for evaluating food security and guiding relevant policy.

The definition of food security has changed over time, but it has also shifted in spatial scale. Initially, food security was understood in terms of the statistically available amount of food on a global scale. Food security was understood as the responsibility of each state and its provision for people within its borders. That is, it was understood that it was the responsibility of each state to obtain a sufficient amount of the global supply in order to feed its populace. As more careful attention was given to the definition of food security, it became clear the availability of food at the global scale or even at the state scale was not sufficient to ensure food security to all people. After all, famines occur in countries where food is plentiful.

The definition of food security has shifted from availability of food to individual access. Recent work on food security reflects this trend and has considered, for example, gender dimensions of food security such as ways that societal differences between men and women contribute to different levels of access to food. Research has considered gender inequities in different societies, such as women's limited entitlement, education, and expenditure as well their role as care givers, as factors of food security (Ramachandran 2007). Women's status influences children's food security (Guha-Khasnobis and Hazarika 2007). Other work has considered urban–rural differences in individuals' access to food. For example, supermarkets are the retail end of the food commodity chain. They influence the food security of both rural food producers who supply urban markets and urban consumers who rely on supermarkets for their food supply (Arda 2007). Just looking at these few examples, we begin to appreciate that food security involves power: which groups in society have control over their own food supply or that of other people? Who is in a position to make decisions about who gets to eat and what they are eating?

Beyond considering multiple spatial scales of access to food, the question of nutrition, not just sufficient food, has also been examined in contexts of humanitarian crises (Webb and Thorne-Lyman 2007). As long as people get sufficient food during a crisis, is that enough? Probably not. Food security is not just about quantity of food, but it is also about quality of food. Micronutrients are especially important during times of crisis and stress since malnutrition is likely to contribute to disaster mortality through disease:

Disorders such as scurvy (deficiency of vitamin C), pellagra (niacin deficiency), beriberi (thiamine deficiency) and angular stomatitis (riboflavin and other deficiencies) have all emerged as problems in humanitarian settings over the past decade – despite the fact that these were long thought of as historical curiosities.

Today, if just one individual is diagnosed with these disorders it is assumed that a population-wide threat must exist, usually because of restricted access to certain types of food.

(Webb and Thorne-Lyman 2007, p. 249)

Malnutrition in the first 2 years of life has irreversible health effects, and hunger is recognized by the World Health Organization as the single most significant threat to the world's public health (see Figure 4.1). There are several ways to fight hunger and malnutrition including food supplements, improved hygiene to prevent the spread of diseases exacerbated by malnutrition, and breast feeding advice and support. In terms of international aid to address hunger and malnutrition:

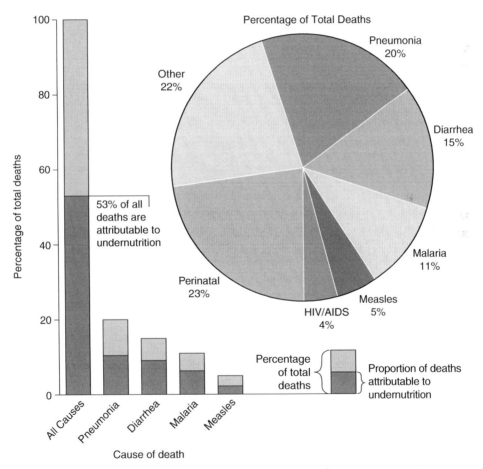

Figure 4.1 Child deaths attributable to undernutrition in comparison to other causes. World Health Organization (2003) Caulfield, L. E. *et al.* (2004).

... money for improving nutrition would be the most effective sort of aid around. At the moment, roughly $300m of aid goes to basic nutrition each year, less than $2 for each child below two in the 20 worst affected countries. In contrast, HIV/AIDS, which causes fewer deaths than child malnutrition, received $2.2 billion – $67 per person with HIV in all countries (including rich ones).

(The Economist *2008b*)

Improving food security would not seem to be an insurmountable challenge compared to other public health issues, and a first step would be to identify who is most food insecure.

Who is vulnerable to food insecurity? Poor people are the most vulnerable. In an early contribution to the literature on food security, Amartya Sen examined how poverty and famine are linked (Sen 1981). He discussed poverty as a complex category that requires us to think about how we identify "the poor" (Is poverty absolute? Is poverty relative?) and the fact that there can be different groups of poor in a given society. Sen also differentiated between starvation and famine. In his work he describes starvation as an ongoing condition of people living on inadequate food, but famines involve widespread death resulting from inadequate food. He argues that "Famines imply starvation, but not vice versa. And starvation implies poverty, but not vice versa" (p. 39). He continues:

A food-centered view tells us rather little about starvation. It does not tell us how starvation can develop even without a decline in food availability. Nor does it tell us – even when starvation is accompanied by a fall in food supply – why some groups had to starve while others could feed themselves. The over-all food picture is too remote an economic variable to tell us much about starvation. On the other hand, if we look at the food going to *particular* groups, then of course we can say a good deal about starvation. But, then, one is not far from just describing the starvation itself, rather than explaining what happened. If some people had to starve, then clearly, they didn't have enough food, but the question is: *why* didn't they have food?

(Sen 1981, p. 154)

Sen promotes a focus on entitlement, or the variation in conditions of ownership and exchange, rather than on food supplies. Food supply is easier to quantify than entitlement which in part explains why it is easier to focus on issues of food supply. However, entitlement allows insights into power dynamics in a given society and enables an analysis of who is able to have sufficient access to food supplies and who is vulnerable to inadequate food supplies and why.

As we consider the issue of food security, it is useful to examine the idea of vulnerability more closely. We can think of vulnerability as a continuum of uncertainty (Løvendal and Knowles 2007). Since people move in and out of poverty, especially in conflict-prone areas, it is important to assess vulnerability over time rather than at one point in time. This kind of approach exposes a longer term dimension of food insecurity than does a focus on poverty alone. Existing food insecurity requires *ex post* efforts to deal with an already existing situation. Examining vulnerability, on the other hand, is a forward-looking approach that encourages us to consider who faces the most uncertainty or who is most likely to fall and remain below a threshold of food security. A focus on vulnerability motivates *ex ante* strategies to identify who is likely to be food insecure in the future, why they are likely to be food insecure, and what policy options or mitigation efforts could address these risks before they are manifested. In sum:

Availability, access and stability: together these three pillars cover all aspects of food security, from production, transport, storage and distribution, to final consumption. Food security involves practices and measures related to the assurance of a regular supply and adequate stocks of foodstuffs of guaranteed quality and nutritional value... Food insecurity, by contrast, is a component of the general state of human insecurity, fuelled by inequality and poverty, often expressed in terms of income levels. It denies minimal conditions for the exercise of citizenship and is detrimental to the concept of human dignity.

(Cavalcanti 2005, pp. 153–154)

Several factors contribute to vulnerability to food insecurity (Herrmann 2007). Political instability and conflict that is either armed or unarmed are leading causes of food crises particularly when these conditions lead to human displacement, destruction of infrastructure or land, and constrained economic productivity. Natural disasters such as floods, storms, and droughts can result in humanitarian and food crises. The destructiveness of natural disasters is often a factor of the level of preparedness and emergency management capacity in particular places. Warning systems, evacuation plans, back up supplies of electricity, water, food, and other supplies including medical support can help to alleviate the effects of natural disasters and associated public crises. Vulnerability may also be reflected in dependency ratios in a population. The dependency ratio of a society is the number of people who are not economically self-sufficient, for example, children and older people, compared to the number of wage-earning people in a society who must support them financially. How many people does one wage-earner have to support? The dependency ratio is higher in places where birth rates and life expectancies are high and where disease or political conflict depletes the workforce. In addition to understanding these factors of vulnerability to food security, we can also think in terms of trigger causes (e.g., natural disaster events or the outbreak of conflict) and how conditions may be made worse by underlying, systemic causes of vulnerability.

Challenging food security

How we define food security will shape how we go about identifying solutions and policy approaches. Two critiques of the concept of food security suggest that food security, as generally understood, is not the best guide for policy. Food sovereignty and food justice perspectives argue that the dominant definition of food security does not lead to useful discussions or to sound policy outcomes. In the policy world, food security is about maximizing supply or availability. It is also about increasing access to food at multiple scales beyond the state to include the region, the community, the household, and the individual. Critiques offered by food sovereignty and food justice perspectives, however, point to the limited usefulness of a food security approach: "Food security's focus on accessibility and hunger is further problematized by viewing individuals, or even households, as mere containers for calories" (Huish 2008, p. 1392). A focus on availability of and access to food miss other, important dimensions of human well-being. We have already seen this idea in the promotion of good nutrition, not just adequate calories. Food justice perspectives go further and view food not as a commodity but as a human right. Food, like other human rights, is often at the center of political struggle. Fundamental ideas of a food justice movement include:

- The rights of consumers must be fought over, maintained or expanded, not merely assumed.
- Human health and environmental health are tightly intertwined.
- There is no such thing as an average consumer.
- It is important to look beyond what is eaten to consider how it is produced and distributed.
- It is worthwhile to work to change policy, but policy is often influenced through creative activism outside of predetermined political channels (Lang 1997).

Food justice movements aim to create political spaces or networks through which people can be supported in their resistance of corporatized agriculture and globalization. Food justice movements seek to reconnect people with their food supply.

In Toronto, for example, activists have created a new political space – beyond and in between existing venues for input into the policy process to address concerns about community food security. This food justice movement involves networks of various groups and individuals rather than being formally institutionalized within the established political infrastructure. The movement engages citizens in a "bottom up," citizen-initiated planning process to address local hunger, poverty, and urban agriculture. Different elements and stages of Toronto's food justice movement have focused on emergency food provision, community gardens, and local economic development paying attention to ways in which these features are influenced by policy decisions and are linked to other spatial scales:

Working together, FoodShare and the Toronto Food Policy Council, and the coalitions and networks that have formed in Toronto, have created a new political space that operates at a multiplicity of scales—the global, national, and regional scales of networks and flows of information that incorporate the Global Food Summit in Rome and community gardens and bake ovens at the neighborhood level.

(Werkle 2004, p. 385)

Food justice movements are a type of social movement aiming to generate societal change and support everyday acts of resistance in relation to food supply: what and how much food is available, who controls the supply, and who benefits from it? Even if food justice movements do not alleviate all food insecurity, they can foster the development of skills and experience in participatory citizenship and strengthen bonds of local community (Levkoe 2006). As noted earlier, Michael Mann has observed that a significant obstacle to public dissent tends to be the inability of the public to organize collectively (Mann 1986). Yet food justice movements, like other types of social movements, encourage participatory citizenship and provide groups and individuals with experience in collective organization and critical thinking about political processes. These movements can help public groups to build their power and capacity to bring about change. Although food justice movements may be primarily focused on the community or local spatial scale, they often "jump scales" (Smith 1992) to connect their efforts with processes at other scales such as regional distribution systems, federal farm policies, local, small farms, individual consumption choices, etc. Groups and organizations may be empowered by their ability "to jump scale to organize themselves at the scale with the most promising opportunities to achieve their goals" (Mamadouh *et al.* 2004, p. 458; see also Jonas 1994 and Staeheli 1994). When food justice movements are able to link their efforts to different spatial scales, they can enhance their own knowledge base and their capacity to bring about change in the system.

Food justice movements may be described as "bottom up" projects since they tend to focus on empowering local food security initiatives by connecting them to other spatial scales. Food sovereignty perspectives may be described as "top to bottom" views since they tend to look at ways in which larger scale international connections have impacts on food security in specific places. Food sovereignty, which also critiques the focus on food security, sees the push for increasing the global food supply as inflicting negative consequences on less economically developed countries (Huish 2008). For example, when Haiti obliged World Trade Organization regulations and allowed the import of rice grown in the US, the result was "food dumping": US-grown rice dominated the domestic market and made it impossible for Haitian rice farmers to compete. Local rice farms were abandoned, and the Haitian economy suffered downward spiral effects. Rather than enhancing Haiti's food self-sufficiency and ability to meet local needs, World Trade Organization regulations, like international trade agreements often do, strengthen global markets while causing detrimental, local effects in particular places. A food sovereignty perspective views this process as backwards and would instead encourage us to consider how well poorer countries can feed themselves, to what extent they have control over their food supply, and how that food supply might serve to enhance their domestic economy and culture.

In other words, food justice and food sovereignty expand our understanding of food security by bringing our attention to different spatial scales. More than the availability or quantity of food, these views emphasize access to food at household, community, and the state level. These views encourage us to think about the influence of power at different spatial scales and ways in which policy decisions in one place or at one scale can affect other places or create other spatial scales of connection and activity.

Consider this observation on policy and food insecurity:

The main reason why there are more food insecure people today than ... 20 years ago is not that the required action is unknown or that the world does not possess the resources to assure food security for all, but rather that food security for all is not an important priority among most policymakers.

(Pinstrup-Andersen and Herforth 2008, p. 58)

If food security is not a top priority concern, does that mean that a society's political leaders and institutions have failed? Or is the lack of attention to food security a temporary condition that will be overcome as economic development proceeds? The next section considers this question about the relationship between a society's wealth and its food security.

Wealth and food security: do things get worse before they get better?

Does food security improve as a society becomes wealthier? One might argue that addressing food security requires not just agricultural development but a comprehensive approach to economic development. Successful economic development, it is generally thought, includes the accumulation of wealth and involves the development of institutional means of distributing wealth within a society. Distributing wealth presumably alleviates poverty which is generally recognized as the main factor causing food insecurity (Tweeten 1999). This line of thinking assumes that economic development occurs in tandem with sound political development. We can point to the most vulnerable states, often the poorest, that do not have the relative autonomy that would allow them to pursue food self-sufficiency (Cavalcanti 2005). They are not only poor, but they are often politically weak. Political failure can result from weakness or from the refusal by the elite to allow sufficient reform and change to the system that is causing uneven access to food. Political failure, more than weakness, can mean that a country or government does not adopt policies that would be appropriate for enhancing the national economy. Political failure can be said to go hand in hand with institutional failure:

> Food insecurity and economic stagnation are not the result of limited natural resources, lazy and fecund people, greedy corporations, environmental degradation, or rapacious rich nations. Rather, they are the result of misguided domestic public policies, which in turn are the product of weak, mismanaged, and corrupt institutions, especially national government.
>
> *(Tweeten 2005, p. 665)*

This view of economic stagnation and political failure subscribes to a view of economic development that can be summed up as "things get worse before they get better." This view of economic development would suggest that, eventually and with continued accumulation of wealth, economic development, and diversification and coordination of economic sectors, a society will emerge more economically and politically robust. A model for this way of thinking is the Environmental Kuznets Curve which hypothesizes that increased wealth in a society leads to lower levels of environmental degradation. This model is worth exploring here, even though its focus is not directly on food security per se, and applying to the question of food insecurity. This way of thinking, that things get worse before they get better, is prevalent and not often critiqued for its assumptions about how benefits of economic and political development are distributed throughout a society.

The Environmental Kuznets Curve, as a model, depicts the idea that as wealth accumulation and economic development proceed, environmental degradation initially worsens until it reaches a threshold or turning point at which point the level of environmental degradation declines (see Figure 4.2). That is, the Environmental Kuznets Curve suggests that as societies become wealthier, they have less of a negative impact on the environment. This model follows the idea that Simon Kuznets put forward in 1955 (Kuznets 1955) suggesting that economic development first leads to an increased level of social inequality followed by greater equality as societies became wealthier. The reduced impact is thought to result from the fact that wealthier societies do not have to worry so much about survival and can turn their attention to

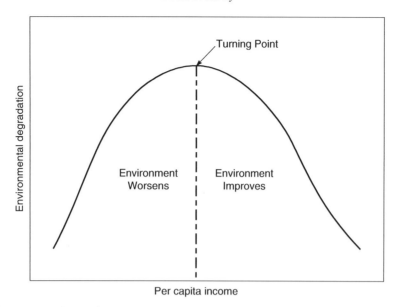

Figure 4.2 The Environmental Kuznets Curve. A graphic illustration of the assumption that as societies become wealthier their negative environmental impacts decrease, but the argument is misleading.

taking better care of the environment (or promoting social equality). Also, richer societies have access to or can generate better technologies that are less polluting or that utilize fewer environmental resources. This model reinforces the notion that economic development should be prioritized since it leads to positive ripple effects throughout society and for the environment. Indeed, in the 1990s, the World Development Bank adopted this idea and promoted economic development, among other reasons, to ease environmental degradation.

The Environmental Kuznets Curve represents a popular though rarely questioned way of understanding how economic development influences the environment. This model, however, may be critiqued on several points. First, it appears as though economic development returns a society to a pristine environment since the upside-down "U" seems to end at about the same level where it began. Yet this observation raises the question of how environmental degradation is measured. Sooty air from burning coal, such as that which plagued Industrial Revolution-era Britain (think of Charles Dickens' novels) or China today, tends to give way to different forms of environmental degradation and pollution. For example, how are we to compare the degradation from burning coal to the environmental degradation from transuranic waste from spent nuclear fuel? Does environmental degradation really decrease, or is it more accurate to say that it shifts in form? We might also observe that wealthier societies tend to consume more resources in fuel and commodities and generate more waste than do poorer societies that cannot afford high levels of consumption. Second, the Environmental Kuznets Curve implies that economic and environmental changes that a society experiences are limited to the geographic location of that society. In reality, societies consume resources from other places and distribute waste in various forms to distant places as well. Indeed, one of the reasons that wealthier societies may seem to enjoy cleaner environments is because dirtier activities such as mining and smelting are outsourced to distant places as are shipments of waste from industrial activities. Poorer societies, on the other hand, have fewer options and are more likely to be stuck with environmentally degrading economic activities and unwanted waste. Transfers of waste and environmentally degrading activities from richer to poorer countries represent a "race to the bottom" as economically developing countries take on environmental (and human health) burdens in the interest of promoting economic development. For example, in 1972 the pesticide DDT was banned in the US as hazardous to the environment and to human health. However, the US continued to manufacture this chemical and export it to places such as Ecuador where it is used on banana crops destined for the US. In this case, US production and consumption is contributing to environmental degradation elsewhere. These kinds of linkages are overlooked by the Environmental Kuznets Curve since it summarizes trends only in one location.

A third critique is that empirical research on the Environmental Kuznets Curve demonstrates that the assumed relationship between economic development and environmental degradation is based on flimsy and unconvincing evidence from the real world (Dasgupta *et al.* 2002; Stern 2004; Copeland and Taylor 2004). There is little actual evidence that countries have followed the inverted U-shape of environmental degradation as they develop economically. This relationship appears to be more hypothesized than real despite the fact that it is a popular argument to point to economic development as a benefit to the environment. It may be true that some types of environmental impacts are abated as societies develop economically. Soil erosion, desertification, species depletion, acid rain, deforestation, and water quality may indeed get worse before they get better, but there are many types of environmental impacts that do not follow the projected inverted U-shape of the Environmental Kuznets Curve. There are several ways in which economic development actually worsens environmental problems. First, carbon dioxide accumulation in the atmosphere continues. Second, solid waste generation continues as a reflection of consumption levels. Third, global and regional stockpiles of fossil fuels and other non-renewable resources continue to decline as societies develop economically (Tweeten 1999). Pollution emissions and concentrations, overall, do not appear to decline alongside economic development. In fact, some developing countries outperform more economically advanced countries in terms of environmental standards (Stern 2004).

If the assumption of "things get worse before they get better" does not necessarily hold for environmental impacts, how well does it capture trends in food security? Does food security improve as societies become wealthier? Do wealthier societies tend to adopt policies that promote access to food supply or encourage a higher quality food supply? An examination of The Food and Energy Security Act of 2007 (also known as The Farm Bill of 2007) demonstrates why this question about food security is oversimplified. The US Farm Bill not only shapes agricultural productivity, food policy, and patterns of food security in the US, but its impacts on food security reach well beyond the US.

The US Farm Bill, agribusiness, and food security

Why is it that a pound of red bell peppers costs more than a pound of Twinkies? Red bell peppers involve minimal processing – perhaps some washing, minimal trimming – and they are usually sold without packaging. Twinkies, on the other hand, are the epitome of processed food. Each Twinkie is individually wrapped, as if untouched by human hands, and further packaged in a brightly colored box. Whereas the single, simple ingredient in bell peppers is quite obvious, it is less clear what kinds of ingredients make up a Twinkie. An inspection of the ingredient label of a Twinkie would reveal a dizzying list of more than 25 materials that only raises more questions about what goes into this snack cake (Ettlinger 2007). "Materials," rather than "foods," is an appropriate description since some of the ingredients in a Twinkie, such as sodium acid pyrophosphate, monocalcium phosphate, and calcium sulfate, like baking soda and salt, are mined and processed minerals. The FD&C Yellow No. 5 and Red No. 40 colorings in Twinkies that give the "golden" sponge cake its color and suggest a richness of butter and eggs beyond which Twinkies actually have, are both derived from benzene, a by-product of oil refining. Polysorbate 60 and cellulose gum, two other Twinkie ingredients that are also common to other processed foods, are emulsifiers that may be traced back to ammunition and gunpowder production. So how is it possible that a pound of Twinkies, in all of their complex, individually wrapped, placeless mystery, are cheaper than a pound of humble red bell peppers? Much of the answer has to do with the US agricultural system and policies maintaining that system.

The US Federal government has a longstanding interest in supporting agriculture in the US. US Federal efforts to support agriculture and improve farm income go back to the establishment of the Federal Farm Board in 1929. Since that time, emphasis has shifted from improving markets for agricultural products to establishing direct payments and subsidies for farmers. Institutional arrangements and policy initiatives have also changed over time with each 5-year renewal of the bill (Tweeten and Zulauf 2008). Most recently, The Food and Energy Security Act of 2007 (The Farm Bill of 2007) has continued the tradition of previous farm commodity programs in its support of producers of a short list of commodity crops: corn, soybeans, wheat, rice, and cotton. This focus concentrates over half of US farm spending in just seven states. It is no surprise that the Congressional committees with the most influence over the Farm Bill include representatives from those states in which the production of these few commodities is economically dominant. The Farm Bill shapes the agricultural system of the US:

The effect of designating certain crops as program crops is shown by the effect in Iowa. In 1945, Iowa's farmers grew seventeen commercial crops, including potatoes, cherries, peaches, plums, pears, strawberries, raspberries, and wheat. Now the commercial crops are down to four: corn, soybeans, hay, and wheat. Three of these four are subsidized program crops, and the fourth is hay, which farmers need to feed livestock. In 2005, 82 percent of harvest acreage in the United States was these four crops.

(Blatt 2008, pp. 11–12)

The resulting abundance of a few crops provides motivation to find new uses for them and integrate them into the food system. For example, corn syrup is a highly processed food product that, just a few decades ago, was too expensive to compete with sugar as a sweetener. However, as corn has become a prioritized and subsidized crop, corn and corn-based products have become cheaper, and manufacturers are encouraged to find ways to integrate corn products into the food system. These products have infiltrated the food system to such an extent that the very cellular structure of North Americans has been altered. Michael Pollan (2006) has described how corn has a unique carbon signature. When corn and a few other plants, known as "C-4" plants, photosynthesize, they create compounds that have four carbon atoms, instead of three like most other plants. These plants cannot afford to be selective about the type of carbon isotopes that they take in, and they tend to have more carbon-13:

One would expect to find a comparatively high proportion of carbon 13 in the flesh of people whose staple food of choice is corn – Mexicans, most famously . . . But carbon 13 doesn't lie, and researchers who have compared the isotopes in the flesh or hair of Americans to those in the same tissues of Mexicans report that it is now we in the North who are the true people of corn. "When you look at the isotope ratios... we North Americans look like corn chips with legs."

(pp. 22–23)

This is one reason why Twinkies are inexpensive despite their complex ingredient list. Many of those ingredients are highly processed food products that are competitively subsidized.

The institutionalized arrangement of government agencies and subsidies that maintains the current system of agriculture in the US faces challenges from different directions (Miller 2009). A few concerns about the Farm Bill worth mentioning here can be summarized as concerns over the size and influence of big agribusiness as opposed to small, independent farms, concerns over ways in which the US food system and public health are affected by the Farm Bill, and concerns about negative environmental impacts fostered by the Farm Bill. First, it is becoming more difficult for corporate agriculture to justify its demands for government subsidies. Corporate agriculture, which is closely linked to the food processing industry, has been making significant profits since the 2002 iteration of the Farm Bill. In other words, the Farm Bill may be said to be too successful in its support of big agribusiness. The Farm Bill concentrates power among relatively few players:

Today five major seed companies dominate world-wide: Monsanto, Aventis, DuPont, Syngenta, and Dow. In the US, four firms slaughter 81 per cent of the beef; four firms own 60 per cent of the terminal grain facilities, and three firms export 81 per cent of corn and 65 per cent of soybeans. In addition, four firms have 46 per cent of the total sows in production and four firms slaughter 50 per cent of all American broilers.

(Morgan et al. 2006, p. 55)

These firms are able to influence a range of activities tied to agriculture such as research and development in biotechnology, distribution of agriculture supply such as seeds, fertilizers and pesticides, food processing, marketing, and more. This vertical integration and control through all stages of agricultural productivity gives agribusinesses greater leverage and ability to bring power to bear on a range of activities and decision-making processes. Additionally, the drive to make agricultural activities more efficient as an industry contributes to a decline in mixed farming practices and increases the tendency towards regional specialization. The trend for larger landholdings is to expand one activity over others which creates "geographies of concentration and integration" (Morgan *et al.* 2006, p. 60). "Super regions" of production and processing have come to define regional landscapes and economies such as those resulting from pork production in Iowa and broiler farms across the American South. The concentration of industrial agriculture horizontally – creating regions dominated by a specific agriculture activity – and the vertical integration of corporate agribusiness reinforces the power of the actors involved.

At the same time, other supply chain actors such as farmers working on smaller, independent farms may be unable to compete directly with the economies of scale that benefit conventional agribusiness. If conventional agribusiness is driven by the motive of producing greater quantities at relatively low cost, alternative agricultural producers find ways to compete that focus consumer attention on other qualities of agricultural commodities. Rather than emphasizing price or cost, alternative producers might aim to educate consumers about how their food is produced, the places it comes from (provenance), and why these features make a difference in the quality of food products. Alternative food networks that offer short food supply chains tend to concentrate on the benefits of organic farming, the quality of food production, or the value of direct selling (Renting *et al.* 2003). They emphasize the importance of face-to-face purchasing of local products (for example, at farmers' markets) and the value of being able to trace food to its source. The focus of alternative agriculture is on the value-added of local and regional production and on supporting local farms and farmers (Morgan *et al.* 2006).

This contrast between conventional agribusiness and alternative agribusiness highlights both power and scale. Larger farms and agribusinesses that produce key, subsidized commodities receive sufficient benefits to make it worthwhile to invest the time, energy, and funds to lobby politicians and make significant contributions to political campaigns (Tweeten and Zulauf 2008). They are motivated and have the capacity to influence governmental decisions about agriculture, and their ability to organize positions them at the center of agricultural policy. As Mann stated "Power is the ability to pursue and attain goals through mastery of one's environment" (Mann 1986, p. 6). Agricultural policy and commodity support programs are institutionalized through government structures established to oversee agricultural programs. These structures benefit from the continuation of agricultural policies. For example, the US Department of Agriculture, the Natural Resources Conservation Service, the Risk Management Agency, and the Farm Service Agency help to support large farms and agribusinesses and mutually reinforce them. Other components that play into a network of support for agricultural policy include land grant colleges of agriculture, the Farm Bloc agricultural interest group within Congress, and elected farmer committees at the local level. It is difficult for smaller, widely dispersed farmers to organize and command this degree of power and influence in the established political system. It is difficult to change the status quo when so many components benefit from its continuation.

The promotion of competitive trade beyond the US, in agreements such as the North American Free Trade Agreement (NAFTA), can also be seen to empower large agricultural corporations over farmers. As agribusiness is empowered by these agreements, through indirect subsidies and reduced international competition, they are able to consolidate their control of supplies and stages of production further increasing their power and influence. At the same time, the US has seen economic and social decline in rural areas. The 2002 Farm Bill did little to change the status quo and the embedded power structures in the agricultural system:

Meanwhile, net income for the U.S. farmers – even including the near tripling of subsidies – fell 16.5 percent, and an estimated 300,000 U.S. farmers were forced out of business. Rural communities died as storefronts were boarded up, churches were closed down, people were forced from their homes by the toxic fumes of industrial animal factories, and a methylamphetamine epidemic swept the countryside.

(Olson 2008, p. 421)

Rural communities are not alone in paying the price of commodity support programs geared towards benefitting corporate agriculture: "US taxpayers losing from agricultural commodity support programs vastly outnumber US producers who gain from commodity programs, but each taxpayer loses too little to motivate organizing and funding opposition" (Tweeten and Zulauf 2008, p. 155). Elsewhere, though, people have not been so complacent. As the US negotiated details of The North American Free Trade Agreement (NAFTA) with its neighbors, one of the concessions required by Mexico was to ease its production of corn so that the US could more easily dominate this market. Mexico adjusted its land tenure policies to alter who had access to land and farming which contributed to rural decline in agricultural areas of Mexico. As NAFTA was implemented in 1994, the Chiapas region was particularly affected, and people's livelihoods there were at risk. People of Chiapas formed the Zapatista movement to protest government land tenure policies and to preserve their traditional culture as farmers. They were led by the mysterious Subcomandante Marcos. Subcomandante Marcos, always hidden by a dark balaclava and smoking his signature pipe, was just the charismatic figure to capture global media attention and bring awareness to the plight of the people of Chiapas. Although the focus of the Zapatista movement was Mexican government agricultural policy, those policies had their roots in US agricultural policy and the so-called logic of international trade (see Figure 4.3).

Figure 4.3 Coffee cooperative in Chiapas, Mexico. Small farmer cooperatives in Chiapas, Mexico provide the means for small farmers to sustain themselves, to improve the well-being of their community, and to expand their economic activity beyond what they might otherwise achieve. Photo: Rita York.

Another challenge to the current arrangement of the Farm Bill comes from interests associated with specialty crops such as fruits, vegetables, tree nuts, and nursery plantings. These crops have not historically received much support from the Farm Bill, but groups associated with them are gaining strength and the ability to organize politically. One of the key arguments that has helped these groups to gain attention and mobilize support is that these specialty crops are key to improving public health in the US. Agricultural policies tend to prioritize the interests of producers rather than the interests of the public at large. Arguably, these policies have been successful in delivering inexpensive, reliable food, but issues of sound nutrition have not been a priority. As a result, another way in which US residents are paying for the US Farm Bill is with their health.

The food industry, and the processed food industry in particular with its linkages to corporate agribusiness, has been influential in shaping public food choices and in promoting certain kinds of foods over others. Even in economically developed countries, the dominant food supply system results in an overabundance of processed foods and simultaneous undernutrition.

Public health concerns center on obesity, cancer, coronary heart disease, and type II, late-onset diabetes as well as other non-communicable diseases associated with poor nutrition. Rather than address upstream, structural issues of what kinds of food crops are subsidized and promoted by government agricultural policies in the US and elsewhere, efforts on public health tend to focus on downstream issues of consumer choice (Caraher and Coveney 2004). Public education efforts in places such as the US, the UK, and Australia focus on encouraging physical activity, consuming more fresh fruits and vegetables, and reading labels to foster greater awareness of ingredients in processed foods. These lifestyle interventions are useful on their own, but a more reasoned approach would question the structure of the dominant food system and who is benefitting from its continuation. One way to engage with power structures underlying the dominant food system is to take collective, political action: "Tactically, public health nutrition, health educators and promoters could take this opportunity to move away from the emphasis on the consumer and build on the experience of alliances and lobbying" (Caraher and Coveney 2004, p. 595). Such efforts could realistically help to develop a model of food citizenship in which the public is actively engaged in the decisions that influence our food choices as opposed to the current model based on food consumerism which only requires the public to respond to a predetermined set of options. In organizing collectively, citizen groups and professionals could garner power to shift conversations about local, national, and even global food supply to a more appropriate scale that challenges powerful actors such as industrial agriculture, the food processing industry, and policy makers in a position to influence basic components of the food supply.

Finally, another challenge to the Farm Bill stems from environmental concerns. The power arrangements institutionalized by successive Farm Bills are challenged by groups concerned about environmental effects of industrial farming. These groups have been increasingly effective in promoting conservation and more sustainable forms of agriculture, but they are far from being a dominant force in the overall agricultural system of the US. The vast size of industrial farms concentrates the use of energy, chemicals, and water as well as the output of solid waste and wastewater.

We can look at the example of Smithfield Foods, the largest pork processor in the world, which operates multiple subsidiaries across the US and which is rapidly extending its business practices in Europe as well. Smithfield Foods exemplifies a vertically integrated system that controls pork production from artificial insemination and birth until each pig passes through the slaughterhouse and is turned into cellophane-wrapped packages of meat. In 2005, Smithfield Foods killed 27 million hogs:

That's a number worth considering. A slaughter-weight hog is fifty percent heavier than a person. The logistical challenge of processing that many pigs each year is roughly equivalent to butchering and boxing the entire human populations of New York, Los Angeles, Chicago, Houston, Philadelphia, Phoenix, San Antonio, San Diego, Dallas, San Jose, Detroit, Indianapolis, Jacksonville, San Francisco, Columbus, Austin, Memphis, Baltimore, Fort Worth, Charlotte, El Paso, Milwaukee, Seattle, Boston, Denver, Louisville, Washington, D.C., Nashville, Las Vegas, Portland, Oklahoma City and Tucson.

(Tietz 2006)

To accomplish such a monumental feat, Smithfield Foods uses a vast amount of antibiotics, vaccines, and insecticides. Without these chemicals, factory pigs would not be able to survive their living conditions:

Smithfield's pigs live by the hundreds or thousands in warehouse-like barns, in rows of wall-to-wall pens. Sows are artificially inseminated and fed and delivered of their piglets in cages so small they cannot turn around. Forty fully grown 250-pound male hogs often occupy a pen the size of a tiny apartment. They trample each other to death. There is no sunlight, straw, fresh air or earth. The floors are slatted to allow excrement to fall into a catchment pit under the pens, but many things besides excrement can wind up in the pits: afterbirths, piglets accidentally crushed by their mothers, old batteries, broken bottles of insecticide, antibiotic syringes, stillborn pigs – anything small enough to fit through the foot-wide pipes that drain the pits. The pipes remain closed until enough sewage accumulates in the pits to create good expulsion pressure; then the pipes are opened and everything bursts out into a large holding pond.

(Tietz 2006)

The amount and type of waste generated by Smithfield Foods at its pork raising facilities is a major environmental concern. First, the volume of waste is considerable. In one year, Smithfield Farms generates an estimated twenty-six million tons of waste which would fill the Yankee Stadium four times over. This waste is held in vast holding ponds which are up to thirty feet deep. The liquid in them is pink from blood, afterbirths, and chemical interactions with animal waste, and it is also highly toxic. All of the drugs administered to the pigs, as well as other toxic substances such as cyanide, heavy metals, and large concentrations of nitrates, methane, and fecal coliform bacteria, eventually make their way to the holding ponds. When these unlined holding ponds threaten to overflow – not unlikely when it rains – the waste is pumped out and sprayed over nearby fields which become puddled with toxic pig waste. The Environmental Protection Agency (EPA) has reported that Smithfield's Tar Heel, North Carolina facility ranks fourth among all industrial facilities in the US, of any kind, in the amount of toxic waste it adds to the country's water systems. Yet fines that the EPA has imposed on Smithfield

Foods to penalize such egregious breaches of environmental standards are barely noticeable when compared to the huge profits that the company enjoys and are insufficient to motivate a change in behavior. Smithfield Foods demonstrates the kinds of practices and environmental disregard enabled by the current institutions of US agricultural policy. The Farm Bill is central to the continuation of that system and is at the same time promoted by that system.

This discussion of the US Farm Bill helps us to return to the idea of whether or not "things get worse before they get better" with food security. As we saw with the Environmental Kuznets Curve, the assumption that social or environmental conditions get worse before they improve does not actually stand up well to scrutiny. How well, then, does this kind of assumption capture trends in food security? Does food security improve as societies become wealthier? Do wealthier societies tend to adopt policies that promote access to food supply or encourage a higher quality food supply? The Farm Bill, integral to the operation and continuation of the US agriculture and food systems, would seem to be the kind of policy positioned to improve food security, access to food, and quality of food while mitigating negative impacts of agricultural practices. This discussion has highlighted ways in which the Farm Bill and supporting institutions exert influence over farming practices, land use, what kinds of crops are grown and how, what kinds of food are produced, processed, and promoted, public consumer options, public health impacts, environmental impacts, international trade and livelihoods beyond the US. What we see is that this system is becoming more entrenched and less flexible. The vertically integrated food production system, from corporate development of seeds and matching pesticides to the marketing of standardized food products, shapes consumer choices and expectations within a limited window of possibilities. Environmental practices associated with agriculture are having long-lasting and probably irreversible effects on the environment (recall the example from Chapter 1 of nitrogen loads in the Mississippi watershed and eutrophication in the Gulf of Mexico). The example of Smithfield Foods emphasizes the extent to which "business as usual" can and does result in degradation far beyond the reach of environmental oversight such as EPA fines or penalties.

Unlike the Environmental Kuznets Curve which suggests responsiveness to economic conditions and flexibility or adaptability within a system, The Farm Bill and the US agricultural system appear to be becoming less flexible and more rigid. This is true for both the horizontal and vertical scope of the current agricultural system. The horizontal scope of the farm system, evidenced by large, corporate farms, concentrates production on a limited number of commodities, draws on significant energy, water, and chemical inputs, and generates a waste stream that affects water and ecosystems well beyond the farm itself. The vertical integration of the farm system, in which a relatively few corporations wield significant influence over all stages of production from seed and pesticide development to marketing of processed foods, is also rigid since the vested interests that benefit from this arrangement are able to shape, maintain, and expand these institutions to consolidate power. Rather than promoting core objectives of food security such as improved access to food or improved nutritional quality of food, the US Farm Bill and the agricultural system into which it is integrated, instead have been promoting activities that might be said to hinder food security. Two trends that we can look at to see how agricultural policies are not progressing towards objectives of food security are the expansion of biofuels production and the promotion of genetically modified organisms (GMOs). These trends reinforce the power of established systems without improving food security for all or even some groups of people.

In Chapter 3, biofuels and ethanol were discussed as being promoted by the Farm Bill. In addition to concerns about environmental degradation, chemical and energy inputs required for ethanol production, and overarching concerns about the efficiency of using biofuels for transportation energy, the promotion of biofuels can also be said to hinder food security. Consider how increased demand for ethanol is linked to food security even beyond the US:

The World Bank has estimated that in 2001, 2.7 billion people in the world were living on the equivalent of less than $2 a day; to them, even marginal increases in the cost of staple grains could be devastating. Filling the 25-gallon tank of an SUV with pure ethanol requires over 450 pounds of corn – which contains enough calories to feed one person for a year. By putting pressure on global supplies of edible crops, the surge in ethanol production will translate into higher prices for both processed and staple foods around the world. Biofuels have tied oil and food prices together in ways that could profoundly upset the relationships between food producers, consumers, and nations in the years ahead, with potentially devastating implications for both global poverty and food security.

(Runge and Senauer 2007, p. 41)

The promotion of ethanol and the subsidizing of corn for ethanol production are examples of agricultural policies that diminish food security and people's access to food both in the US and beyond its borders. Another example of the promotion of biofuels having a negative effect on food security comes from China. There, constraints on production of biofuel crops within the country's borders have increased the demand that China is placing on the global supply of these crops (Naylor *et al.* 2007). In particular, China's demand for cassava as a biofuel crop is expected to lead to higher prices for this crop and possible food insecurity for people who rely on cassava as a food crop. In the Democratic Republic of Congo and Ghana, for example, cassava represents a significant portion of calories consumed, but people there are unlikely to be able to afford cassava if prices increase. This example further illustrates how agricultural policies in an economically advancing country can contribute to food insecurity beyond its borders. Promoting biofuels over food crops can be seen as a temporary solution for the rich that will not stave off inevitable decline of our current mechanistic, industrial lifestyle (Shiva 2008). Similar to the Environmental Kuznets Curve, we must look beyond the scale of the state or a single society to understand linkages between or among places that hinder food security.

Another example of policy rigidity rather than responsiveness to food security in US agricultural policy is the widespread use of genetically modified organisms or GMOs. Unlike the plants that result from cross-fertilization between like species of plants, GMOs have been genetically altered with material from completely different species. For example, fish genes have been added to tomatoes to help them freeze better. The Bt gene, which comes from a naturally occurring soil bacterium, *Bacillus thuringiensis*, has been integrated into the genetic make-up of plants to serve as a built-in pesticide. GMOs are promoted as a means to increase the food supply, to enhance the nutritional value of staple crops, and to reduce the use of added chemicals to cropland. Yet these claims have been questioned. As an earlier section of this chapter pointed out, availability of food does not ensure food security.

Justifying the use of GMOs for increased food supply, then, is not necessarily a strong argument. Although GMOs may require less of some chemicals, they also may require the use of other chemicals. Bt-transgenic crops, for instance, are inconsistent in the levels of chemical applications that they require (Benbrook 2001). Although GMOs may be enhanced for improved nutrition, even this aspect of GMOs does not translate into food security when we understand food security as promoting the well-being and health of individuals:

The suggestion that genetically altered rice is the proper way to address the condition of 2 million children at risk of Vitamin A deficiency-induced blindness reveals a tremendous naiveté about the reality and causes of vitamin and micro-nutrient malnutrition.... Vitamin A deficiency is not best characterized as a problem, but rather as a *symptom*, a warning sign if you will. It warns us of broader dietary inadequacies associated with both poverty, and with agricultural change from diverse cropping systems towards rice monoculture. People do not present Vitamin A deficiency because rice contains too little Vitamin A, or beta-carotene, but rather because their diet has been reduced to rice and almost nothing else.

(Rosset 2006, p. 87)

Even this brief consideration illustrates why GMOs do not necessarily enhance food security. Why, then, does the US agricultural system promote them so energetically? Returning to the theme of power:

> In the case of genetic engineering, money has been the prime motivator. The reason gene splicing was developed is so that agrobiochemical companies could own their own seed supply and control the means and methods of food production, and profit, at each link in the food chain. The farmer is put in an even more serflike position than would otherwise be possible. The major chemical companies have invested billions of dollars in the technology, have political clout in Washington, and have successfully lobbied government agencies to allow them to be essentially self-regulating and allow GM foods to enter the food chain and the environment without announcing it to the public. The FDA has ruled that GM products are "substantially equivalent" to conventional products and therefore need not be labeled, regardless of what the public wants.
>
> *(Blatt 2008, p. 96)*

By this view, it is clear that support for GMOs in the US is not driven by the motive of improving food security, or even in response to public demand, but instead it is driven from a desire by corporate interests to wield more power over the food system. Rather than put the power of food choices and access to food in the hands of consumers, the promotion of GMOs demonstrates how the US agricultural system serves to collect and organize power at a different scale defined by chemical companies, agricultural policy, distribution systems, and farming practices particularly on larger, corporate farms.

It is this same network of overlapping systems that make large-scale food scares possible. For example, in 2009, *Salmonella typhimurium* was found in products containing peanut butter and peanut paste: cookies, crackers, candy, cereal, pet treats, and more. Over 700 people in the US got sick from this outbreak, and over two thousand products were recalled. Although the source of the contamination was eventually identified as the Texas-based Peanut Corporation of America, this salmonella scare brought to the public's attention how little we know about where our food comes from, who controls it, and points of risk along the commodity chains that bring our food from field to table. Similarly, a tainted milk incident in China in 2008 sickened more than fifty thousand children and brought to light that dairies were adding melamine to milk to boost the appearance of its protein content. This practice had been ongoing for several years and had been maintained by a powerful system of the Chinese dairy industry, economic pressure, lack of oversight, and limited media access. Again, we see that these systems gain and organize ideological power and use it to control public relations. These systems are also able to organize economic power to pressure farmers to generate products that meet government standards that rely on quantitative rather than qualitative measures. As food commodity chains become longer and as corporate interests are able to influence control over supplies, products, standards, and monitoring systems, it becomes less clear who has control over the food supply, where our food comes from, and what our options are for alternative food sources. In short, the current system of food production, distribution, and marketing may be said to constrain rather than enhance food security in very basic ways. Rather than policies evolving to improve food security for all or even most people or groups, we see how policies and control of power in the food system become more rigid, less transparent, and have increasing influence across a wider space with deeper reach into our food choices and food quality.

Another aspect of agriculture policy that does not necessarily get worse and then get better has to do with energy inputs in industrial agriculture. The very practice of industrialized farming requires huge energy inputs:

> Corn, rice and wheat are especially adapted to catastrophe. It is their niche. In the natural scheme of things, a catastrophe would create a blank slate, bare soil, that was good for them. Then, under normal circumstances, succession would quickly close that niche. The annuals would colonize. Their roots would stabilize the soil, accumulate organic matter, provide cover. Eventually the catastrophe niche would close. Farming is the process of ripping that niche open again and again. It is an annual artificial catastrophe, and it requires the equivalent of three or four tons of TNT per acre for a modern American farm. Iowa's fields require the energy of 4,000 Nagasaki bombs every year.
>
> *(Manning 2004, p. 39)*

Food products such as meat, milk, and dairy products require even greater energy inputs than do grain crops. As wealth in countries and societies increases, there tends to be an upward trend in the consumption of meat and other forms of protein such as fish or eggs and dairy that require the support of livestock. These types of calories require greater energy input in the form of fossil fuels. Studies have calculated that for every kilocalorie of food delivered to the US consumer, between 7 and 10 kilocalories were used in its production, packaging, and transport (Heller and Keoleian 2000; Pfeiffer 2006). After food is delivered to or purchased by the consumer, additional energy is required for its storage and preparation. Fast-paced Western lifestyles encourage the consumption of more processed and prepared foods that require more energy to transport and process through each stage of its commodity chain, to package, and to store. One response to this shift towards processed food is that refrigerators in North America are increasing in size to accommodate the expanding availability of frozen foods and ready-to-cook meals which time-pressed individuals and busy families turn increasingly to at mealtime. The supersizing of major appliances (Barkenbus 2006), in turn, requires still more energy. The amount of energy that it takes to sustain food systems in Western or richer parts of the world relates to food security because it quickly becomes clear how vulnerable these systems are to disruptions in energy supply either in agriculture, transport, or storage. Societies that have become accustomed to a variety of energy-intensive foods may find that such consumption is not sustainable in the long run.

Local fish, international trade, and food security

Food security is not just a terrestrial concern. Fishing and fish farming are critical sources of calories and protein for much of the world's population. In 2006, world fish production reached 143.6 million metric tons with about 110 million metric tons going towards human consumption and the rest being used for animal and poultry feed in the production of meat, milk, and eggs (*The Economist* 2009a). Almost half of all fish eaten by people is farmed through aquaculture rather than caught in the wild, and the amount of fish caught in the wild is decreasing. Although China is the dominant producer of both wild caught fish and fish produced through aquaculture, many countries turn to fishing of either kind as a way to supplement their food supply and make up for a shortage of arable land. In the 1960s, Georg Borgström coined the term "ghost acres" to refer to the amount of land that a country would have to cultivate to generate the same amount of animal protein that it could otherwise obtain through fishing and international trade (Borgström 1965; Talberth *et al.* 2006; Bodley 2008). The idea of ghost acres gained through fishing recognizes that many countries have extended their carrying capacity by supplementing their food supply with fish. Countries such as Japan and the United Kingdom have managed to sustain larger populations through fishing and trade than they could based solely on food production from their own farmland. A concern about relying on ghost acres to support a population, however, is that global fisheries are in danger of collapse from over-exploitation (Loh 2008). Here we can draw upon the idea of an ecological fishprint to think about the impact of relying on fishing as a supply of protein and an input into the food industry. The ecological footprint of a country or an activity measures its environmental impact such as the environmental impacts of producing a hybrid car, the downstream effects on water and soil quality of growing an acre of genetically modified corn, or extracting enough gold for a typical wedding ring which can generate three metric tons of mining waste. In a similar way, the ecological fishprint assesses how a country's fish catch has an impact on global fisheries:

... the world was taking 157 percent of global marine biocapacity in 2003. At that time Japan was using more than 6 times its ecological footprint biocapacity, and its ecological fishprint was nearly 8 times its fisheries biocapacity. The fishprint takes into account the trophic level of fish harvested and reductions in capacity as overfishing occurs. Trophic level matters because for example it takes over 1.7 million tones of primary biological productivity to produce 1 ton of Bluefin tuna at the top of the marine food chain, but only 79 tons to produce 1 ton of anchovies near the bottom of the food chain.

(Bodley 2008, p. 180)

Using lower trophic level fish as feed for higher trophic level fish is energy inefficient. A basic rule of thumb is that approximately 90% of energy is lost from one trophic level to the next. That means that only 10% of available energy from lower level fish will be used by the Bluefin tuna that eat them. The rest of the energy, following the first law of thermodynamics, the principle of conservation of energy which states that energy can neither be created nor destroyed but only changes form, dissipates as heat. The same process holds in terrestrial ecosystems. Only 10% of the available energy in grass is used by herbivores, such as rabbits, that consume the grass. A carnivore that eats the rabbit will only get 1% of the energy that had been available in the plants eaten by the rabbit.

The question we need to ask, if we are to understand power dynamics and spatial relationships shaping global fish production and consumption, is "Who or where is benefitting from the harvesting of fish?" *The Economist* newspaper recently made this statement about the fishing industry in Africa:

The future increase of production is predicted to be greatest in Africa. Growth rates here are already high, albeit from a low base (in 2006 the continent produced less than 1% of the world's farmed fish). Between 1995 and 2005, production rose by 11.4% a year in sub-Saharan Africa and 21.9% in north Africa, with much of the growth being supported by outside injections of investment and expertise. The growing commercialization of African aquaculture offers tremendous potential for the continent.

(The Economist 2009b)

This statement sounds very positive for the people of African countries where fishing is an expanding economic activity. However, we gain sharp insight into the realities of fishing in Africa when we consider the documentary, *Darwin's Nightmare*. This film takes us to Tanzania and a village, Mwanza City, on Lake Victoria. Years ago the Nile Perch was introduced into the lake's ecosystem. As a predatory, exotic species with few obstacles to its survival, the Nile Perch has come to dominate the ecosystem to the detriment of native species of fish. Since Nile Perch grow to be quite large and offer palatable fillets, a booming fish processing and packaging industry has sprung up in the village. The bulk of these fillets, however, are exported to Europe. Locally, poverty is rife. Men who fish sell their catch to the fish processing plants for money rather than eat the fish themselves. The fish processing plant dumps "fish frames" – the bones left after fillets have been cut away – and locals with few other options pick over these remnants to survive. Refugees from nearby wars, particularly orphaned children, populate the village. The film follows these children as they spend their days looking for food, trying to avoid violence, and turning to drug use such as sniffing gasoline to numb the reality of their existence. We are introduced to young women who have turned to prostitution to survive. Their clients are the pilots and fishermen who are drawn to the economic activity around Lake Victoria. These young women risk violence and exposure to HIV/AIDS but have little or no prospects for advancing their education or pursuing other careers.

The documentary shows us airplanes, flown by Russian pilots, which land on rugged, dirt runways to pick up the frozen fillets and fly them to consumers in Europe. The question running through the documentary is "Do the planes arrive empty? If not, what do they bring?" We learn by the end of the film that the planes arrive laden with weapons to fuel ongoing wars in the region. The starting point of the documentary is the local fishing industry and the lack of food security among the people living near this incredible food supply. We see the contrast between fish production for human consumption, as captured in country-level statistics for food production, and the harsh realities of life in Mwanza City. More importantly, we begin to understand how food security is linked to other forms of security. Income from fish exports is somehow translated into a supply of weapons, and neither end of this equation benefits locals. Clearly, power is organized at a level and by people whose interests are served by exporting locally needed food to Europe in exchange for a thriving arms trade.

If European consumers were aware that the fillets came from Africa, might they think, as *The Economist* statement suggests, that they are helping an African economy to expand and to improve? Europeans who consume the perch fillets from Lake Victoria likely have no idea where they come from since their provenance is a mystery. It matters little if at all to consumers whether or not these fish fillets were wild caught or farmed. The case of the Nile Perch in Lake Victoria is but one example of how the logic of international trade creates an uneven distribution of food (in)security:

Scarce protein resources in the form of meat, fish and fish products, nuts, and oilseed cakes move with bananas, cocoa, coffee, and tea from protein-poor, hungry nations to rich, well-fed nations, propelled by the exigencies of the world's financial markets... Peruvian traders, for example, instead of satisfying the obvious needs of

Peru's protein-deficient people, find it more profitable to ship Peru's rich fish meal resource to the United States, where it is fed to chickens to subsidize energy-intensive egg industries. Likewise, Indian oilseed cakes are fed to European cattle while millions of Indians are starved for protein and Indian cattle scavenge for refuse.

(Bodley 2008, p. 180)

Food in these instances is not a human right. It is a commodity like any other. Its production draws from ecosystems, and it has implications for the livelihoods and well-being of people who live close to those ecosystems as well as people who live at a distance from those places. Like other commodities, food often appears placeless as it moves closer to the consumer, but as a resource that is drawn from specific places, it has place-specific as well as economic, political, and cultural implications at multiple spatial scales.

Conclusion

Like other commodities, food is controlled by those who have economic power over its production and distribution, by those who have political power over the use of state-level resources such as agricultural subsidies or trade agreements (legitimate or illicit), and those who have ideological power to maintain and promote the system without being subject to question. Food security, clearly, involves spatial scales of global trade, state power, corporate systems, and networks of production, distribution, and marketing. Each of these systems uses different forms of power to advance specific interests and maintain or expand influence and control over particular processes. Food security has also been discussed in this chapter as individual access to adequate and appropriate food supplies. Increasing consumer awareness about food sources does not necessarily mean bringing food supply systems into a smaller or more local spatial scale. As the discussion on food justice and food sovereignty movements suggested, improved food security may involve linkages among multiple spatial scales. Food security is not about making food systems and food choices more local, but it is about demystifying processes of food production and prioritizing human well-being over corporate profit or entrenched government policies that maintain an unjust status quo. Current policies even in economically advanced countries do not necessarily foster food security at international, state, community, or individual scales but may in fact put more control of the food system into the hands of a limited number of corporations and decision-makers.

5

Garbage and waste

Tons of active pharmaceutical ingredients dumped into the environment by medical-supply companies since 1988: 421,500
— Harper's *Index, August 2009*

Backlog, in years, of retired U.S. nuclear warheads waiting to be dismantled by the Federal Government: 13
— Harper's *Index, August 2009*

Introduction

On the website "365 Days of Trash: One man's attempt to throw nothing "away" for a year . . . and beyond," the creator of the site writes:

The idea for this project came about six months ago as I was throwing something away in the garbage. It occurred to me that I was doing nothing more than that. I was making it go away, not dealing with it, not accounting for it, simply removing it from my sight. When you think of it in simple terms like that, it's really quite insane. I came to the realization that if we were all accountable for our waste, if we couldn't simply make it disappear, we'd have to deal with some pretty ugly truths about the way we live. And in so doing, it would cause us to start making better decisions about what we buy, where we buy, and what's left over when we are done with that purchase. So starting tonight at midnight, I am not going to throw anything away for 365 days in order to see what my impact is . . .
(http://365daysoftrash.blogspot.com, accessed 17 June 2009)

The website is rich with information and ideas about using fewer plastic bags, switching to non-toxic cleansers, reaping the benefits of local farmers' markets, using worm composting, and stopping junk mail among other things. Another close inspection of one person's garbage generation is captured in *Garbage Land: On the secret trail of trash* by Elizabeth Royte (2005). She decides to follow her trash to the dump to see the impacts of burying trash, she learns what happens to recyclable items, and she tracks what happens when we flush something "away." Expand these explorations up to the global scale, and we can look at the trash floating in the ocean as an indicator of the state of the planet's garbage. Circling ocean currents have captured a growing collection of rubbish (Moody 2006). Scientific study has traced the origins of some of these gyres of garbage to the specific loss of steel containers from cargo ships (Ebbesmeyer and Scigliano 2009; Tabor 2009). For instance, the Columbus Gyre cycling around the Atlantic Ocean every 3.3 years carries over 800 000 Lego pieces lost off a ship at Land's End, England in 1997. The Turtle Gyre carries Nike shoes and hockey pads on a route between the US Pacific coast and the Pacific Islands and takes 6 years for each orbit. 17-inch computer monitors, dumped off a ship in 2000, are dropped off on beaches along the Northern Pacific coast after being carried by the Aleut Gyre. More generally, though, the Pacific Ocean between Hawaii and California is home to a gyre of flotsam so large that plastic is over one hundred times more prevalent than naturally occurring plankton (*The Economist* 2009d).

How we deal with the garbage and waste we generate would seem to be a matter for policy makers. Yet policy outcomes are not always the most economically effective or the most reasonable:

> ... governments seldom get the rules right. In poorer countries they often have no rules at all, or if they have them they fail to enforce them. In rich countries they are often inconsistent ... They are also prone to imposing arbitrary targets and taxes. California, for example, wants to recycle all its trash not because it necessarily makes environmental or economic sense but because the goal of "zero waste" sounds politically attractive. Britain, meanwhile, has started taxing landfills so heavily that local officials ... are investing in all manner of unproven waste-processing technologies.
>
> (*The Economist* 2009e, p. 5)

This chapter considers power and scale dimensions of garbage and waste. The goal of this chapter is not only to consider what society does about garbage but to look at garbage as a flow of resources. From extraction to manufacture to consumption to the point of being thrown "away," garbage and waste are moderated by different forms of power and can be seen to have important spatial dimensions. First, this chapter examines ideological power underlying consumption patterns in the rich world and how dominant under-standings of waste change over time. Electronic waste provides an illustration of different spatial scales involved in the production of garbage and waste. A discussion of bottled water, rights to resource use, and national sacrifice zones looks at ways in which power is implicated in the defining of and dealing with waste and environmental degradation. The discussion on power continues by considering how decisions about garbage and waste are made in the policy process. The chapter closes with thoughts about the meaning of garbage and waste as a reflection of society's values.

The meaning of garbage

Garbage and waste are not contemporary innovations. Archeologists have observed that even ancient societies were inefficient in their use of materials (Rathje and Murphy 2001):

Many ancient civilizations piled up mountains of garbage. At a spot in America called Pope's Creek, on the shores of the Potomac river, oyster shells discarded by the pre-Columbian inhabitants cover an area of 30 acres (12 hectares) to an average depth of ten feet.

(The Economist *2009c, p. 4*)

Societies generate waste. As societies change, their forms of waste change. The industrial revolution, for example, changed relationships between people and their immediate and distant environments. It extended the rate and reach of how people drew upon natural resources and how they generated waste. Innovations in transportation and communication altered the influence that people in North America and Europe had on resource bases and ecosystems in far away places and closer to home. Viewed from a designer's perspective, the Industrial Revolution may be seen as a process of imposing a one-size-fits-all approach to local economies and environments:

If the first Industrial Revolution had a motto, we like to joke, it would be "If brute force doesn't work, you're not using enough of it." The attempt to impose universal design solutions on an infinite number of local conditions and customs is one manifestation of this principle and its underlying assumption, that nature should be overwhelmed.

(McDonough and Braungart 2002, pp. 30–31)

A dominant design model left over from the Industrial Revolution is a linear "cradle-to-grave" model in which the bulk of raw materials used to construct products ends up being thrown "away." In the US, almost 90% of the materials extracted and used to make goods end up as waste. However, much of that waste has been or could be reintegrated into the commodity stream (see Lipsett 1963). The Industrial Revolution, for instance, was in many ways enabled by innovative uses of wastes as input. For example, until the mid-1800s, paper was made not from wood pulp but from rags. An entire rag industry emerged as paper manufacturing developed (O'Brien 2008). The demand for paper expanded, and international trade in rags expanded throughout Britain, the US, and Europe in the late 1700s. The increased availability of paper contributed to the development of newspapers, books, paper money, and other forms of written communication including legal documents and standardized law. Mostly women were employed in the work of finding rags to sell for use in paper making. At the same time, the leather producing industry was expanding and relied on dog waste, known at the time as dog "pure," as a key material in the tanning process. The astringent and alkaline qualities of dog waste served to clean goat hides at that time before synthetic chemicals were used for tanning hides. Men were employed to collect dog waste to sell to tanneries. These two examples demonstrate that:

From the inner material upon which words of wisdom were written to the protective outer shell that kept the words of wisdom intact, rags and pure were two components of a waste management machine that enabled nineteenth-century Europe to materialize a revolution in scientific and social thought ... In an even wider sense, rags and pure demonstrate beyond any doubt that the incorporation of so-called wastes into social and economic life has impacts on international trade, government policy, industrial innovation, occupational structure and the gendering of labour relations.

(O'Brien 2008, p. 63)

Another waste product for which new applications were found was coal tar which was used to make synthetic products ranging from aspirin to indigo. Animal fat, instead of being thrown out, was used to create a host of products including cream cheese and nitroglycerin, the latter of which led to the development of subways and skyscrapers thanks to its explosive properties. Petroleum spirit was an inconvenient waste product of paraffin refining. There was no use for this by-product, and so it was burned in open pits until a combustion engine was designed that could use petroleum spirit, or petroleum, as fuel. The resulting shift to petrol-powered combustion engines gave rise to the US-dominated airplane industry and signaled the end of Britain's coal-powered hegemony. Even today, we can see how waste, or otherwise unused resources, are infused with new usefulness. For example:

A single human body that has been 'abandoned' to medical research or over which no-one claims possessory rights of disposal is worth in excess of $70,000 to the cosmetic surgery industry. Corpse tissues are used in lip-enhancement, breast augmentation, penis-enlargement and in treating wrinkles. Ounce per ounce, human tissue in this industrial complex, is as valuable as diamonds.

(O'Brien 2008, p. 78)

Present day industrial agricultural practices use sewage as fertilizer and rendered animals in animal feed. Many pharmaceutical products also rely on human or animal "waste" for their effectiveness. Erythropoietin, or EPO, a performance-enhancing substance which has been used (illegally) by many professional athletes, is distilled from human urine, and "If making a fortune from urinating is not the height of ingenuity in waste reclamation then nothing is" (O'Brien 2008, p. 79). Indeed, it is clear that economic motivation and power drive ways in which waste is revalued, reintegrated into product life cycles, and used to create new products.

Ideological power determines the acceptability of such use or reintegration of waste in a given society. Even in twentieth century US, we can see the influence of ideological power shaping public perceptions of consumption and waste. During World War II, it served the interests of the government, gearing up to supply and strengthen the military, to promote conservation and recycling of materials such as scrap metal, rubber, rags, and paper. Public messages in the form of propaganda posters, pamphlets, and radio announcements relayed the values of recycling and conservation to the public. Most of these messages were issued by the US government, but the private sector, such as manufacturers and energy companies, also distributed their own posters and public service announcements to encourage conservation.[1] The availability of drop off centers for recyclable materials and the promotion of a general sentiment that conservation equated to support for the war effort all served to reinforce the practice of conservation and recycling. Before long, though, public sentiment shifted towards the idea of disposability and obsolescence.

As new and improved products become available, old products lose their appeal and are replaced. This process is known as technological obsolescence or innovation and is the first stage of obsolescence. Corporations took the idea of obsolescence further by changing products, such as unveiling new models of cars, new fashions or other items, and encouraging repetitive purchasing. This type of obsolescence can be referred to as psychological or progressive obsolescence. Manufacturers further realized that they could manipulate product durability by using inferior materials and thereby shorten the lifespan of their products. This practice is usually referred to as planned obsolescence. Overall:

As obsolescence became an increasingly useful manufacturing and marketing tool, an eclectic assortment of advertisers, bankers, business analysts, communications theorists, economists, engineers, industrial designers, and even real estate brokers contrived ways to describe, control, promote, and exploit the market demand that obsolescence created. What these approaches had in common was their focus on a radical break with tradition in order to deliver products ... and in the process to gain market share and make a buck.

(Slade 2006, p. 6)

The shift towards disposability and the growing acceptance of obsolescence complemented the promotion of progress and the rejection of tradition. Early critics of this transition pointed to marketing and advertising as efforts to manipulate people into consuming more and generating more waste. (Packard 1963; McLuhan 1964).

Whether it is by government-supported efforts, manufacturers, or advertisers, ideological power may be seen as an influence on public opinion and the range of acceptable or expected behavior. When Rachel Carson published her watershed book, *Silent Spring*, (Carson 1962), she drew public attention to the risks of pesticides and other widely used chemicals. She rejected the idea that chemical and technological innovation could make the waste products of society disappear, and she promoted the idea that waste actually imposes unwanted costs on society. Yet as popular as this notion may have been, and may still be in some circles, we can find cases where forms of garbage or waste generation is acceptable. For instance, the American public generally accepts that fluoride is added to public water supplies because it promotes strong tooth enamel. After all these years of advertising and being told that fluoride is good for us, would we really want to know that fluoride is a waste by-product of the nuclear and aluminum industries? Although it can be naturally occurring in some places, there is reason to believe that known effects of fluoride were not communicated openly before non-naturally occurring forms of it entered into water systems (accidentally, in some cases) (Bryson 2004).

Ideological power determines much of what the public knows about waste and garbage and what the public views as appropriate or inappropriate ways to deal with waste and garbage. We tend to think, for example, that recycling is an environmentally responsible thing to do. Most everyone would recognize the recycling logo, but few would suspect that it was developed by the packaging industry. Indeed, "the Container Corporation of America commissioned the design a few months after the first Earth Day [in 1970] to advertise its reprocessed products and left the logo in the public domain for others to adopt" (Rogers 2005, p. 171). Manufacturers, in this way, were at the forefront of shaping public perception of this new concept of recycling and played a critical role in promoting recycling over reducing consumption or reusing products. Now, we rarely question the process once we have put materials into the recycling bin. Yet even by the mid-1990s:

...recycling did not minimize the creation of discards. Instead, this back-end refuse management strategy left wasteful mass production and consumption unaltered and even encouraged. People started believing that their trash was now benign. Today it's likely that more Americans recycle than vote – yet greater amounts of rubbish are going to landfills and incinerators than ever before ... Just because materials are hauled away in a recycling truck doesn't mean that they actually get reprocessed. Almost half of discarded newspapers and office paper is buried or burned, while two-thirds of glass containers and plastic soda and milk bottles are trashed instead of recycled.

(Rogers 2005, pp. 176–177)

Ideological power, such as that exercised by the manufacturing industry in forming public perceptions of recycling, can serve to focus attention or hide from public view aspects of consumption and resource use that are less than appealing or that might lead people to question what happens to the waste we create.

E-waste

E-waste, or electronic waste, illustrates dynamics of power dimensions and overlapping spatial scales of garbage and waste. E-waste comprises not just personal computers and cell phones, but also includes:

> ...last year's Palms, Blackberries, Notebooks, printers, copiers, monitors, scanners, modems, hubs, docking ports, digital cameras, LCD projectors, Zip drives, speakers, keyboards, mice, GameBoys, Walkmen, CD players, VCRs, and DVD players... PlayStations, Xboxes, and Ipods are not far behind.
>
> *(Slade 2006, p. 2)*

The number of discarded, old televisions with cathode ray tubes (CRTs) will likely increase in response to a new US law that will shift the country to high definition television (HDTV). A thriving industry of electronics recycling has emerged in response to this swelling waste stream (Grossman 2007). Several hundred businesses in the US alone, ranging in size, extract metals from e-waste that are re-entered into commodity chains, or they refurbish and update equipment that may then be used in schools. The Environmental Protection Agency (EPA) does not regulate or license electronics recycling, so there are no standards or guidelines. Not everyone has access to or awareness of e-waste recycling facilities, so recycling levels are still relatively low. A lot of these electronics end up in landfills. There is concern that toxins and heavy metals in e-waste including lead, cadmium, mercury, chromium, beryllium, barium, and arsenic, will leak and contribute to poisonous leachate – or "garbage juice" – flowing from landfills (O'Rourke 2007; see Gattuso 2007 for an opposing view arguing that scientific research on leachate has been misunderstood and misrepresented). Incineration of e-waste generates similar concerns since these toxins and other dioxins released from burning plastic become airborne and could lead to contamination and health problems.

Not all of this waste from electronic gadgets goes to landfills within the US, however. E-waste and other forms of toxic and hazardous waste are traded internationally. The Basel Convention on the Control of Transboundary Movements of Hazardous Wastes and their Disposal, known simply as The Basel Convention, is an international agreement intended to minimize the creation of hazardous waste in both quantity and hazardous quality, to reduce the transboundary movement of hazardous wastes, and to encourage the disposal of such wastes as close to their source as possible. The Basel Convention was originally signed by 35 countries in 1989 and came into force in 1992 once the required 20 countries ratified it or implemented legislation to conform to the requirements of the agreement. Three states that signed the treaty but have not yet ratified it are the US, Afghanistan, and Haiti (see The Basel Convention website at http://www.basel.int/, accessed 21 July 2009). The Basel Convention came about largely due to the efforts of non-state actors such as environmental non-governmental organizations that were concerned about negative, environmental effects of global-reaching, private economic activities. The idea was to get states involved in managing and restricting the flow of hazardous waste. Trade in hazardous waste, however, can be very lucrative. Countries that do not have the proper facilities to dispose of hazardous waste still accept hazardous waste from other states. One significant weakness of the Basel Convention is that it does not outright ban the trade of hazardous waste from richer countries to poorer countries. There are also several ways to get around the guidelines of the treaty (Clapp 2001). For example, if materials might be considered recyclable, it is not clear that they are subject to treatment as hazardous materials. Hazardous materials are also defined differently by different states. There are no clear consequences for illegal hazardous waste trade such as trade between participating and non-participating members.

Asia and Africa are main destinations for e-waste from richer countries. In Asia, the volume of waste is large enough to make the recovery of materials economically worthwhile for some people. Unfortunately, recovery often involves "…women and children laborers who cook circuit boards, burn cables, and submerge equipment in toxic acids to extract precious metals such as copper" (Schmidt 2006, p. 235). The local health and ecological effects of these recovery practices are significant but mostly ignored. African port cities also receive large volumes of e-waste. Shipments of e-waste from used electronics exporters may be negotiated to include a specific number of usable items such as Pentium III processors, but shipping containers are often topped off with unusable items. One coordinator of the Basel Action Network, an environmental organization, visited the port city of Lagos which receives an estimated five hundred shipping containers of used electronics monthly and observed:

We saw people using e-waste to fill in swamps … Whenever the piles got too high, they would torch them … Residents complained about breathing the fumes, but the dumps were never cleaned up. We saw kids roaming barefoot over this material, not to mention chickens and goats [which wind up in the local diet].

(quoted in Schmidt 2006, p. 234)

The flow of hazardous waste from richer to poorer countries would seem to follow a line from more to less economically powerful. Yet economic power alone does not determine which countries send or receive hazardous waste from other countries. Richer countries also trade hazardous waste among themselves. Considerable trade in hazardous waste flows between rich countries where the difference in economic or even political power is not so great. In these cases, the difference between which states send or accept hazardous waste has more to do with procedural differences within those states such as their regulatory structures, how issues of hazardous waste are interpreted, at what spatial scale they are defined, the degree and directionality of risk tolerance or risk averseness, and the role of national lobbies (O'Neill 2000). All of these factors highlight ways in which different forms of power and different spatial scales come into play on the single theme of international trade in hazardous waste.

The Basel Convention is clearly not achieving the goals of keeping hazardous waste close to the source or minimizing international trade in hazardous waste and the threat it poses to particular communities. In that sense, we might view it as a failed policy. However, we can also see that the Basel Convention serves the interests of actors or agents who benefit from the export or import of electronic waste because it enables this trade to occur. The guidelines and restrictions of the Basel Convention are vague enough to permit trade in e-waste to continue. It serves as a placeholder. It is unlikely that another policy will emerge to address the shortcomings of the Basel Convention, so we are left with this policy as the dominant institution shaping the way that second hand electronics move around the world. This policy, then, serves to hold power relations stable. It also maintains the transboundary spatial scale of e-waste movement and reinforces our perception that as we purchase new gadgets we can simply throw the old ones "away."

Waste from the information technology industry does not only occur at the end-of-life stage of gadgets. Mining the metals that go into these products itself is a process that generates several kinds of waste. Coltan, for example, is a key mineral which is processed into tantalum powder and used to make capacitors for a variety of high-tech electronics. Although approximately 80% of the coltan used today is mined in Australia, significant, untapped reserves are located in Africa, particularly in the Democratic Republic of Congo (Grossman 2006). Coltan mining there has become yet another funding source for ongoing, armed conflict in the region. Mines are unsafe and largely unregulated, the industry contributes to a weakened social fabric, agricultural land is overwhelmed by mining activities leading to a shrunken food supply, and ecosystems and habitat are destroyed. A movement of non-governmental organizations has initiated a campaign to bring public awareness to the destructiveness of the coltan mining industry in the Democratic Republic of Congo and encourages consumers and companies to boycott coltan mined there. However, it is nearly impossible to discern the provenance or source of coltan sold on the world market:

> ... the trail of Congolese coltan is circuitous. The UN report traces coltan mined in the Congo under the auspices of an American company called Eagle Wings Resources – a subsidiary of another American company called Trinitech that is associated with a Dutch company called Chemie Pharmacie Holland (with headquarters in Ohio) – to Kazakhstan, where the mineral was processed at the Ulba Metallurgical Plant, and to the Ningxia smelter in China...Other reports gathered by the UN team follow coltan mined in the eastern Congo across the border into Uganda, where it was flown to the United Arab Emirates and then to Kazakhstan for processing. The report also traces coltan mined in the Congo moving in and out of Europe through Belgium ... Some countries listed as sources or producers of tantalum on the USGS [US Geological Survey] annual fact sheets for the mineral industry, are merely transshipment points – countries (for example, the Bahamas) without tantalum mines or processing facilities – something that adds to the difficulty of independent tracking of the ore's world travels.
>
> *(Grossman 2006, p. 50)*

The spatial scale of coltan, a key, front-end mineral in the eventual generation of e-waste, ties together many places and activities (mining, shipping, manufacturing). This example illustrates the complexity of waste even if we are only looking at the input end of the production process. It demonstrates the difficulty of managing waste not only because it affects many places but also because it takes many forms from destroyed mining landscapes to quickly outdated, difficult-to-dismantle electronic devices. We could (and probably should) add to the list of complicating factors the physical and social damage done to communities in places like the Democratic Republic of Congo – men leaving their families and farms to work in unsafe mines, women and children seeking work in the mines in order to survive, and the role of coltan and other minerals in the continuation of armed conflict in the region. These are unexpected, destructive side effects of our consumption that are often hidden from view by various forms of ideological power including advertising and entertainment, social reinforcement, and product obsolescence.

Bottled water, wise use, and national sacrifice zones

Ideological power drives consumption as has already been discussed. The desire to have the latest gadgets or styles with little thought to the effects of that consumption is an effect of this power. Another example is the popularity of bottled water. In her book *Bottlemania: How Water Went On Sale and Why We Bought It*, Elizabeth Royte (2008) explores the recent bottled water phenomenon throughout the world and particularly in the US. Powerful companies such as Nestlé and Coke sign contracts with governments to pump water out of lakes and groundwater supplies to bottle and sell, usually at locations distant from the source. This shifting control over natural resources is happening in the US, where, for example, Coke and Pepsi have arranged with Michigan to bottle water from the Great Lakes. It is also happening in places like India where rural water supplies are in decline as globe-spanning, corporate control wields influence. Bottled water was originally promoted for having healthful, spa-in-a-bottle qualities, but more recently a message driving consumption of bottled water is that it is safer or of a more consistent quality than tap water.

Economic and ideological forms of power are clearly at play in the expansion and promotion of bottled water. This power extends to the control of physical infrastructure:

Well-maintained fountains are becoming about as scarce as working pay phones... Cynically, I think "Why not?" If I were in the containerized-water business, I'd do everything in my power to either hide the bubblers or make public supplies look wildly unattractive. A new football stadium in Orlando, Florida, was built without a single water fountain; one hot afternoon, a dozen people were treated for heat exhaustion after the concession stands, which charged three bucks for a bottle of water, ran out. After the scandal hit the papers, fifty water fountains were quickly installed. At Lehigh University...the dining-services company removed the free waterspouts from its Pepsi soda machines, steering students to bottled water. Only after much student protest did the spouts re-spout.

(Royte 2008, p. 210)

If we examine the issue of bottled water more deeply, we arrive at questions of political power as well. Is water a human right? Who has the right to control this resource that all people need in order to survive? Consuming bottled water may be a convenience or a perceived or real improvement on other water supplies, but some people go further and take the view that "drinking bottled water is a far more political act: it's an affirmation that water is a commodity, and that it's okay for corporations to control it" (Royte 2008, p. 209). The implications for garbage and waste are significant here. When we pay for water, what are we paying for? Are we paying to maintain a locally controlled, democratically managed, not-for-profit water system that the public may use, or are we paying for the decline of distant water supplies, corporate profit (Snitow *et al.* 2007), and the generation of a considerable volume of containers that may add to landfills or require energy to recycle (see Figure 5.1)?

Figure 5.1 Frozen assets. An art installation at the University of Kansas used hundreds of recyclable water bottles to demonstrate the generation of waste from the consumption of bottled water. Student artist: Matthew Farley. Photo: Jaclyn Lippelmann.

The question of who owns natural resources – and who is responsible for addressing the waste generated by the extraction, processing, and consumption of those resources – is a critical question for the issue of garbage and waste. Waste can take the form of environmental degradation and the generation of by-products from industrial resource use. These forms of waste are justified as acceptable through the exertion of ideological power. One illustration of ideological power exercised in the interest of resource extraction is the Wise Use Movement. The Wise Use Movement is often described as a backlash against a growing environmental movement in the US starting in the 1990s. The Wise Use Movement includes a diverse membership, but it comprises mostly industrialists and entrepreneurs who seek to remove or limit government restrictions on the use of public lands. The name "Wise Use" is a reference to Gifford Pinchot, a leader in the early years of the US Forestry system at the turn of the previous century, who is attributed with initiating the idea of conversation (see Chapter 1). Pinchot (1947) wrote about conservation as "the use of the natural resources for the greatest good of the greatest number for the longest time" (p. 326). The Wise Use Movement draws upon this idea to emphasize that resources should be used for their economic potential.

The Wise Use Movement was established to promote a broad agenda:

... that included developing oil and gas reserves in the Arctic National Wildlife Refuge; eliminating restrictions on wetlands development; opening all public lands, including national parks and wilderness areas, to mineral and energy production, redesignating 70 of the 90 million acres of the National Wilderness Preservation System for motorized trail travel, limited commercial development, and commodity use; instituting civil penalties against anyone who legally challenged economic action or development on federal lands; and recognizing private rights to mining claims, water, grazing permits, and timber contracts on federal lands.

(Layzer 2002, p. 241)

The Wise Use Movement is often described as being anti-environmentalist (see Echeverria and Eby 1995) and as waging a "war against the greens" (Helvarg 1994) in an effort to promote unlimited exploitation of natural resources. The Wise Use Movement is seen by its critics as anything but "wise" since it rejects government oversight and restrictions on how public lands are used for private profit by ranchers and the timber and mining industries, among others. Without accountability for what they leave behind, these groups are able to maximize their profits at the expense of the quality of public lands and wilderness areas. Members of the Wise Use Movement view themselves as true environmentalists since they are the ones who extract resources upon which society depends for food, clothing, and material comforts. In addition to referring to the "unavoidable environmental damage that is the price of our survival" (Arnold 1996, p. 23), one self-description of the movement goes so far as to explain:

We only learn about the world through trial and error. The universe did not come with a set of instructions, nor did our minds. We cannot see the future. Thus, the only way we humans can learn about our surroundings is through trial and error. Even the most sophisticated science is systematized trial and error. Environmental ideology fetishizes nature to the point that we cannot permit ourselves errors with the environment, ending in no trials and no learning.

(Arnold 1996, p. 24)

When read carefully, this passage can be seen to excuse any damage resulting from "trial and error." Even science, Western society's gold standard for establishing facts and truth, is indicated as a process of mistake making. Humans are only trying to learn about our environment, and how else can we do that if there is no room for error? What kind of environmental errors might this passage refer to? One form of error might be the devastating effects of large-scale strip mining in places such as Appalachia and the Rocky Mountains that has destroyed vast areas and left toxic mine tailings exposed and seeping into headwaters of major rivers. Other public lands are devastated by all manner of motorized recreational vehicle when wilderness paths are opened up as roads for the purpose of timber harvesting or mining.

Garbage and waste

No one may have intended to cause vast soil erosion and habitat loss, but uncontrolled use of public lands can lead to precisely that kind of damage. The above passage justifying trial and error omits mention of the fact that someone is profiting from the resource use and, moreover, from not having to be accountable for the environmental damage caused or the waste generated by resource extraction. The Wise Use Movement borrowed Gifford Pinchot's words about wise use, but they may well have missed his sentiment. Later in the same work in which he wrote about wise use, Pinchot also wrote that "... monopoly of natural resources was only less dangerous to the public welfare than their actual destruction" (Pinchot 1947, p. 326). Clearly, Pinchot was not advocating placing control of public natural resources in the hands of private interests but thought that government oversight was necessary to ensure that the greatest good truly was distributed to the greatest number of people over the longest possible time. That is a lofty goal, but it is not clear how society is supposed to deal with waste or environmental damage resulting from our interactions with the physical environment.

Military power and national sacrifice zones

The case of the Wise Use Movement highlights a contrast between political power reflected in state control of resources and economic power which is demonstrated by corporate or private control of resources. Sometimes these forms of power align such as when private interests sign contracts with state entities to use public resources. For example, private ranchers might graze their livestock on public lands managed by the Bureau of Land Management. In that case, the state maintains control of the resources and the ranchers benefit from publicly owned resources. Ideological power comes into play as both sides persuade the public on how best to manage, use, preserve, or benefit from public lands as well as how to manage the damage or waste left behind by this use. Taking a feminist approach to environmental degradation, Joni Seager (1993) questions assumptions underlying dominant institutions that influence society's use of the environment. She observes that:

The environmental crisis is not just a crisis of physical ecosystems. The *real* story of the environmental crisis is a story of power and profit and political wrangling; it is a story of the institutional arrangements and setting, the bureaucratic arrangements and the cultural conventions that *create* conditions of environmental destruction. Toxic wastes and oil spills and dying forests, which are presented in the daily news as the entire environmental story, are the symptoms – the symptoms of social arrangements and especially of social *derangements*. The environmental crisis is not just the sum of ozone depletion, global warming, and overconsumption; it is a crisis of the dominant ideology.

(Seager 1993, p. 3, emphasis in original)

She focuses on militaries as a particularly insidious type of institution in terms of inflicting environmental damage since "Their daily operations are typically beyond the reach of civil law" (p. 14). Environmental damage done by militaries is often overlooked since that is the least of transgressions for which militaries tend be held responsible. This chapter has already considered how different forms of power – ideological, economic, and political – shape society's relationship to garbage and waste, but we can also see how military power can be related to the generation and perception of waste. The military is another institution that exerts its power, which overlaps with ideological and political power, to justify the use of resources and the physical environment in ways that are not necessarily sustainable.

An outstanding example of military and nationalistic justification of environmentally destructive and waste-generating practices may be seen in the Soviet Union's approach to development. The Soviet leadership's ambition was to be a world power, and that objective motivated aggressive steps towards development. Power, in that context, had a significant military component. Achieving that military power meant overcoming vast physical challenges. The Soviet Union stretched across eleven time zones. Its natural resources were unevenly distributed and often difficult to reach due to extensive frozen or perma-frost covered areas. In the late 1920s, the Soviet leader, Joseph Stalin, initiated the first of 13 5-year plans which set goals for development in multiple areas: agriculture, education, communication, transportation, and the military. The first 5-year plan in 1920 focused on making significant advancements in and expansion of military artillery, tanks, aviation, and chemical weapons. Subsequent 5-year plans set guidelines to expand agricultural productivity, literacy rates, urban development, resource extraction, and industrial productivity. Soviet leadership pursued ambitious and aggressive plans for development and emphasized meeting goals and production quotas at any expense. A particular example of how nature was viewed as a stockpile of resources to be utilized for national development was Stalin's Great Plan for the Transformation of Nature. In the late 1940s, this plan was launched as a means of overcoming constraints imposed by nature. Major projects included the reversal of rivers in northern regions so that instead of draining "uselessly" into the Arctic Ocean they would be redirected to the Central Asian steppe where water was needed for agricultural and urban expansion.

What is still obvious to anyone living or working in most of the former Soviet realm is that the Soviet disregard for the environment in favor of development has left a powerful, lingering legacy of environmental damage and toxic waste (see Figure 1.1). Thanks to the Soviet predilection for large-scale and vertically integrated industries, environmental damage was

(a)   (b)

Figure 5.2 Nuclear memorial at Semey, Kazakhstan. The poignant *Stronger than Death* memorial, depicting a mother shielding her infant from a 30m black marble mushroom cloud, commemorates the innocent victims of the nuclear testing grounds near Semipalatinsk, Kazakhstan. Photos courtesy of Cristin Burke.

concentrated, multi-layered, and resulted in the creation of toxic "hot spots" wherever economic activity was most intense. For example, the city of Sumqayit in Azerbaijan was home to a vast chemical industry during Soviet times. The concentration of poorly managed chemical waste resulted in high infant mortality rates, and high rates of cancer and birth defects. One may still visit the children's cemetery in Sumqayit, itself a sobering reflection of the effects of the chemical industry there, and see that fresh flowers still grace graves of children who died years ago. Another example of how Soviet decision-makers laid waste to the environment may be seen in Semipalatinsk in present day Kazakhstan. Semipalatinsk was the primary Soviet nuclear weapons proving ground. Between 1949 and 1989, 459 nuclear explosions were conducted there (Takada 2005). People in nearby villages were rarely evacuated prior to these tests and were exposed to radioactive fallout. Around 1.7 million people have been severely affected by radiation. Cancers, leukemia, heart, cardiovascular and bone diseases, and children born with physical or mental handicaps have increased dramatically since the testing started. Soviet prioritization of military power and rapid, large-scale economic development had, and continues to have, spatially uneven effects (see Figure 5.2a and b). Again, we can see why it is useful to understand that power takes different forms and generates complex geographies of garbage and waste.

In the US, the case of Tooele County, Utah aptly illustrates another example of a military installation becoming a national sacrifice zone or wasteland created in the pursuit of national interests. Reaching across the southern Great Salt Lake Desert, Tooele County was home to Dugway Proving Ground which served as the central testing ground for incendiary, chemical, and biological weapons (Davis 1998). Napalm was developed there, and an anthrax bomb was tested there in the 1940s along with atomic bombs such as those dropped on Hiroshima and Nagasaki. A series of experiments with live human subjects was also conducted there. In the 1950s and 1960s over 1600 field trials of nerve gas were conducted with minimal public oversight (or notice). In the 1990s, Tooele County was designated as "the nation's first officially zoned "hazardous industry area" for the disposal of medical waste, deadly industrial chemicals, and uranium tailings" (Davis 1998, p. 35), and *Outside Magazine* has labeled Tooele County "the most polluted site on Earth."

How can such devastation and pollution be considered acceptable? The activities conducted in Tooele County, like those conducted in Semipalatinsk or Sumqayit, were likely justified in the interest of national or state security. By invoking the scale of the state, military institutions identify with state power. In this way, political power and military power reinforce each other. Military activities are justified on the spatial scale of the state as protecting the state's territorial integrity and political sovereignty. The benefits – knowledge, skills, and capacity acquired through weapons development and testing – arguably accrue to the whole state. That idea assumes that the political power of the state serves the interests of the majority of citizens. The spatial scale of the damage and waste, however, is concentrated in "sacrifice zones" such as Tooele County and other military installations. The costs – environmental degradation and devastation, negative health impacts, limitations or constraints on using that space for other purposes – are unevenly distributed.

Returning to Gifford Pinchot's perspective, we can see how the creation of environmental sacrifice zones for the expansion of military capacity could arguably serve the interests of "the greatest number for the longest time" (Pinchot 1947, p. 326). Yet the fact that the military industrial complex operates with minimal public input or oversight raises similar concerns we might have about the way other industries operate:

When the public has no say in manufacturing – which materials get used; how they are extracted from nature; what kind of production process is employed; and levels of toxicity in manufacturing, use, and disposal of materials – the democratic utilization of our common natural resources is fundamentally undermined. Just as the airwaves belong to the people, so too is the rest of the natural world part of the public commons. It is only fair that since we share the responsibility for and consequences of wastes, we should also participate in the choices made during production, the real source of trash. U.S. industry's largely unfettered access to natural resources is the mark of a deeply undemocratic system.

(Rogers 2005, p. 229)

It may be argued that when it comes to protecting the state's territorial integrity and political sovereignty, democracy has already been exercised when citizens elected their leaders. How elected leaders use their power on issues of environmental decision-making goes back to a point made in the introductory chapter of this book about the difference between the political and politics. There, it was noted that the political moment is the point at which values and ideals are competing. Once institutional norms have been determined and leaders have been elected, we witness politics and the carrying out of procedures within the institutionalized order (Edkins 1999). Activity at that point, the point of politics, is limited to the constraints of the system and has been effectively depoliticized.

Back to Tooele County, when the state of Utah proposed to retake control over a road used for the transport of spent fuel rods to try to control the flow of waste into the county:

... the county commissioners erupted in self-righteous fury. Despite growing citizen opposition to further hazardous dumping in their backyards, the majority of Tooele County's elected politicians – now addicted to hefty campaign contributions from hazardous waste industries – continue to claim a divine design for their toxic open door. Referring to the County's vast arid hinterland, one commissioner told a Salt Lake City reporter: "It's a resource that the Good Lord intended us to use for exactly the purpose we're using it for."

(Davis 1998, p. 39)

Is the wasting of the physical environment, or the generation of physical waste itself, then, an inevitable side effect of politics in action as established actors, stakeholders, and governments maneuver to maintain power?

Rational decision-making

The problem of garbage or waste would seem to be a relatively straightforward one that could be dealt with by subjecting it to an established policy-making process. Anyone who has interacted with institutional bureaucracy (e.g., university administration, city government, etc.) is aware that for any given situation (e.g., applying to college and enrolling in classes, paying a parking ticket, or registering to vote) there is usually a protocol or process that one must work through in a stepwise fashion to achieve the desired end. Institutions, as bodies that organize and maintain the structure of society, serve to channel certain processes towards recognized outcomes while at the same time prohibit other types of processes or actions. We tend to look to these institutions to solve problems, but they can only solve problems that they were established to address. An analogy might be computers. Computers can only do tasks and solve problems they were programmed to address. Despite what HAL 9000 in Arthur C. Clarke's *Space Odyssey* series might think, computers cannot think for themselves. Just because an institution or set of rules is in place, however, does not necessarily mean that it is the best tool for resolving problems. It may be the current or established tool, but it may not be the most effective or even the most appropriate means of resolving problems.

Consider the Environmental Protection Agency (EPA). Most Americans, if they are at all familiar with this institution, likely assume that this regulatory agency protects them from pollution and other hidden, environmental dangers by setting and enforcing rules about how we interact with the environment. Most people may be unaware, however, that when the EPA was established in 1970, it was given no Congressional charter or clear organizational mission. A result of this lack of focus is that the EPA's responsibilities are very broad and relatively unprioritized. Additionally, the EPA's budget and staffing fluctuate with changing White House administrations. In addition to its role as both a regulatory agency and a distributive agency (e.g., allocating federal funds for waste treatment grants), the EPA is also under constant pressure to provide scientific findings to policy makers. Policy makers, however, operate on time scales that often curb or hinder the scientific process. Election cycles rarely match the timeframe of environmental research and investigation. One telling example of the challenges that the EPA faces in doing its job is the gap in data on toxins that the EPA is required but unable to provide due to constraints in time, funding, and personnel. For instance, there are 168 chemicals on the EPA's list of airborne toxics of concern, but the EPA has only been able to study 27 of those. Similarly, there are 476 chemicals in urgent need of testing under the Toxic Substances Control Act, but the EPA has only been able to study 10 of those chemicals. These are but a few tasks that fall under the EPA's responsibilities along with studying and regulating air quality, water quality, hazardous waste, pesticides, and nuclear waste (Rosenbaum 2008). The example of the EPA illustrates how

environmental degradation is a twenty-first century problem resolved according to eighteenth-century rules: fundamental government arrangements such as institutional checks and balances, interest group liberalism, federalism ... are explicitly created by the Constitution or are implicit in its philosophy ... environmental management has become a permanent new policy domain within federal and state governments with its own set of institutional and political biases.

(Rosenbaum 2008, p. 61)

Why, then, do institutions or protocols persist even if they are largely inefficient or ineffective? Part of the reason institutions and their established processes persist is that they are place holders for power as has already been discussed in the case of the Basel Convention. Governing and policy-making institutions reflect power in society. They recognize some issues as relevant and worthy of consideration, and they render other issues or concerns as irrelevant. They provide channels and parameters for the resolution of certain problems. Institutions and the rules which organize society also reflect power by determining whose views, perspectives, and input is recognized as legitimate. Recent debates over whether or not to make official documents such as tax forms available in multiple languages and whether or not same sex marriage is legally legitimate are a few examples of ways in which institutions can prohibit the considerations of certain issues and in so doing exercise a form of power.

Here, it is useful to look at the rational decision-making process as an example of how we might reasonably expect decisions to be made about how to deal with environmental problems such as garbage and waste. This model outlines a linear means of evaluating a situation and identifying the most appropriate response to that situation. It is a template for a process that is often used in governing bodies to make decisions. It is useful here as a starting point for understanding complexities and power dimensions of the decision-making process. We will see how this process works and how it may be seen to present a reasonable, measured, and, yes, rational, approach to solving problems. It is a guide to evaluating an issue through multiple stages of a decision-making process. We will also consider limitations of this model to illustrate how established institutions and protocols may actually limit our thinking about environmental problems such as garbage and waste. The purpose in examining this model is to consider how different forms of power and different spatial scales come into play in or are sidelined from a problem-solving process.

The model for rational decision-making outlines a set of steps of evaluation in the planning process to clarify objectives, consider multiple alternatives, and evaluate feasibility and effectiveness associated with possible solutions (see Figure 5.3). The first step is to identify the problem to be addressed or resolved. This step may seem straightforward and uncomplicated, but as we will see below, it can be very difficult to clarify what "the" problem is. The second step encourages brainstorming possible solutions and assessing different plans to resolve the problem. At this stage multiple

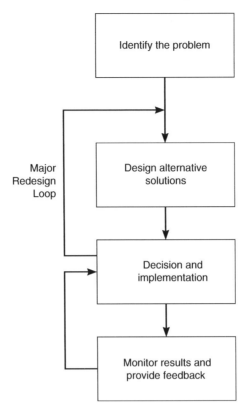

Figure 5.3 A model for rational decision-making. Adapted from McAllister (1988), p. 80.

variables of costs, benefits, and risks would be considered for each alternative plan. Third, a decision is made about which plan to pursue, and that plan is implemented. At this stage, it may become clear that more information is needed to make the decision or that an additional alternative might be considered. Finally, the implemented plan is monitored, and feedback may encourage a reconsideration of how the plan was implemented, if the decision has proven to be effective, or if the correct problem was identified initially.

This linear process appears to work like a checklist towards resolving a problem. For example, a municipality might be interested in promoting, say, the recycling of aluminum cans. If that is the problem that has been identified (i.e., not enough people are recycling cans), we can see that the second step of exploring alternatives might look at different forms of economic incentives to encourage recycling, the provision of drop-off facilities or curbside pick-up options for collecting cans, and options for ways to encourage the public to take the initiative to recycle aluminum cans. From there, benefit–cost analyses of each option could be weighed to discern its advantages and costs. Comparing costs and benefits can be a transparent way to determine which approach to the problem is most feasible in terms of economic costs, political attractiveness, resonance with the local population, and so forth. This simple scenario is complicated, however, when we recognize that there are opposing views as to whether or not recycling is a useful practice. Although recycling is a popular idea that most people associate with being environmentally responsible, it has been argued that recycling is just another manufacturing process that requires considerable energy and water inputs and that has a negative environmental impact in the pollution that it generates (Benjamin 2007). Mandatory curbside recycling programs are viewed by some people as wasting household members' time to sort their trash and as a waste of energy used to gather and process recyclables (Janney 2007). Landfilling or inciner-ating garbage may indeed look like a cheaper option than recycling depending on how the numbers are calculated, and using virgin materials may also seem less expensive than reprocessing recyclable materials depending on how the calculations are done. For example, any benefit–cost analysis comparing recycling to other options should consider that resource extraction is often supported by government subsidies in one form or another. Calculations should also consider that the prices of materials and processing may fluctuate over time, so drawing on data for just a few years may not lead to an accurate assessment. Spatially, recycling programs for some materials might make sense in some places and not in others. Recycling efforts in densely populated urban areas might make more economic and environmental sense than landfilling, but this might not be the case in sparsely populated, rural areas. Instead of conceptualizing blanket policies for recyc-ling, it is helpful to consider how "Recycling, when it comes down to it, is a very geographically narrow activity, and its costs and benefits vary accord-ingly. Like politics, all garbage is local." (Clement 2007, p. 92).

Identifying a problem to be solved is not enough. We also need to under-stand how success will be measured. To continue our example of recycling aluminum cans, if recycling is the goal, are we measuring success in terms of the rate of public participation, the volume of collected material, the economic benefit to the municipality, or some other objective? Technical understanding of the identified problem is also key. For example, recycling aluminum cans probably strikes most people as a more environmentally friendly alternative than, say, throwing away aseptic drink boxes. Such drink boxes may be described as a "monstrous hybrid" (McDonough and Braungart 2002, p. 98) of materials that defies dismantling to basic components that may be recycled. Yet given the right incentives, it may be cheaper to landfill drink boxes than to recycle aluminum cans (Porter 2002, p. 152). Part of the problem with recycling aluminum cans is that they are made of different types of aluminum. The sturdy top of aluminum cans is made of aluminum magnesium alloy, but the sides are made of a combination of aluminum, magnesium, magnesium alloy, and coatings. When aluminum cans are melted for recycling, the materials mix and result in a downgraded, or downcycled, and less useful material (McDonough and Braungart 2002, p. 57). Whether or not the objective is to arrive at the cheapest solution is also up for debate: cheapest for whom and measured in what kinds of costs? Clearly, even a seemingly straightforward garbage issue such as promoting recycling can quickly become a complex decision-making challenge.

Power – political, economic, and ideological – underlies how a problem or policy issue is defined. Political power may be applied with the objective of garnering yet more power, control, and influence:

Key to advocates' success in building a coalition substantial enough to overturn the status quo is their ability to promote a compelling definition of the environmental problem. Although conventional tactics, such as lobbying legislators and donating money to political campaigns, remain important means of influencing policy, scholars increasingly have recognized the importance of strategically defining problems in determining the outcome of policy contests. For environmentalists, those efforts entail generating scientific information and framing it in ways that emphasize the risk of inaction. When advocates succeed in translating the scientific explanation of a problem into a compelling causal story ... they are much more likely to attract support.
(Layzer 2002, p. 350)

In other words, those actors with the power to define or frame the environmental problem under consideration can often set the decision-making agenda in such a way that they garner yet more power. One study has looked at what kinds of groups appear to have the most influence on rulemaking on major policies (Kamieniecki 2006). Environmental policies tend to be written in vague language and without explicit directions for how a given policy should be implemented. Rules are required to interpret the substance of laws and to establish an understanding of how to attain the policy objective. The study tracked public comment periods on proposed adjustments to rules for major pieces of US environmental legislation. The study examined rule changes for proposed revisions to arsenic standards in drinking water, proposed revisions to criteria for solid waste disposal facilities, proposed revision of the extremely hazardous substance list, proposed revision to the roadless area conservation rule in US forests, and a proposal to adjust the gray wolf's classification as an endangered or threatened species. These particular rules were selected as a good test of how much influence business interests have on the rulemaking process. The study compared the time windows for public comment on each proposed rule change, the types of groups that submitted comments on the proposed rules (e.g., business, utilities, citizens' groups, government agencies, academics, etc.), the number of comments submitted, and the amount of change (e.g., none, minimal, some, a great deal) between the proposed and final rules in each case. In short, this study examined how various stakeholders contributed input at the second step of the model for rational decision-making, above.

The study found that interest groups, environmental organizations, or business interests did not have a major impact on final rules. Economic considerations only had a significant impact on the outcome of the arsenic standards rule change. What the study found is that in cases where business strongly opposed a proposed rule change (e.g., timber companies opposing bans to the development of forestry roads), they engaged in agenda blocking so that the proposed rule would be retracted and never even reach the public comment stage. The study concludes that the important part of rulemaking occurs earlier and often away from public view:

As far as rulemaking on environmental and natural resources issues is concerned, public and business input plays only a small role in shaping final policy. The kind of rules that are initially proposed is more critical and probably a better indicator of the amount of influence business has in the rulemaking process ... In particular, the degree to which business has access to the executive branch will help determine the nature and contents of rules that are proposed under new and existing legislation. The more access business lobbyists have to important members of the administration, the more business is likely to get its way.

(Kamieniecki 2006, p. 18)

The point is that setting the agenda, identifying and framing the question on which a decision-making process will proceed, reflects a great deal of power and influence. The steps that follow may or may not actually make much difference. Michael Mann argues that a significant obstacle to public dissent is the inability of the public to organize collectively (Mann 1986). Here, however, we see that even if the public does organize, the effort may be fruitless if the public, including various forms of civic organizations, cannot truly challenge other forms of power. When we look at decisions made about garbage and waste, it is critical to look at which problems are identified and pursued. Similarly, we can also gain insights by considering what kinds of issues pertaining to garbage and waste are *not* on the agenda.

In this example of environmental policy rulemaking, we see how a variety of stakeholders and actors – not just government agencies – are involved in environmental decision-making. This point raises the issue of governance.

In her work on garbage governance, Davies explains that a governance analysis:

> ...permit[s] attention to the various scales, from the local to the global, that may influence the way waste matters are addressed and to the interventions in waste management that emanate from civil society groupings and the private sector as well as public authorities. Essentially a governance perspective allows for consideration not only of technical matters or scientific analyses, but also of the social, cultural, political and economic contexts and networks that shape waste landscapes.
>
> *(Davies 2008, p. 15)*

Environmental issues such as dealing with society's garbage and waste tend to attract the attention and energy of public, private, and civil society actors (multiple "spheres") operating at different spatial scales (multiple, overlapping "tiers"). Here, it is helpful to reiterate that geographic scale is understood in this book not as predetermined containers for social activity (e.g., counties, states, etc.), but as interconnections among processes and places. A governance analysis is suited to this approach to scale since it looks at ways in which different groups of people, places, processes, and agendas intertwine in decision-making.

In her work on garbage governance, Davies examines how the same issue in two different places may be addressed at different spatial scales depending on the governance structures brought to bear on defining and addressing the problem. She compares how Ireland and New Zealand have dealt with waste management policies and practices. She finds that the evolution of environmental policy-making has led to differences in the location of decision-making and enforcement of environmental policies in each country. In New Zealand, the national level Ministry for the Environment sets broad environmental policy guidelines, but local authorities arrange conditions and make decisions related to resources. Ireland, too, has a national environmental protection agency, and it plays a central role in establishing nationally uniform policies on pollution control and enforcement that are compliant with European Union directives. In Ireland, local authorities have limited input into environmental policies in large part because European Union standards or guidelines are prioritized. In both countries, the private sector, involving national and international waste companies, is an important actor in waste management and particularly in municipal waste collection. In New Zealand, contracts are often determined by arrangements with local authorities, but in Ireland, local authorities have less control over the collection and disposal of waste. In each country, the role of civil society organizations also differs:

> Ireland's waste related civil society organization – be that community based recycling organization, anti-incineration campaigns or organized protests surrounding waste

charges – are few in number, weakly networked and generally marginalized from decision-making circles. In contrast New Zealand has hundreds of community resource or recycling organizations that provide a whole range of services and contribute significantly to local waste management strategies in particular areas.

(Davies 2008, p. 165)

This comparison illustrates why "all garbage is local" (Clement 2007, p. 92), as stated earlier in this chapter. In the countries compared in the study, different stakeholders (e.g., levels of government agencies, private interests, and civil society organizations) have different degrees of power and influence on decision-making processes having to do with garbage. In each case, the problem is defined and pursued differently depending on the actors involved: Ireland's approach is guided by EU policies and standards, and New Zealand's approach reflects a strong history of social activism at local levels. Each country's policies on waste management reflects a different set of networks and connections among the "spheres and tiers" of actors. It follows that the outcomes, or the narratives created to conceptualize waste, are different in each country. That study is an excellent example of how spatial scale and power intertwine in unique contexts to generate geographies of garbage and waste management. In other words, the model for rational decision-making provides a useful template to understand a linear process to break decision-making into component steps. However, it is important to recognize that decisions pertaining to garbage as well as other environment-related policies are influenced at different stages by multiple forms of power and are reflected in unique and complex spatial relationships that are not necessarily captured by labels of "state," "city," or any other pre-existing spatial container.

Conclusion

This chapter began with an acknowledgement that garbage and waste are not recent phenomena. We might even consider that "waste is a necessary condition for society" (Thompson 1979, p. 11). This chapter has considered how political and economic power shape resource use and consumption. It has also considered how ideological power shapes what we understand about garbage, what we find acceptable about resource use and recycling, and why we might make particular purchases or decisions about consumption. It is worth taking these ideas a step further to see consumption not just as buying a product but as a way that we "buy the self" (Scanlon 2005, p. 13):

...products are simply garbage in waiting, temporarily refashioned into a useful or desirable form out of some primary matter to meet any of a countless number of ideas that are usually symbolic of the opposite of death or decay – youth, beauty, machismo, athleticism, sex, and so on. Can desire ever be fulfilled under conditions where the want itself is what ultimately confers death on the object?

In reinforcing our self and the values that structure our society, we are affirming an understanding of life. Particularly in Western society where fashion or attachment to novelty drives consumption, we can see that "the creation of garbage in modern society [is] the result of a *positive affirmation* of the self" (Scanlon 2005, p. 134, emphasis in original). As we strive to affirm the values and ideals communicated to us by various forms of ideological power:

> We consume and discard more than consumer products, however. And we degrade more than spaces, places and things. The truth is that these behaviours and the processes they set in motion are also directed towards the incorporeal objects of knowledge. Thus corruptibility spills over from the material world of objects into the imperfection of useless knowledge and beliefs, where defective knowledge, at the extreme, may represent a threat to life.
>
> *(Scanlon 2005, p. 38)*

Garbage is a way to see how we distinguish culture, knowledge, order, value, and meaning from nature, ignorance, chaos, and worthlessness. There is power in the way we differentiate the value of material things and what those things signal about our culture. The above passage suggests that we should pay attention to how these distinctions spill over into ways in which we set unequal values on places or groups of people. What is genocide, for example, if not an act based on the labeling of a group of people as "garbage" to be removed? In other words, what kinds of power are exercised or reinforced in the definition of what is valuable?

Here, it is useful to give careful consideration to whom or what is shaping our sense of what is desirable and what is disposable. What could we learn by paying attention to the forms of power driving and directing our use of resources, our patterns of consumption, what we waste, what we value, what we find acceptable to destroy or important to salvage? What would our response to those observations be?

> When we hear stories of dying rivers or see images of mountains made of garbage, nature is framed as dead or definitely on its last legs, and it's difficult not to feel a sense of despair or grief. While the political intention of these stories might be to shock us into action, their impact is often overwhelming and immobilizing. They can perpetuate the very relation to nature they seek to challenge: alienated distance and disinterest. When the exploitative force of economic power and human destruction is so overcoded why bother contesting it? You may as well just keep shopping.
>
> *(Hawkins 2006, p. 9)*

Hawkins refers to these narratives about the environment as "disenchantment stories" (p. 9) which demonstrate dualistic thinking and draw a clear boundary between human culture and non-human nature. Broad, general categories offer little potential for the consideration of specificities of garbage and waste ("Poor waste; environmentalism infuses it with a metaphysical dimension that makes it stand for death" (p. 13)). These narratives simplify waste and crystallize it as a negative, contaminating influence on both culture and nature. If we accept that storyline, how are we to imagine political change on issues of garbage and waste? Devaluing waste and setting it apart from meaningful culture is not conducive to creating thinking about human–environment interactions or about power dynamics shaping society.

Individual choices are often criticized as being too minor to make any real difference in the face of powerful, established institutions such as capitalist production or overconsumption. Hawkins (2006) argues that individual actions should not be pitted against the power of the state or capitalism or valued only if they lead to widespread, revolutionary change. Individual actions play out in the interstices between political and economic institutions. In the terminology of this book, individual actions reflect different spatial scales of activity that are not necessarily "local" or "national." Individual actions can be part of networks and interactions involving different kinds of actors in different kinds of places. Therefore, these "everyday actions of cultivating the self would seem to be crucial for understanding how new waste habits and sensibilities might emerge" (p. 7). This chapter has highlighted other ways that paying attention to spatial scale could expand our understanding of garbage and waste: At what point spatially and in the lifecycle of electronic gadgets does e-waste actually begin? How does the popularity of bottled water affect water supplies both locally and at a distance? How are national sacrifice zones justified, and whom do they benefit? If we truly embrace the scale of garbage, that is, if we look at garbage and waste not just as something to throw away or distance ourselves from, we may come to a better appreciation of power dynamics embedded in garbage and in our society.

Endnote

1 With thanks to Imagene Harris and her undergraduate research project "Conservation During World War II: A Temporary Sacrifice."

6

Toxins

Projected percentage change by 2050 in the amount of mercury in
the Pacific Ocean: +33
— Harper's *Index, August 2009*

Percentage of fish samples from 291 U.S. streams for a recent study
that were found to be contaminated with mercury: 100
— Harper's *Index, November 2009*

Introduction

There is renewed energy to ban aspartame, commercially known as Equal,
Nutrasweet, and Canderel, on the basis that it causes cancer. Aspartame is
the second most widely used artificial sweetener in the world after saccharin.
It was initially approved by the US Food and Drug Administration in 1974,
but its approval process is a dramatic story of high-level politics and
corporate involvement in the policy-making process. When faced with the
ubiquitous pink (saccharin), blue (aspartame), and yellow (Splenda or
Sucralose) packets of sweeteners, many people already have a sense that these
artificial sweeteners are not good for human consumption … are they right?
How would we know?

Another similar but less widely known case of possible toxins intentionally
included in our food supply is diacetyl. Just because you have never heard
of it does not mean you have not eaten it. It is not required that this chemical
be listed on any packaging by name, and even if it were, few people would
know about the serious lung disease attributed to inhaling this chemical
(Michaels 2008). Diacetyl safely (or ominously, depending on your view-
point) is suggested only by the ingredient "butter flavor" in microwave
popcorn. Inhaling diacetyl, either in the process of manufacturing microwave

popcorn or simply in opening a freshly popped bag of popcorn, is the most dangerous form of exposure to this toxin.

It is easy to assume that if artificial sweeteners and other food additives, as well as ingredients in drugs, cosmetics, or other items such as building materials and paint, have been approved by a government, then surely these chemicals are safe. Aspartame and diacetyl highlight two particular features of toxins. First, they are usually invisible to the public. People are often unaware of chemicals they are consuming or using in a wide array of products. Unless they are avid readers of product labels and have educated themselves about chemicals that may be considered risky, they probably have no idea that they are exposed to a wide range of toxins on a daily basis. Second, since most toxins are invisible to the public, the public tends to trust that appropriate research has been done and that measures have been taken to ensure a safe, non-toxic environment. Toxins raise the issue of risk assessment and the question what is safe or at least what kind of risk is acceptable. It would be impossible to create a risk-free world due to economic, technical, and logistical realities. At some point in a decision-making process, someone has determined what will be considered a risk and what level of that risk is acceptable. There are clear power implications in any risk assessment process: Who is assessing the risk? Who decides how much and what kinds of risks will be tolerated or faced and by whom? What if something goes wrong?

Toxins are a concern at multiple spatial scales that represent different kinds of interactions and exposures. For example, this chapter will discuss persistent organic pollutants (POPs) which literally travel the globe as cross-media pollutants that move through air, water, soil, and organisms. Yet due to their chemical nature, these pollutants tend to concentrate in specific regions. The example of DDT was discussed in Chapter 4: Food security. That pesticide was banned in the US but is still produced there and shipped to other places such as Ecuador for use on crops to be imported back into the US. DDT is widely recognized as being toxic to humans (as well as an excellent means to fight mosquito-borne malaria), and the commodity chain or lifecycle path of DDT illustrates the spatial scale of that particular toxin: Where is it produced? Do its handling and transportation affect people and places along the way? Where is it used and for what purpose? Who is affected (for better or worse and in the long run) by the use of this chemical? Different state policies for toxins generate spatial patterns of toxins that are banned, controlled, traded, and tracked. For example, the US–Mexico border has come to be referred to as "La Frontera Química" (the Chemical Border) since the production, transport, and disposal of various toxic and hazardous materials near the border exacerbate existing, uneven patterns of environmental health and degradation (Varady *et al.* 2001). Borderlands can be vague frontiers where lax policies encourage dumping or other forms of mishandling of toxic materials. Other types of borders differentiate distinctive spaces with very different regulations for toxins. Later in this chapter, differences between toxins regulation in the US and in the European Union will be discussed as creating a spatial scale of toxins sloping towards the US where less stringent regulation enables international dumping of toxic products that do not meet Western European standards. Even though the US and the EU do not share an actual border, toxins regulations between these regions has established a clear borderline in the geography of toxins.

Toxins also have important spatial dimensions at other scales such as the scale of the body. The body is a spatial scale that reflects culture, economy, and politics. For example, the wearing of religious symbols, women wearing a chador, tattoos, piercing, and scarring, male and female circumcision, the cultural significance in Western societies of a diamond ring – all of these examples are ways that we use our bodies to reflect our identity, status, and beliefs. Toxins draw our attention to how these chemicals affect the health and well-being of individual bodies of actual people as they interact with a particular environment or lifestyle. As we think about how toxins may be affecting us in the air we breathe, in the water we drink, in the foods we consume, in the products we use, or in the home and workplace, it becomes clear that the spatial scale or administrative level at which decisions are made about toxin regulations is often quite removed from the spatial scale of toxic effects.

Toxins basics

People in Western societies did not always know about germs largely because germs are invisible to the naked eye. Physicians did not always wash their hands prior to performing surgery. Similarly, people were not always aware of toxins. In 1962, Rachel Carson published her book *Silent Spring*, which drew public attention to the dangers of using DDT as a pesticide and its effects on wildlife and human health. Her book is often cited as the starting point of a widespread realization of toxins in the environment and risks associated with long-term exposure. We have a better understanding now of how many chemicals are in use. A study in 1980 identified "1500 active ingredients of pesticides, 4000 active ingredients of therapeutic drugs, 2000 drug additives to improve stability, 2500 food additives with nutritional value, 3000 food additives to promote product life, and 50 000 additional chemicals in common use" (Zakrezewski 2002, p. 108). That was 30 years ago. The volume, not to mention the number, of chemicals in use is no doubt greater now. With this many chemicals in use, it would be a phenomenal task to understand the toxicity of each one as well as possible combinations of chemicals that are toxic. There is still a lot we do not know about toxins.

Of particular concern among this boundless selection of chemicals is a group of toxins known as persistent organic pollutants, known by the shorthand POPs. The pesticides DDT and toxophene are POPs as are industrial chemicals such as dioxins, furans, and polychlorinated biphenyls (PCBs). POPs represent hundreds if not thousands more toxins since these chemicals break down into other chemicals, many of which are unknown or untested (Visser 2007). The Green Revolution in the 1960s contributed to the diffusion of the use of agricultural POPs since it encouraged the use of genetically modified crops in less economically developed countries. Those crops required the use of chemical pesticides and fertilizers, many of which contained POPs, for maximum production. Although some countries such as Canada and the US have banned agricultural POPs, other countries such as Russia, China, and India continue to use them. Other POPs, such as dioxins, are released when heavy metals, such as those found in computer components, are burned for disposal.

Individual country bans on POPs help to reduce the overall level of POPs in the environment, yet it matters that POPs are still in use in many places. One of the reasons these chemicals have earned their name is that not only do they persist for a long time in the environment, but they also are a cross-media pollutant. That means they can travel long distances in air, water, soil, and in living organisms. POPs are lipophilic which means they concentrate in fatty tissue within living organisms. This trait allows them to move easily up the food chain in a process known as bioaccumulation. At each trophic level, for example as small fish are eaten by large fish which are then eaten by seals, POPs reach higher concentrations in an animal's fatty tissue. The higher up the food chain an organism is, the greater the concentration of POPs in their system.

In 2001, The Stockholm Convention on Persistent Organic Pollutants was adopted and signed, although not yet ratified and implemented, by 150 countries. The motivation behind this international agreement was the recognition that no state working alone could protect its population from persistent organic pollutants. The Stockholm Convention recognizes 12 POPs the hazards of which far outweigh their industrial or agricultural benefits (see Table 6.1). The Convention requires an end to the production and use of nine of these chemicals. DDT, however, is permitted for use in some places for controlling disease vectors for malaria until suitable substitutes are found. The convention requires governments to develop plans for the appropriate transport and disposal of unintentionally produced POPs such as dioxins and furans.

Table 6.1. *The dirty dozen POPs of the Stockholm Convention*

Aldrin	A pesticide applied to soils to kill termites, grasshoppers, corn rootworm, and other insect pests
Chlordane	Used extensively to control termites and as a broad-spectrum insecticide on a range of agricultural crops
DDT	Perhaps the best known of the POPs, DDT was widely used during World War II to protect soldiers and civilians from malaria, typhus, and other diseases spread by insects. It continues to be applied against mosquitoes in several countries to control malaria
Dieldrin	Used principally to control termites and textile pests, dieldrin has also been used to control insect-borne diseases and insects living in agricultural soils
Dioxins	These chemicals are produced unintentionally due to incomplete combustion, as well as during the manufacture of certain pesticides and other chemicals. In addition, certain kinds of metal recycling and pulp and paper bleaching can release dioxins. Dioxins have also been found in automobile exhaust, tobacco smoke, and wood and coal smoke
Endrin	This insecticide is sprayed on the leaves of crops such as cotton and grains. It is also used to control mice, voles, and other rodents
Furans	These compounds are produced unintentionally from the same processes that release dioxins, and they are also found in commercial mixtures of PCBs
Heptachlor	Primarily employed to kill soil insects and termites, heptachlor has also been used more widely to kill cotton insects, grasshoppers, other crop pests, and malaria-carrying mosquitoes
Hexachlorobenzene (HCB)	HCB kills fungi that affect food crops. It is also released as a by-product during the manufacture of certain chemicals and as a result of the processes that give rise to dioxins and furans
Mirex	This insecticide is applied mainly to combat fire ants and other types of ants and termites. It has also been used as a fire retardant in plastics, rubber, and electrical goods
Polychlorinated biphenyls (PCBs)	These compounds are employed in industry as heat exchange fluids, in electric transformers and capacitors, and as additives in paint, carbonless copy paper, sealants, and plastics
Toxaphene	This insecticide, also called camphechlor, is applied to cotton, cereal grains, fruits, nuts, and vegetables. It has also been used to control ticks and mites in livestock

Source: Stockholm Convention on Persistent Organic Pollutants, http://www.pops.int/ documents/pops/default.htm, accessed 30 September 2009.

One way to assess how toxins bioaccumulate in humans is to study breast milk. In the 1980s, researchers wanted to look at the accumulation of toxins in the breast milk of women living in cities. The researchers needed a control group and sought women who were unlikely to be exposed to toxins on a daily basis. The researchers analyzed samples of breast milk from indigenous women living in Arctic communities thinking that these women would be far removed from toxins. To their surprise, the researchers found that women in the Arctic had among the highest recorded levels of POPs in the world (see Downie and Fenge 2003). This seemingly unlikely concentration of toxins is explained by another feature of POPs:

> Because POPs are semi-volatile compounds, they can travel from lower to higher latitudes through a series of volatilizations and condensations – volatilizing in warmer climates, condensing in colder climates, and repeating the process with the seasonal cycles. This process, known as the "grasshopper effect", tends to move atmospheric POPs poleward.
>
> *(Eckley 2001, p. 28)*

Entire Arctic ecosystems and food chains are contaminated with toxic POPs. One researcher commented that "The Arctic is contaminated to the degree that wildlife reproductivity and survival is compromised, and humans are consuming food so toxic that it would be prohibited from placement in a modern landfill" (Visser 2007, p. 121).

Scientific research on and public understanding of health risks associated with toxic chemicals were based on the assumption that greater exposure led to greater risk. In 1996, the book *Our Stolen Future* challenged that assumption by drawing attention to endocrine disruptors (Colborn *et al.* 1996). Research indicated that males were at particular risk. These chemicals mimic hormonal activity in the body and do not behave like other cancer-causing toxins:

> Not only do they not resemble structurally the hormones which they are mimicking, or with whose action they interfere, but frequently they do not bear any structural similarity among themselves. In other words, in contrast to carcinogens, where in many cases structure-activity relationship can be identified, no such relationship exists among compounds with hormonal activities.
>
> *(Zakrezewski 2002, p. 100)*

Even a brief exposure to endocrine disruptors can have a serious negative impact, and the effects of endocrine disruptors can be latent and not become apparent for years. Given that there are so many unknowns about toxic chemicals, how do we measure, communicate, and understand risks that they pose to human health?

Risk assessment

In the late 1980s, Ulrich Beck's book, *Risikogesellschaft*, was already famous in Germany. In 1992, right after the Chernobyl nuclear plant disaster in Ukraine and Belorus, his book was published in English as *Risk Society: Towards a New Modernity* (1992) and became instantly famous in the English-speaking world. In that book he coined the term "risk society" which referred to the dangers that globalization and modern technology pose to the planet:

> In advanced modernity the social production of *wealth* is systematically accompanied by the social production of *risks*. Accordingly, the problems and conflicts relating to distribution in a society of scarcity overlap with the problems and conflicts that arise from the production, definition and distribution of techno-scientifically produced risks.
>
> *(Beck 1992, p. 19)*

Put another way, industrial society generates new forms of risk:

> Today's risks, such as global warming, the hole in the ozone layer, ionizing radiation, or the contamination of foodstuffs by pesticides tend to be invisible, and can only be assessed by scientific methods and culturally represented by scientific and media knowledge systems. Moreover, Beck argues, these risks often reflect the dangers posed by science itself.
>
> *(Tulloch 2008, p. 146)*

Modern society's scientific advances and capitalistic activities have generated risks that are unevenly distributed and which are often invisible. Indeed, unlike tornadoes or mountains of trash, toxins are often imperceptible, and their effects are not necessarily obvious. Their production, distribution, and use tends to be controlled by agencies that have access to the best possible scientific understanding of toxic materials and the political power to shape, implement, enforce, and possibly ignore policy.

The danger of toxins is usually determined through a process known as risk assessment which involves a systematic evaluation of the "likelihood of an adverse effect resulting from a given exposure" (Greim and Snyder 2008, p. 2). Objectives of risk assessment include:

1. Balancing risks and benefits (e.g., drugs and pesticides)
2. Setting target levels of risk (e.g., food contaminants and water pollutants)
3. Setting priorities for program activities (e.g., regulatory agencies, manufacturers, and environmental and consumer organizations)
4. Estimating residual risks and success of steps taken to reduce risk (Faustman and Omenn 2008, p. 109)

In the US, the Environmental Protection Agency (EPA) follows a widely accepted, four-step procedure to assess risk:

1. Hazard assessment

This initial step identifies sources of risk and hazards that might result in harmful exposure. We are not always aware of the source of risks. As already mentioned, the books *Silent Spring* and *Our Stolen Future* drew public attention to chemicals and exposures that had previously not been thought to be dangerous. Lead in paint and gasoline, asbestos, and Bisphenol-A plastics are other toxic hazards that have been at the forefront of public and scientific attention at different times.

Although the hazards of many toxins are universal, some chemicals pose more of a hazard to some people than to others. For example, anyone who reads labels has probably noticed the warning on beverages containing aspartame that the product contains phenylketonurics. Most people cannot pronounce the name of that chemical never mind know why they might be concerned. People with phenylketonuria, a metabolic disorder involving a deficiency of an enzyme required to metabolize an amino acid called phenylalanine, however, know to avoid that chemical as much as possible. For most people, the presence of phenylalanine in their diet pop does not pose a problem, but it is a case for special labeling since, for some people, it poses a hazard.

2. Dose-response assessment

Paracelsus, a Renaissance alchemist, physician, and botanist, said "In all things there is a poison, and there is nothing without a poison. It depends only upon the dose whether a poison is poison or not" (Greim and Snyder 2008, p. 1). How much exposure or how great a dose will lead to a toxic effect? Two main ways to assess exposure and effect are through animal studies and through epidemiological studies. Animal studies allow for controlled experimentation, the results of which are extrapolated to humans. Animal studies may be critiqued in terms of biological extrapolation and in terms of numerical extrapolation: Can the system of a mouse, guinea pig, or rabbit realistically stand in for a human system? Is it realistic to study the effects of extremely large doses given to animals over a short time frame and assume that smaller doses in humans over a longer time period will have similar effects? Animal studies do provide a way to conduct research on toxins without harming humans, but they raise the question of the ethics of inflicting harm on animals for human benefit. Animal studies cannot test real world human exposures to toxins, but epidemiological studies can. These studies are done after the fact of exposure. For example, if a known site is contaminated, an epidemiological study would identify people known to have lived near that site and assess symptoms or reactions that those people present from that exposure. One problem with epidemiological studies is that the exact level of exposure to a suspected toxin is unknown. Additionally, it is unknown what other substances a person has been exposed to that might exacerbate or ameliorate the effects of the chemical in question. In both animal studies and epidemiological studies, it is nearly impossible to study with any accuracy the latent effects of a suspected toxin in humans since latent effects can show up years after exposure.

3. Exposure assessment

Controlled laboratory experiments do not tell us about real world exposures. This step of risk assessment aims to identify and measure our actual interactions with toxins or other hazards. Who is likely to be exposed? Under what circumstances? Calculations of exposure are made based on standard human body mass, skin surface area, and resting respiration rate to estimate exposure through drinking, inhalation, or contact with contaminated air, water, or food (Zakrezewski 2002, p. 117).

4. Risk characterization

Assessing dosage and exposure provide valuable measures for understanding risk, but the scale or scope at which risk is characterized and communicated is also important. Is risk described in terms of "individual lifetime risk" or as "societal risk"? Measuring risk in terms of the "loss of life expectancy" recognizes a difference between risk for older people and risk for younger people who might be expected to live many more years.

An ideal outcome in risk assessment is the identification of a bright line or threshold that divides safe exposure from dangerous exposure. A bright line provides a sense of certainty and brings clarity to policy. Speed limits, for example, are a type of bright line that make it possible to set a policy on which to base decisions: How fast is it safe to drive on this road? Driving how much faster than the speed limit is likely to result in a speeding ticket? Yet a bright line is also arbitrary depending on how safety or danger is defined and for whom, for how long, and under what conditions the bright line is established. For example, Table 6.2 shows guidelines used by the US Food and Drug Administration on acceptable levels of natural defects in food. How was it determined that fewer than four rodent hairs is an acceptable number to have in 100 grams of apple butter but more than that is not? Similarly to the questions about risk assessment listed above, these bright

Table 6.2. *Acceptable levels of natural food defects*

Apple butter	Average of 4 or more rodent hairs per 100 g of apple butter
Asparagus, canned or frozen	10% by count of spears or pieces are infested with 6 or more attached asparagus beetle eggs and/or sacs
Berries, canned or frozen	Average mold count is 60% or more
	Average of 4 or more larvae per 500 g
	Average of 10 or more whole insects or equivalent per 500 g
Broccoli, frozen	Average of 60 or more aphids and/or thrips and/or mites per 100 g
Chocolate	Average of 60 or more insect fragments per 100 g when 6 100 g subsamples are examined
Mushrooms, canned and dried	Average of over 20 or more maggots of any size per 100 g of drained mushrooms and proportionate liquid or 15 g of dried mushrooms
Peanut butter	Average of 30 or more insect fragments per 100 g
	Average of 1 or more rodent hairs per 100 g
	Gritty taste and water insoluble inorganic residue is more than 25 mg per 100 g
Popcorn	1 or more rodent excreta pellets are found in 1 or more subsamples, and 1 or more rodent hairs are found in 2 or more other subsamples
Red fish and ocean perch	3% of the fillets examined contain 1 or more copepods accompanied by pus pockets
Tomatoes, canned	Average of 10 or more fly eggs per 500 g
	5 or more fly eggs and 1 or more maggots per 500 g
	2 or more maggots per 500 g

Source: US Food and Drug Administration. (2009) *Defect Levels Handbook: The Food Defect Action Levels* (Levels of natural or unavoidable defects in foods that present no health hazards for humans). http://www.fda.gov/Food/GuidanceComplianceRegulatoryInformation/GuidanceDocuments/Sanitation/ucm056174.htm#CHPTA, accessed 13 December 2009.

lines illustrate the arbitrariness of risk assessment in terms of where we look for risk and how we identify hazards.

In addition to these standard steps of risk assessment, we can stand back and ask broad questions about how risk assessment is put into practice:

1. How do we determine "how safe is safe enough"?
2. How good are the knowledge base and methods for estimating the risks associated with different technologies?
3. How are estimates of risk incorporated into decision-making?
4. How do decision-makers treat uncertainties associated with different risks and hazards?
5. How do features of the institutional context affect decision-making bodies concerned with risk and uncertainty?
6. What factors influence individual perceptions of risk and benefit?

7. How are perceptions of risk and benefit incorporated into public policies?
8. How does society cope with risks that are unacceptable to some segments of the population?
9. How are normative considerations such as equity and social justice balanced in decision-making about risk?
10. What are the criteria for comparing and evaluating different management policies?
11. How do we inform people about risk?
12. How do different societies and cultures perceive, understand, and tolerate risk? (Golding 1992, pp. 27–28)

When we start asking these kinds of questions about how information enters into the decision-making process or whose perceptions and values are considered in the process, we are really asking who has power to direct or influence decision-making. We can look at these questions as pointing to ways in which power shapes the risk assessment process and, in turn, ways in which power shapes the kinds of toxins or other hazards that we face or avoid on a daily basis depending on who we are, where we live, where we work, and what we buy.

The four steps of risk assessment, discussed above, are one way of understanding risk and how to deal with uncertainty (Zinn 2008, p. 5). That standard approach reflects a realist perspective that views risk as an objective reality. It views risks and dangers as events or situations that can be identified, measured, and quantified through objective science. That perspective acknowledges a range of human response to risk, but it promotes the idea that there is an ideal, rational way to respond to risk based on objective knowledge (Zinn 2008). This view can be summarized as "safety is quantifiable" (Frank 2008, p. 5). This type of understanding of risk might be seen in the work of engineers, actuaries, and other people trained to apply a quantified, scientific approach to understanding risk.

Another perspective on risk and uncertainty, a psychometric approach, focuses on risk perception and what kinds of risks people worry about (see, for example, Slovic 1992). This kind of approach is demonstrated in a comparison of government approaches to the nuclear industry in the US and in France (Jasper 1990; Slovic 2000a). In both countries, public perception of risk associated with nuclear power is high. In France, government control over the nuclear industry is centralized and the public has less input but more trust in experts and in the government. The system in France allows people to exercise power on the basis of merit: scientific training and certification. In the US, the public also has a high degree of risk perception associated with nuclear power, but there is general distrust of government, science, and industry. In the US, the public tends to believe it has some control over risks. The system allows for the public to intervene, to question expert opinion, and to litigate. Public risk perception, in this example, shapes and reinforces how the nuclear industry is managed in both countries. This nuanced understanding of risk would not be captured by a realist approach that would more likely focus on exposures to nuclear radiation and other tangible hazards.

Risk may also be approached with a sociological perspective that views risk as socially mediated. Real dangers may exist, but social factors and values determine which dangers emerge as key concerns within a society and how institutions generate responses. The risk "out there" is only one component of how society understands and responds to risk:

> The relationship between the present and the future depends on how society feels about itself today. Fears about the future are linked to anxieties about problems today. And, if the future is feared, then reaction to risk is more likely to emphasize the probability of adverse outcomes. As a result, the very meaning of risk is shaped by how society regards its ability to manage change and deal with the future.
>
> *(Furedi 2005, p. 18)*

Other views see risk and uncertainty as socially constructed and not necessarily reflecting an actual, objective danger. This view is captured by the idea that "Uncertainty does not simply exist 'out there in the environment', but is constructed and negotiated in human society" (Dovers *et al.* 2008, p. 249). As Slovic (2000b) has noted "danger is real but risk is socially constructed" (p. 411). He goes on to explain that:

> Whoever controls the definition of risk controls the rational solution to the problem at hand. If you define risk one way, then one option will rise to the top as the most cost-effective or the safest or the best. If you define it another way, perhaps incorporating qualitative characteristics and other contextual factors, you will likely get a different ordering of your action solutions ... Defining risk is thus an exercise in power.
>
> *(p. 411)*

A similar view comes from Lee Clarke and his work on worst case scenarios and catastrophes, arguably the kinds of situation people want most to avoid. Clarke has observed:

> Disasters, even worst case ones, aren't special. Destruction is no more special than construction. Political struggle is also normal, even when the subject is large-scale devastation. Everyday life is political. So are worst cases. If we care about what produces them, how we should respond to them, how we might prevent some of them, we must understand the distribution of power that permeates societies.
>
> *(Clarke 2006, p. 128)*

Indeed, as we examine toxins and see how risk is – and is not – associated with particular chemicals and exposures, we begin to see how dimensions of power shape our perceptions of what is toxic.

Power in risk assessment

An excellent illustration of ways in which economic and political power shape the detection, identification, and policy process associated with toxins is the case of atrazine. Research showed that this common fertilizer has serious hormonal effects on frogs at very low doses. In his investigative work on this controversy, William Souder introduces atrazine as follows:

Atrazine is among the world's oldest and most effective herbicides – the aspirin of weedkillers. It was developed during a period of intense innovation in the chemical industry that began with the Second World War and the invention of 2,4-0, the first "selective" herbicide: it could kill weeds without killing the crops. (It was later mixed with *2,4,5-T* by the military to make the decidedly nonselective defoliant Agent Orange.) Syngenta, a company with roots dating back a couple of centuries that also gave the world DDT and LSD, introduced atrazine to the market in 1959 ... Syngenta does not divulge sales figures for individual products, but atrazine continues to contribute a significant portion of the company's U.S. revenues from selective herbicides, which last year totaled $1.9 billion worldwide.

(Souder 2006, pp. 61–62)

Souder tells the story of Tyrone Hayes, a biologist at the University of California, Berkeley who served on a panel for Syngenta to assess the safety of atrazine. Hayes, a specialist in frogs, conducted a study that exposed developing tadpoles to very low doses of atrazine. His results showed that doses as low as one tenth of one part per billion (0.1 ppb) altered hormonal activity and led to "chemical castration and feminization" (Souder 2006, p. 61). To emphasize how low that dose is, it helps to think of it as approximately the same concentration as one grain of salt dissolved in ten gallons of water. In the USA, "safe" levels for atrazine in drinking water are set at 3 ppb which is 30 times greater than the concentration that altered sexual organs in frogs and caused some of them to become hermaphrodites. Atrazine is widely used as an industrial scale agricultural fertilizer, and it finds its way into rivers, lakes, aquifers, rain, and fog. Levels of atrazine in surface water in the Midwest are often greater than 10 parts per billion, and atrazine levels in post-treatment drinking water in some agricultural communities have surpassed 2 parts per billion or twenty times the level that caused sexual abnormalities in frogs (see Figure 6.1). The implications of Hayes's research were significant:

From a research standpoint, Hayes's discoveries added up to a holy shit moment. The findings, though preliminary, implicated atrazine in two of the most debated

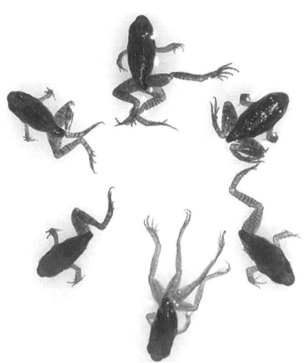

Figure 6.1 Frog deformities associated with pesticides. Photo courtesy of Joseph Kiesecker, The Nature Conservancy.

issues in science: the causes of a shrinking amphibian population and the effects of chemicals that disrupt the intricate functions of hormones. Not only did the studies suggest that atrazine was a likely factor in the decline of amphibians worldwide, they also raised disturbing questions about how atrazine, at background exposure levels, impacts animals and the environment ... Scientifically speaking, Hayes had opened up an exciting path for research. Financially speaking, Syngenta had a vested interest in blocking it.

(Baker 2008, pp. 65–66)

As an herbicide, atrazine is one of Syngenta's best selling products and is applied to a range of crops including corn, sorghum, sugarcane, winter wheat, guava, and macadamia nuts. It is also used on golf courses and as a lawn fertilizer. Souder (2006) describes how Syngenta funded additional research by other scientists to see if Hayes's findings could be replicated. These additional studies were fraught with complications: researchers could not keep the frogs alive, tadpoles did not metamorphose, or water in control tanks was contaminated. These problems meant that researchers were unable to replicate Hayes's work but not because his results were questionable. The EPA analyzed new data submitted for review, and Syngenta continued to submit the inconclusive findings of researchers who were unable to replicate Hayes's results. These additional studies were given equal weight to Hayes's work and detracted from the impact of Hayes's findings. Loading the EPA with spurious research allowed Syngenta to delay an action to change the approval status of atrazine and maintain the flow of profit. Meanwhile, the frogs, as a sentinel species – a biological canary in the coal mine – are telling us something about what is happening to the environment (Souder 2000).

Here we can see how economic and political power become intertwined in toxins-related policy. For example, the EPA has fostered nearly collegial relationships with pesticide manufacturers, and these same companies have excelled at building strong alliances with farm advocacy groups. Those groups, in turn, speak for agricultural interests and wield influence in government circles in Washington. As a large corporation, Syngenta is able to exercise political influence through these channels. It has the capacity to organize and establish an ideal political situation in which atrazine maintains its legal status and therefore continues to generate significant profit. Syngenta can fund additional research to stall the EPA while simultaneously promoting its products to farmers and other consumers. To question negative effects of this popular herbicide could challenge its predominance and profitability. Delay becomes a political tactic: "With delay comes uncertainty. Thus for those who wish to oppose a policy process, delay can be an effective tool for creating uncertainty" (Moore 2008, p. 179).

Syngenta's use of scientific uncertainty to promote political delay reflects a shift in political tactics: "Industry has learned that debating the *science* is much easier and more effective than debating the *policy*" (Michaels 2008, p. xi). Nowhere has this tactic been used more dramatically than the tobacco industry:

> For almost half a century the tobacco companies hired consultants and scientists – swarms of them, in times of greatest peril – initially to deny (sometimes under oath) that smokers were at greater risk of dying of lung cancer and heart disease, then to refute the evidence that secondhand smoke increases disease in *nonsmokers*. The industry and its scientists manufactured uncertainty by questioning every study, dissecting every method, and disputing every conclusion. What they could not question was the enormous, obvious casualty count – the thousands of smokers who die every day from a disease directly related to their habit – but no matter. Despite the overwhelming scientific evidence, the tobacco industry was able to wage a campaign that successfully delayed regulation and victim compensation for decades – and it is still doing so.
>
> *(Michaels 2008, p. 4)*

Powerful companies have developed their organizational capacity to exert influence on the policy process. One important way that they are able to do that is through the use of public relations, or PR, firms. These firms can quickly mobilize a range of scientific experts to prepare papers that look like peer reviewed research. The aim of their published studies is to support the position of the corporate sponsor both in the policy-making process and in terms of public opinion. These studies, like the ones generated by Syngenta's funding but which were not scientifically robust, overload regulatory agencies and grind any forward-moving policy process to a halt. Instead of providing objective information to guide the policy process, science for hire becomes a tool to leverage policy outcomes and frustrate litigation.

As Michael Mann (1986, p. 6) argues "Power is the ability to pursue and attain goals through mastery of one's environment". Here we can see how chemical manufacturers and other corporations are able to influence the policy process by supporting bogus science, by forging alliances with industry groups, and by mastering the policy process not on its own terms but by understanding how the process can be derailed and delayed. These same actors are able to gain and maintain economic power by monopolizing control over systems of production, distribution, and consumption. By eliminating obstacles such as prohibitive policies, it becomes easier to promote products and ensure a broad consumer base. This influence on toxins policy clearly has impacts at the scale of the body, at the scales of particular economic sectors (e.g., agriculture, manufacturing, food processing, etc.) and at multiple environmental scales from localized toxic phenomena to the global reach of POPs. Industry's influence also shapes state-level policy on toxins and on state competitiveness in global trade.

Toxins and international trade

The previous discussion illustrates how policies related to toxins have impacts at multiple spatial scales, but toxins policies also have implications for power at spatial scales at and beyond the scale of the state. Mann's definition of political power notes that "political power heightens boundaries, whereas the other power sources may transcend them" (p. 27). State-level policies on toxins demonstrate this territorializing dimension of power.

In 1976 the US passed the Toxic Substances Control Act (TSCA) which allowed the government to track and ban industrial chemicals thought to be harmful to humans or to the environment. At the time, these regulations set the international standard of toxins policy, and countries such as France, Germany, Britain, and Japan brought their industries in line with these regulations in order to maintain favorable trade relations with the US. A loophole in this policy, hard won by industry efforts, was that any chemical in commercial use prior to 1979 was exempt from testing to determine its toxicity or impacts on the environment.

Currently, some 42 billion pounds of chemicals are produced in or brought to America each day, but because of TSCA exemptions, fewer than 200 of all the chemicals on the market have ever undergone any serious risk assessments. Among the 62,000 chemicals the act excused from testing or review were thousands of highly toxic substances.

(Schapiro 2007a, p. 80)

The TSCA encourages the status quo rather than the development of newer, less toxic substitutes for chemicals that are already in use. The lack of toxicity data for so many chemicals not only protects business-as-usual practices in chemical-reliant industries, but the public has no way of discerning sources of toxins or of voicing a preference for less toxic alternatives.

In 1998, Greenpeace International released a report condemning the use of DINP (diisononyl phthalate) in products and toys that children could chew. DINP is one of a group of plasticizers known as phthalates, and it is similar in chemical composition to a compound that has been shown to cause liver damage in animal studies. DINP is used in children's items such as rubber ducks and pacifiers, but it is also used in the production of medical equipment, packaging material, and food containers. The media quickly latched on to this news of a toxin in everyday products, and public outcry against the use of this chemical soon followed (Rosenbaum 2005, pp. 111–113). The incident prompted people in the US and Europe, especially, to consider how interactions with unseen toxins were affecting their health and their children's health.

Biomonitoring confirmed these fears. Biomonitoring involves analysis of blood, urine, exhaled air, breast milk, and tissues such as fat, hair, and nails to assess human exposure to chemicals in the environment. The chemical itself may remain in these fluids and tissues, or it may leave another marker such as a broken down component of the chemical in question or affects on the body caused by the chemical. Biomonitoring is a direct measure of exposure from multiple sources (e.g., air, food, etc.), but specific sources of chemicals cannot necessarily be traced from biomonitoring data.

The World Wildlife Fund used biomonitoring to study chemicals in the bodies of Europeans across three generations. They analyzed blood samples from grandmothers, mothers, and children in the same families to gauge the presence of man-made chemicals found in everyday products:

107 different man-made chemicals were analysed in the families' blood: 12 organochlorine pesticides (including DDT), 44 polychlorinated biphenyls (PCBs), 33 brominated flame retardants including 31 polybrominated diphenyl ethers (PBDEs), hexabromocyclododecane (HBCD) and tetrabromobisphenol-A (TBBP-A), 8

"non-stick" perfluorinated chemicals (PFCs), 7 artificial musks, 2 antimicrobials (triclosan and its breakdown product, methyl triclosan) and the polycarbonate plastic monomer, bisphenol-A. The results of these surveys show that every family member, from grandmothers to children, is contaminated by a cocktail of at least 18 different man-made chemicals, many of which can be found in everyday consumer items. Some of the identified chemicals such as PCBs and DDT, have been banned for decades but persist in the environment and continue to contaminate new generations with every passing year. Moreover, the results of this survey show that for certain chemicals the extent of contamination in younger generations can equal or exceed that of their elders. The grandmothers are the generation most contaminated with older, banned chemicals such as organochlorine pesticides and PCBs, but "newer" chemicals in widespread use such as the brominated flame retardants, perfluorinated chemicals and artificial musks can be found more frequently and at higher levels in the younger generations.

(World Wildlife Fund 2005, pp. 6–7)

These findings underscore the reality of lax chemical regulation policies. Moreover, they demonstrate how policy at the state level can have a direct influence on the scale of the body.

In 2003 the European Commission had issued a proposal called Registration, Evaluation, and Authorization of Chemicals known as REACH. The main target of this proposed legislation was the glaring loophole of the TSCA legislation in the US that grandfathered 62 000 chemicals and protected them from screening for their impacts on environmental and public health (Schapiro 2007b). Not only does REACH require screenings for toxicity, it makes toxicity data widely available to the public on the Web. This dissemination of toxicity information is intended to inform consumers about choices they can make to curb their exposure to toxins in consumer goods.

As a chemical producer, Europe controls approximately 33% of the chemical market surpassing the US which controls 28%. Countries around the world sell chemicals and chemical-containing products to Europe, and REACH requires them to meet European toxicity screening standards. Global competitors such as the US and even the World Trade Organization complained that REACH was, in effect, a trade barrier. The EU pointed out, however, that it held its own manufacturers to the same rigid requirements. The approach of REACH is radically different from US policy on toxins. Instead of assuming that chemicals are safe until proven otherwise, a basic implication of TSCA, REACH is rooted in the precautionary principle that requires chemical manufacturers to demonstrate a chemical's safety before it is acceptable for use. It was a bold move: "It was the first time the EU wielded the political muscle that goes with its economic power. And it worked" (Schapiro 2007b, p. 140). Indeed, policy to regulate toxins reflects a shift in global power. The European Parliament approved REACH in December 2006. Within months, the US Department of Commerce was assisting US businesses in how to comply with the new European standards. These changes reflect an earlier time:

Shortly after the EPA was founded, the United States imposed domestic restrictions on some of the most dangerous pesticides and other chemicals, and U.S. companies responded by exporting millions of pounds of these toxins to Third World countries, where such regulations didn't exist. The irony is that our nation's steady retreat from environmental leadership means it may soon become a dumping ground for chemicals deemed too hazardous by more progressive countries.

(Schapiro 2007a, p. 83)

By 2008, an expansive list of chemicals of concern was under consideration for removal from the market unless their safety can be proven. There are also predictions that chemical-reliant industry groups will be at the forefront to promote higher standards in the US to ensure that US producers remain competitive on the world market. If "Power is the ability to pursue and attain goals through mastery of one's environment" (Mann 1986, p. 6), European toxins regulations arguably demonstrate how Europe's power extends beyond European borders. This power is not only political and economic, but it is also ideological as consumers become more aware of the presence of toxins and are able to exercise a choice between screened goods and untested products.

Perhaps in response to the threat of declining competitiveness in world trade, the Obama Administration is supporting more stringent regulation of chemicals under proposed revisions to the TSCA. In September 2009, the EPA announced that updating chemical regulations was a top priority of the agency and identified several changes to current law that will be put before Congress. Both new and existing chemicals would have to be reviewed for both environmental and for public health safety. Proposed legislation would shift practice away from the assumption that chemicals are safe until proven otherwise. Until such legislation passes and is implemented, however, consumers are left to do their own research on products they use if they are interested in taking responsibility for their exposure to toxins.

Toxins compete with many other product features in the public mind, and it can be difficult to prioritize toxins when they are invisible and largely undiscussed. Consumers might assume that if a product is environmentally and socially responsible in some ways, then it poses no risks. For example, The Body Shop is the second largest cosmetics and personal care products company in the world. The franchise, now part of L'Oréal, emphasizes environmentally and socially responsible values to draw thoughtful consumers to its product lines. The company promotes environmental sustainability, community (fair) trade, rainforest preservation, and takes a stand against media stereotyping of women and animal testing of any kind for its products. The Body Shop also sponsors campaigns against HIV, domestic abuse, and other forms of exploitation and injustice. The Body Shop emphasizes these campaigns to portray itself as a company with ethics to appeal to consumers and investors alike. However, The Environmental Working Group, a non-profit organization established to protect public health through public information, brings a different perspective to The Body Shop's operations. The Environmental Working Group tracks, among other activities, company compliance with The Compact for Safe Cosmetics. The Compact aims to increase product safety of signatory companies and requires them to disclose full information to the public about ingredients used in cosmetics. The Environmental Working Group points out that although The Body Shop has signed The Compact for Safe Cosmetics, it is non-compliant due to its use of chemicals that are prohibited by The Compact. In particular, The Body Shop's use of methylparaben in approximately 148 of its products is a significant concern for toxicity associated with multiple, non-reproductive organ systems in the human body. However, unless or until trade restrictions or state-level regulations limit The Body Shop and other manufacturers in their use of toxic chemicals, the company will continue to command economic power that transcends state borders but that has potentially significant impacts at the scale of the body.

Chemical warfare and a nuclear legacy

This chapter so far has examined how three forms of power discussed by Mann (1986) – political, economic, and ideological – intertwine with issues surrounding toxins and the spatial scales at which we see and experience the effects of these forms of power. The fourth dimension of power that Mann discusses as being applied for certain social outcomes is military power. Military power is a form of organization in the interest of physical defense and aggression. Military power is most often centrally commanded by the state, it can be intensive in terms of the involvement of individuals directly involved, and it can be extensive in terms of the physical territories controlled. One way that military power enters into the discussion of toxins is through chemical warfare. Throughout history, chemical warfare has been used to generate a fear of horrifying weapons to deter the enemy and to expand the spatial reach of effective combat and territorial control. Even in the ancient world:

An astounding panoply of toxic substances, venomous creatures, poison plants, animals and insects, deleterious environments, virulent pathogens, infectious

agents, noxious gases, and combustible chemicals were marshaled to defeat foes –
and *panoply* is an apt term here, because it is the ancient Greek word for "all
weapons." Many of these bio-weapons and stratagems, some crude and others
quite sophisticated, were considered fair, acceptable ruses of war, while others were
reviled. The ancient tension between notions of fair combat and actual practice
reveals that moral questions about biochemical weapons is not a modern
phenomenon, but has existed ever since the first war arrow was dipped in poison.

(Mayor 2003, p. 30)

In ancient Greece, for example, snake venom and toxic botanicals were used
to make poison arrows. The purpose was not to ensure a swift death; just the
opposite. The intention was to cause gruesome suffering and thereby terrify
the enemy. In the Black Sea region of Turkey and the Caucasus, toxic honey
made by bees drawing nectar from poisonous rhododendron blossoms was
used as a hallucinogen and could incapacitate the enemy for days. Mead
made or fortified with this "mad honey" may have been used against
Russians by Olga of Kiev in AD 946, and then later used by Russians in
1489 against Tatars (Mayor 2003, p. 154). The city of Kirrha was destroyed in
590 BC when the Greeks dismantled the city's aqueduct causing thirst among
the population. When they reopened the aqueduct, they tainted the water
with hellebore, an herbal toxin, to inflict debilitating intestinal sickness
on everyone inside the city walls including the guards and soldiers. Other
historical examples of chemical warfare involved launching clay bombs filled
with venomous bees, poisonous insects such as pederin beetles or scorpions,
or vaulting diseased animal carcasses at the enemy. By World War I and the
advent of mustard gas, for example, toxic warfare reflected changes in scientific understanding of chemicals. Chemical weaponry continued to develop
through the Vietnam War with the use of napalm and Agent Orange which
served as defoliants to eliminate vegetative cover and expose the enemy.

Despite advances in chemical weaponry, compared to other military
technologies, chemical weapons have changed surprisingly little over the past
century. This point raises a concern for another intersection of power and
spatial scale in regards to chemical weapons, namely, the use of chemical
weapons by terrorist organizations. Terrorism is a form of organized violence
the operation and objectives of which are beyond the purview of state
authority. Terrorism may be seen as a form of interstitial emergence, as
described by Mann (1986, p. 16) in that it operates and seeks to consolidate
its capacity in between the already-established power networks of society. For
much of the twentieth century in the US and Europe, terrorism was often
employed by groups such as the IRA, The Red Brigade, and the Black
Panthers to communicate a particular political message through symbolic

violence. The objective was to make a point, shock the public, and gain support for a political agenda. In the 1990s, a shift towards more violent acts motivated by religious extremism occurred. When religious terrorists follow a belief system that permits if not encourages killing as a divine duty, the scale and target of violence become unbounded and limitless. This shift in perspective on the part of terrorist organizations is complemented by the lethality and reach of toxic chemical weapons. Although it is not easy to achieve mass casualty capability, it is possible:

Chemical substances are easily accessible and available, they can be manufactured using simple chemical processes known to any university student and the components are usually simple products that can be obtained in the free market without restrictions. A chemical attack then can be executed using, for example, off-the-shelf pesticides sold in most supermarkets . . .

(Coleman 2005, p. 139)

What is more, many chemical substances are easily transported under cover, and only a small amount may be required. Technology that is used to detect chemical substances, on the other hand, is not as widely available and is therefore of limited use in preventing terrorist attacks. Chemical terrorism, however, is relatively limited in frequency and in spatial scope, and is likely to remain less of a threat than conventional terrorism.

When they are initially deployed, toxic weapons are usually intended to bring about a desired result in a specific time and place, yet a critical aspect of toxic weapons is that once they are unleashed, they tend to resist destruction and can take on a life of their own. Toxic weapons are nearly impossible to contain and can spread across unintended spatial and temporal scales. In this way, toxic and chemical weapons exemplify how concentrated power can become a spatially diffuse threat:

Long before the invention of Greek Fire, and two millennia before the invention of napalm and nuclear bombs, the Greeks and Romans confronted new chemical fire weapons whose awesome powers of destruction could not be checked by normal means. Over and over, the ancient historians repeated the refrain: the only hope of quelling such ghastly fire was to cover it with earth . . . Now those desperate attempts to bury poison and fire weapons seem to foreshadow our own efforts to dispose of dangerous weapons underground, out of sight but never completely out of mind.

(Mayor 2003, p. 53)

Warfare leaves a legacy on the landscape in many forms, and the militarism of the twentieth century is no exception. In the past, states engaged in military efforts to maintain or expand state territorial sovereignty. More recently, however, there has been a shift towards militarism in which economic investment in and profit from armed conflict becomes an end in itself. This shift has changed the nature of conflict and expanded the availability of lethal weapons to groups and organizations outside state militaries. Stores of chemical weapons and areas dotted by unspent landmines are additional relicts of "twentieth century military violence which is distinctive in both its geographic scale and its historical persistence." (Tyner 2010, p. 155).

Today, we still rely on burial and isolation to deal with toxic materials that cannot otherwise be contained. Even burial is not completely reliable. For example, the Soviets tested and dumped bioweapons materials on Vozrozhdeniye Island in the Aral Sea in Central Asia:

The human cost of this, the world's largest bioweapons testing ground, is incalculable. But of the environmental disasters in the region that have been made public, the sudden death of 500,000 steppe antelopes in just one hour in 1988 was one of the most striking.

(Mayor 2003, p. 253)

The Aral Sea has shrunk due to the drawing off of waters from the rivers that feed this water body. It has shrunk so much that it has divided into two much smaller lakes leaving Vozrozhdeniye Island exposed and accessible by land to animals, such as antelopes, that might wander in its direction. The impact of these poorly contained toxic chemicals on human communities living in the area remains to be fully seen.

Another example of our attempt to control toxic material is the burial of nuclear waste at Nevada's Yucca Mountain facility. The US Department of Energy began to plan this facility in 1982 to serve as a national repository for up to 77 000 metric tons of spent nuclear fuel and high level radioactive materials from commercial and defense sources. No Plan B was identified in the event that the Yucca Mountain facility was not completed and put into use. In 2002, Congress and President George W. Bush officially designated Yucca Mountain as the country's nuclear waste repository. President Obama's administration, with the support of Energy Secretary Steven Chu and Senate Majority Leader Harry Reid, has cut funding to Yucca Mountain even though this opposition to the project does not change its legal status (Nuclear Waste Update 2009). Opponents to Yucca Mountain question, among other concerns, the concentration of nuclear waste in one location. An estimate of the additional radiation that Yucca Mountain would bring to Nevada, which has already been exposed to nuclear testing, is 6 billion curies. As a point of comparison, the nuclear accident at Three Mile Island released 15 curies. The lethality of nuclear waste remains for at least 10 000 years. The Environmental Protection Agency requires that the Yucca Mountain site be marked in some way to warn future generations from disturbing the area and possibly releasing its contents. It is a challenge to

Figure 6.2 Yucca Mountain Mausoleum. The Yucca Mountain Warning Sign Competition was sponsored by the Desert Space Foundation. This design entry envisions large blocks of reinforced concrete approximately 100 feet high that sit on top of the nuclear waste sites at Yucca Mountain Nevada. The cubes with international warning signs for "Radioactivity," "No Entry," and "Bio Hazard" – visible even to passing UFOs – are meant to warn people away from the dangerous radioactive site for ten thousand years. Co-designers: Scott A. Ogburn, M.Arch., Temple University and Linda Buzby, M.Ind.Des., Philadelphia University. Image used with permission.

consider how to warn future generations about the toxic legacy of Yucca Mountain. Experts including artists, architects, archeologists, engineers, and linguists have contributed ideas about how to indicate the danger of nuclear radiation on the landscape (see for example Figure 6.2).

A concern about marking the site so that it stands out from the surrounding area is that it could possibly attract the wrong kind of attention and be mistaken for something of great value. The Department of Energy plans to encircle the site with verbal warnings even though the toxic legacy will likely outlast current forms of language. Nonetheless, a poem is proposed to be placed at the site as a meta-message of the toxic danger there:

This place is a message ... and part of a system of messages ... pay attention to it!
Sending this message was important to us.
We considered ourselves to be a powerful culture.
This place is not a place of honor ... no highly esteemed deed is commemorated here ... nothing valued is here.
What is here was dangerous and repulsive to us.
This message is a warning about danger.
The danger is in a particular location ... it increases towards a center ... the center of danger is here ... of a particular size and shape, and below us.

The danger is still present, in your time, as it was in ours.
The danger is to the body, and it can kill.
The form of the danger is an emanation of energy.
The danger is unleashed only if you substantially disturb this place physically.
This place is best shunned and left uninhabited.

> *(Department of Energy: The Monumental Task of Warning Future Generations http://www.ocrwm.doe.gov/factsheets/doeymp0115.shtml, accessed 3 October 2009)*

This communication to future generations captures a sobering commentary on our own understanding of – yet apparent disregard for – the realities of toxins.

Conclusion

This chapter has considered ways in which different dimensions of power – economic, political, ideological, and military – are relevant in a consideration of toxins. This chapter has also discussed multiple spatial scales that are influenced by decision-making related to toxins. A main focus of this chapter has been risk assessment processes since they act as gatekeepers in determining how toxins are identified, permitted into use, or prohibited. Different approaches to risk assessment have been discussed to emphasize that there are many ways to interpret and act on risk associated with toxins.

Since standard risk assessment procedures, or science in general for that matter, cannot really measure effects of exposure to multiple chemicals at once, we might ask if risk assessment can tell us anything about actual exposures and their effects. Perhaps risk assessment provides a false sense of security (Zakrezewski 2002, p. 119). An alternative to risk assessment is the precautionary principle which is demonstrated in the EU's REACH policy on toxins:

> At its most basic, the precautionary principle is a principle of public decision-making that requires decision-makers in cases where there are 'threats' of environmental or health harm not to use 'lack of full scientific certainty' as a reason for not taking measures to prevent such harm.
>
> *(Fisher et al. 2006, p. 2)*

This principle of precautionary action turns risk assessment on its head. It requires that the responsibility of assuring that a policy or action is safe lies with the person or agency advocating that action. Risk assessment reports conditions under which an exposure may be hazardous, but it does not necessarily prove that exposure is safe. A precautionary approach, on the other hand, advocates the principle "Do no harm." More specifically:

> ... the precautionary principle shifts the burden of proof regarding new substances, technologies, or courses of action with potentially significant effects to those who are promoting those new things. There are no forces anywhere that can stop companies

from pushing high technology, the bioengineering of foods, and so on. Globalization and private interests are just too strong. The precautionary principle is a tool that can sometimes be used to make some of those interests consider worst case possibilities. It can push policy makers to be explicit about the values they're pursuing, to specify the uncertainties in their decision processes, and to imagine alternatives they might otherwise ignore.

(Clarke 2006, p. 180)

A key idea here is uncertainty. When potential threats are not well understood scientifically, and when there is insufficient direct experience with these threats, it is more realistic to think in terms of uncertainty management rather than risk management (Kasperson 2008). That is, rather than assume that a limited number of scientific studies or models has adequately estimated the likelihood of risk, and rather than using that information to establish a safety threshold, a focus on uncertainty anticipates negative outcomes. Borrowing from the risk-informed approach adapted by the Nuclear Regulatory Commission (Farber and Weeks 2001), we can think of uncertainty management as asking three questions:

- What can go wrong?
- How likely is it to occur?
- What are the consequences?

Anticipating what can go wrong could result either in not pursuing a particular action or in planning appropriate responses. Either way, this approach would significantly alter decision-making processes around the production, distribution, and use of potentially toxic chemicals. Rather than unleashing risk on the general public and on the environment because the science supporting that decision is "good enough," the person or agency considering the action would face much greater responsibility if or when the worst case scenario was realized. This approach could have significant effects on how power is applied. State laws on toxins regulations would likely become stricter if the state was going to be held accountable for paying for health care costs of exposed or damaged individuals, for example. Corporations and manufacturers might reconsider their economic reach and weigh potential profits against economic loss of being held accountable for inflicting damage. Ideologically, individuals who are informed and who do not blindly trust that "someone" has ensured their safety might take greater personal responsibility in regards to everyday activities that could expose them to toxins. Although Mann (1986) notes that the public masses do not revolt because they lack the organizational capacity to challenge current systems of power, we might look at individual actions designed not to challenge systems of power but to take back the power to control personal toxicity.

An example of ways to exercising personal uncertainty management comes from the Environmental Working Group which offers these suggestions for curbing the effects of everyday exposure to toxins:

Everyday pollution solutions

1. Use cast iron pans instead of non-stick to avoid exposure from toxins released from Teflon.
2. To avoid chemicals leaching into food, minimize consumption of processed, canned, or fast foods. Bisphenol-A is a toxic food-can lining ingredient associated with birth defects. Never microwave plastic.
3. Buy organic, or eat vegetables and fruits that have been treated with fewer chemicals: onion, avocado, sweet corn, pineapple, mango, asparagus, sweet peas, kiwi, cabbage, eggplant, papaya, watermelon, broccoli, tomato, sweet potato. Avoid or buy organic when choosing: peaches, apples, bell pepper, celery, nectarines, strawberries, cherries, kale, lettuce, grapes (imported), carrots, and pears since they tend to be treated with heavy loads of pesticides and herbicides.
4. Pregnant women should use iodized salt to combat chemical interference from the thyroid. A particular concern here is the effect of the rocket fuel contaminant perchlorate in food or water that can cause a serious decline in thyroid hormone levels.
5. Seal outdoor wooden structures. It is recommended that wooden decks, picnic tables, and wood playsets are tested to check for leaching arsenic.
6. Leave your shoes at the door. This cuts down on dust-bound pollutants in the home.
7. Avoid perfume, cologne, and products with added fragrance. Search for personal care products that are fragrance-free.
8. Buy products with natural fibers, like cotton and wool, that are naturally fire resistant to avoid polybrominated diphenylethers (PBDE) which are used as a chemical flame retardant.
9. Eat low-mercury fish like tilapia and pollock, rather than high-mercury choices like tuna and swordfish.
10. Filter your water for drinking and cooking.

The Environmental Working Group offers additional information on each of these suggestions, as well as information on assessing one's personal body burden of toxins, at their website (http://www.ewg.org/, accessed 3 October 2009) as part of an effort to inform the public about health hazards of which they might not otherwise be aware. Although personal decisions made on the basis of this information may not be far reaching and are unlikely to influence, say, state regulations or international standards for trade, they are intended to influence the spatial scale most directly of concern for toxic exposure: the human body.

7

Resource conflict

Minimum number of countries where there have been food riots during the past two years: 30

– Harper's *Index, June 2009*

Percentage change since 2007 in the number of Texas cattle thefts: +300

– Harper's *Index, August 2009*

Introduction

A diamond is forever. De Beers has used this advertising slogan since 1948, borrowing from Anita Loos's book, first published in 1925, *Gentlemen Prefer Blondes*. There, she wrote "So I really think that American gentlemen are the best after all, because kissing your hand may make you feel very very good but a diamond and safire [sic] bracelet lasts forever." (Loos 1992, p. 80). The De Beers marketing campaign is largely responsible for the expectation in Western countries that a bride-to-be will be offered a diamond engagement ring. The symbolism is fitting. Diamonds are a particularly hard gem (which also makes them ideal for use in industrial machinery and drill bits) making them an appropriate symbol for a long lasting relationship. Diamonds are also very expensive. Their price tag is due in large part to the fact that De Beers has at times controlled as much as 80% of the world diamond market through its influence over diamond mines, contracts with suppliers, and the available supply of diamonds. The release of the Hollywood blockbuster, *Blood Diamond*, in 2006 exposed the movie-going public to the violence of the diamond trade. Blood diamonds, or conflict diamonds, originate in areas controlled by rebel groups that are acting in opposition to a country's internationally recognized government. Not only are profits from the unregu-lated diamond trade in African countries such as Angola, Côte d'Ivoire,

Democratic Republic of Congo, and Sierra Leone used to fund armed conflict and purchase weapons, but opposition groups that control diamond mining areas have resorted to mutilating and killing men, women, and even very young children as enticement to work in the mines. Brutal child labor practices are often used in these areas to produce diamonds. Additionally, tens of thousands of people have been forced to flee their homes, have been killed or abducted, or have been mutilated in diamond-producing areas.

In the early 2000s, the United Nations General Assembly began working with governments, civil society organizations, and the international diamond industry to develop a way to control the production and trade of rough diamonds. The Kimberley Process emerged as a way to certify diamonds as "conflict free" and to stem the trade in conflict diamonds. The Kimberley Process went into force in 2003 as signatory countries agreed to steps to bring about transparency and accountability in the diamond trade. This unique certification scheme is credited for helping to stabilize fragile governments by boosting their legitimate income from diamonds, and it is widely thought to be an effective mechanism to ameliorate conflict and to promote peace. However, Human Rights Watch (2009) recently released a report claiming that police and army forces have brutally taken over recently discovered diamond-rich areas in Zimbabwe. The report summary begins:

Zimbabwe's armed forces, under the control of President Robert Mugabe's Zimbabwe African National Union–Patriotic Front (ZANU-PF), are engaging in forced labor of children and adults and are torturing and beating local villagers on the diamond fields of Marange district. The military seized control of these diamond fields in eastern Zimbabwe after killing more than 200 people in Chiadzwa, a previously peaceful but impoverished part of Marange, in late October 2008. With the complicity of ZANU-PF, Marange has become a zone of lawlessness and impunity, a microcosm of the chaos and desperation that currently pervade Zimbabwe.

(Human Rights Watch 2009)

Zimbabwe is a member of the Kimberley Process Certification Scheme which not only means it should comply with the standards of production and certification set out by the agreements, but it also means that other member countries must adhere to guidelines in their trade with Zimbabwe. Human Rights Watch has called upon the members of the Kimberley Process Certification Scheme to respond to these dire conditions by recognizing diamonds from the Marange region as "conflict diamonds" and immediately halt any trade of these diamonds. Human Rights Watch has further called for a broadening of the Kimberley Process Certification Scheme to hold

Figure 7.1 Advertisement for conflict-free Canadian diamonds. Image used with permission from Leber Jeweler Inc.

government bodies, in addition to rebel groups, accountable for violence and abuses committed in the production of diamonds. A different response to conflict diamonds comes from Canada, another diamond producing country. Diamonds produced in Canada's North West Territories are monitored at every step of production and sold with certification of their origin as well as a computer-scanned "gemprint" to identify each diamond. Jewelers advertise these features of Canadian diamonds to assure customers that their purchase is "conflict free" (see Figure 7.1).

Diamonds are but one example of how environmental or "natural" resources become entangled in conflict. Other resources such as oil and drugs are often associated with conflict. "Resource conflicts" grab the public's attention because the association between environmental resources and violent conflict seems clear: there are more and more people on the planet but the stockpile of resources remains relatively fixed. Therefore, this line of thinking goes, conflict over resources is inevitable. This chapter examines this perspective and the large and growing body of scholarly literature devoted to analyzing resource conflict. First, the chapter considers two predominant schools of thought about natural resources and conflict. One view is that resource scarcity leads to conflict, and the other view is that resource abundance leads to conflict. Both of these perspectives, however, oversimplify complexities of conflict. The chapter then examines geographic features of environmental resources and why these characteristics are important for understanding links between the environment and conflict. Finally, the chapter considers the case of Azerbaijan, an oil-rich country where we might expect to see resource-related conflict but do not. The objective of this chapter, as with the examination of other topics in previous chapters, is to encourage the reader to think critically about the forms and modes of power shaping the way we tend to conceptualize resource conflicts and the spatial aspects that we tend to focus on or overlook.

Resource scarcity, resource abundance, and conflict

In the 1980s, during the final years of the Cold War, Arthur Westing (1984) wrote about different ways that the environment could have a role in warfare. He outlined ways in which different aspects of the environment could be brought to bear in "hostile manipulations" (p. 4): the atmosphere (altering the ozone layer in certain places to subject enemy territory to high levels of ultraviolet radiation or manipulating the chemical balance of the atmosphere to interfere with communications), the lithosphere (instigating landslides or avalanches, the destruction of dams to cause floods), the hydrosphere (disruption of sonar properties, the generation of seismic sea waves), and the biosphere (the destruction of forests and other ecosystems or the release of microbiological agents). A few years later, Peter Gleick (1991), an internationally recognized expert on water, took a somewhat different tack to consider the role of environmental features in the post-Cold War world. He wrote a short piece in *The Bulletin of Atomic Scientists* arguing that there are clear connections between the environment and security. He echoed Westing in his argument that the environment can have multiple roles in conflict and therefore should be raised to the level of "high politics" as a security concern for states. Gleick discussed how the environment could be a strategic goal of military endeavors. Hitler's objective of gaining control of Caspian Sea oil resources to fuel his military campaign is an example. Gleick observed that the industrialized countries' disproportionate control over and use of fossil fuel resources contributes not only to environmental degradation around the world but also to a growing gap between the "haves" and the "have nots." A result of this uneven distribution of the use of and benefits from fossil fuel consumption in particular is that "The stage is thus set for continuing misery, despair, and frustration for billions of people – and, inevitably, social and political unrest" (p. 19).

Second, Gleick discussed attacks on resources as another concern for state security. He gives examples of the destruction of dams during twentieth century wars, Israel's attack on the Osirak nuclear plant in Baghdad in 1981, and Iraq's attacks on Kuwaiti energy installations and nuclear facilities in the initial weeks of the Persian Gulf War in 1990. Third, Gleick discussed the environment as a military tool. Scorched earth policies, for example, are a military strategy often used when retreating from enemy territory in which anything that might be useful to the enemy, such as crops or infrastructure, is destroyed. The deliberate spilling of oil in the Persian Gulf War and setting oilfields on fire are also examples of using the environment as a military tool. Finally, Gleick discussed the disruption of ecosystem services as a security concern. Here, he is referring to the overuse of natural resources such as cutting down forests beyond the ecosystem's capacity to recover or polluting water and air. Disruption of environmental services alters the very biological and geological conditions on which we depend for survival. He argued that such damage spills over national boundaries to affect other places and people and can lead to social strife and political tension. Differences between industrializing and industrialized countries over how to address human-induced climate change illustrate this point.

Gleick's early contribution to what has become a large body of scholarly work on resource conflict outlines key concerns about how environmental resource scarcity can lead to conflict. Scarcity, in his writing, is relative, especially when some groups of people enjoy higher levels of resource consumption. The uneven distribution of resources is also a form of scarcity for places that are not endowed with these supplies either due to geography or through international trade. Other scholars also advanced the view that scarcity of resources leads to conflict. Thomas Homer-Dixon (1991, 1994) studied how resource scarcity within states, rather than between states, has contributed to conflict. He refined the idea of scarcity by looking at supply-induced scarcity, demand-induced scarcity, and structural scarcity. Supply-induced scarcity results from environmental degradation that reduces an ecosystem's productivity such as the loss of forest, the destruction of crop-land or fish habitat, or soil degradation. Demand-induced scarcity results when there are more people in need (or want) of a particular resource or when higher levels of consumption place greater demand on resource supplies. This type of scarcity occurs, for example, as new population groups migrate into an area. Structural scarcity occurs when there is uneven distribution of a resource or when the control over a resource is concentrated in the hands of few people (Barber 1998). Famines, for instance, can occur in places where enough food is available but not accessible to everyone who needs it. Resource scarcity itself, researchers have argued, does not necessarily lead to conflict, but it can trigger conflict in places where ethnic tensions already exist (Baechler 1998, 1999b) or where people are able to mobilize around a shared religious, class, or ethnic identity to engage in violent conflict (Homer-Dixon and Blitt 1998). Conflict, in turn, may have negative impacts on the environment and generate feedback in recurring cycles of conflict that coincide with seasonal or production cycles of natural resources (Maxwell and Reuveny 2000).

This line of thinking about resources and conflict has a similar spatial focus as political ecology (see O'Lear 2005). Political ecology is an interdisciplinary field of study that focuses on the land manager and how shortages of, degradation of, and disputes over resources are experienced at a local scale by people who are probably powerless to change these conditions. An important difference though between literature on resource scarcity as a cause of conflict and political ecology is that political ecology traces connections between the immediate ecosystem and larger scale economic and political processes (Watts 1983; Blaikie 1985; Blaikie and Brookfield 1987). Political ecology studies focus on how local scarcity, degradation, or uneven distribution are connected to larger scale economic and political processes. For example, the exploitation of forest resources in Cambodia was a lucrative activity thanks to the global trade in forest products and demand for those products elsewhere. The income from this exploitation has been seen to fund both peace and conflict within Cambodia (Le Billon 2001). As another example, in the Eastern Brazilian Amazon, changes to local land tenure policies in response to internationally encouraged economic development policies have combined to contribute to localized conflict (Simmons 2004). Political ecology not only considers multiple spatial scales and connectivity among places (e.g., international demand for commodities and trade patterns), but it also aims to trace power relations that shape who has control over the management of and benefit from environmental resources. The literature that connects resource scarcity to conflict shares political ecology's focus on the local, but it does not systematically assess multiple scales or explicitly consider multiple and simultaneous forms of power. Additionally, it tends to concentrate narrowly on violent conflict instead of considering social and political forms of conflict.

Another line of research connecting environmental resources to conflict views resource abundance as a contributing factor to violent conflict. Writing in the early 1960s before petroleum had replaced coffee as the world's most widely traded commodity, Mancur Olson (1963) observed that resource wealth can lead to rapid but unbalanced economic growth within a country. Selling off natural resources as commodity exports, as opposed to refining them as export products with greater value added, brings resource "rents" to a country. These quickly gotten funds can widen the gap in the distribution of income within a country, increase geographic mobility as people move from rural areas to cities to find better-paying jobs, and lead to rural decline and the disintegration of the social fabric of society – all of which can be destabilizing (Auty and Mikesell 1998; Auty 2001a). Countries with large supplies of petroleum appear to be uniquely vulnerable to disparities of wealth and to internal economic and political instability (Amuzegar 1982; Gelb 1986, 1988; Karl 1997, 2000). Oil has also been linked, more than other natural resources, to civil wars (Ross 2004a, 2004b). As oil has gained predominance as an energy resource in the world economy, it has become integrated into global power politics (Yergin 1992). Oil is a unique resource in how it serves to concentrate power by maintaining dictatorships in oil-rich countries that do not manage their oil wealth transparently (Bacher 2000). As a counter example, Norway has established an oil fund which serves as a means for managing its oil income in a transparent way and for distributing benefits of the country's oil wealth throughout society. That approach to resource wealth is stabilizing. Other countries may have also established oil funds, but if they are not managed transparently, oil funds can become a conduit for funneling oil wealth into the hands of a few people rather than to the country as a whole. Countries with this approach to managing oil wealth are often referred to as "petro-states" because their governments have a tendency to use their oil wealth to reinforce their own power over the state.

Having an abundance of any natural resource that is in demand as a commodity in the world economy – timber, gems or minerals, drugs – can be a liability if it serves as a means to obtain funds that, instead of being added to accountable government coffers for the public good, may be channeled to superfluous or extravagant projects with no budgetary approval process. The temptation to have access to unrestricted cash flow can encourage governments to waste their country's natural resource stockpile (Ascher 1999, 2000). These arrangements of power encourage corruption by strengthening central control and intimidating the public from dissent or opposing powerful government structures and authority (Auty 2001b; Auty and De Soysa 2006). Resource wealth, in these ways, may be a "resource curse," and it can inhibit the growth and development of other economic sectors thus making a country's economy even more dependent on the export of its resource wealth (Sachs and Warner 2001). Governments that use or abuse resource wealth at their discretion are usually not under pressure to appease their citizens or pursue reform. By not building institutional capacity (e.g., reliable operation of government agencies, or systems of education, health care, public safety or other social safety nets), governments of resource-rich states may increase the risk of instability.

Just as the view linking resource scarcity and conflict shares a spatial focus with political ecology, the view that links resource abundance to conflict takes a similar spatial focus as the field of study known as environmental security. The notion of environmental security is popular in some circles because it tends to focus at the spatial scale of the state and lends itself to thinking about state-level policy. The basic premise of environmental security thinking borrows the assumption from political realism that states are in a zero-sum game of competing for access to resources. Uneven patterns of resource distribution, population density, levels of consumption, and the generation of environmentally degrading waste are all challenges that states must face as they maintain their sovereignty and territorial integrity (Falk 1971; Ullman 1983). Resource abundance, either as something to be protected within one's state borders or as something to be sought outside of one's border, focuses attention on plentiful environmental resources as an issue for state security. Environmental security, as a perspective on how to define problems and identify solutions, has been critiqued for limiting our understanding of both what the "environment" is and what "security" is (Dalby 1992, 1996, 2002; Tennberg 1995; Barnett 2000, 2001) and for promoting a narrowly militaristic view (Deudney 1991; Lipschutz and Conca 1993; Deudney and Matthew 1999). These points are in line with the discussion in the next section.

Spatial scale and conflict

A problem with the debate over whether resource scarcity or resource abundance (or more accurately, dependence on resource exports) sets the ground for conflict is that it sets up a binary which oversimplifies our understanding both of environmental resources and of conflict. By presenting the link between the environment and conflict as an "either/or" choice, we are limited to a view that resource conflict is being determined solely by environmental or resource conditions. We miss the opportunity to ask more refined questions about the nature of conflict, the actors involved, and the different roles that "the environment" may have in conflict. Asking these kinds of questions also allows us to understand more clearly spatial dimensions of resource use and conflict.

What is the nature of conflict?

Much of the research and literature on resource conflict concentrates on violent, armed conflict. Of course it is important and worthwhile to understand such events, but such a narrow definition of conflict limits our understanding of human suffering. One reason that attention stays focused on violent conflict is that the most commonly used databases for analyzing conflict have a threshold for violence – usually measured in battle deaths – for events to be included in the data set. For example, the Correlates of War Project (http://www.correlatesofwar.org/, accessed 1 November 2009) has a threshold of one thousand battle deaths that conflict events must clear in order to be included in its database. Anyone using that database will only have information on conflicts that have resulted in at least one thousand battle deaths, so any conflict that resulted in fewer battle deaths would not appear in the database or in an analysis using that database. The Uppsala Conflict Data Program (http://www.pcr.uu.se/research/UCDP/, accessed 1 November 2009) has a much lower threshold of 25 battle deaths and therefore captures many more conflict events. A focus on battle deaths, however, overlooks the fact that violent conflict contributes to many deaths off the battlefield due to starvation, water borne diseases, and a lack of access to medicine and medical care among other causes. These aspects of widely used datasets are important to acknowledge. Still, an advantage of using large databases to study resource conflict is that they enable an assessment and comparison of many different cases so that trends may be observed (Buhaug 2007).

Earlier in this chapter, political ecology was described as an approach to studying human interactions with the environment, and that field of study also examines conflict. The conflict of interest there has to do with land managers and people working closely to extract and use environmental resources and how those activities are influenced by political economic connections beyond the sites of resource use and extraction. For example, in Bolivia, coca leaves have long been used medicinally by indigenous Andean people. However, since coca leaves are the key ingredient in cocaine, international efforts to eradicate drugs at the source brings international interests to clash with the traditional practices of ritualistic resource use. This conflict of interests explains why coca eradication efforts in Bolivia (and elsewhere) tend to fail since coca is highly valued locally and because there is limited access to profitable markets for other crops.

Although this example is not one of violent, armed conflict, it is a form of conflict nonetheless which involves people, environmental resources, and some degree of political and economic tension. Similarly, Chapter 2 on climate change discussed public dissent by indigenous groups over the assumption by richer countries that carbon offset forests may be planted anywhere. From the perspective of indigenous groups, forested areas are not "empty spaces" to be used for the benefit of people who live at a distance so that arbitrary offsets of carbon emissions may be satisfied. This disagreement is another kind of conflict that, depending on its resolution, could have very real impacts on the livelihoods and well-being of indigenous groups. Another example of a resource-related conflict that would be under the radar of key conflict databases is depicted in the film, *The Golf War*. The film tells the story of the seaside community called Hacienda Looc in the Philippines which the government wants to open up to golf course development. The villagers want to maintain their agricultural way of life on their ancestral lands. If the land is converted to a tourist destination, they know they will have few options for survival other than working as groundskeepers on golf courses or as prostitutes. As the villagers organize and stand up against the government, a few of their outspoken members are mysteriously killed. A group of the villagers takes up the challenge and arms themselves to protect the village. One of these villagers tells the film producer that they have to take up arms because this is a matter of life and death. In poignant contrast, we then see Tiger Woods's father who is participating in a nearby event in the Philippines to promote golf. He says to the crowd of youth gathered around him that golf is a game; it is not a matter of life and death. Again, this conflict situation would not register in the Correlates of War Project or the Uppsala Conflict database, but it still involves a struggle of economic interests, political power, and – yes – even death.

As we consider that the nature of conflict varies greatly, we are also led to the question of who is involved in conflict. Does a conflict over environmental resources involve state-to-state dispute and the use of state-funded military forces? Does it involve opposition forces, militia groups, or rebels who want to overthrow the government or gain control of part of a state's territory? In the above examples, we can see how "conflict" can involve ordinary people trying to maintain their livelihoods without the advantage of much political power. Given our media-saturated society's fascination with violence and "action," it is often assumed that difficult conditions will automatically and naturally motivate people to become involved in dissent, protest, violence, and conflict. This quote by Berndard Brodie reminds us otherwise "The predisposing factors to military aggression are full bellies, not empty ones" (Brodie 1972, p. 14). If we think carefully about sacrifices that individuals must make to be involved in activities of dissent or risks that may be incurred from such involvement, we are reminded that conflict comes at a price. Even involvement in social movements that may seek change or recognition in altogether non-violent ways requires that individuals have sufficient time and resources to commit to the cause. Returning to Michael Mann's (1986) dimensions of power, we are reminded that public dissent is limited by the ability of people to organize collectively. It is a lot to expect that a situation involving environmental resources would automatically lead to public organization sufficient enough to wage conflict.

What is the spatial scale of conflict?

Asking who is involved in conflict leads into another question about resource conflict, namely, where is that involvement? Where is the conflict? These questions lead us to consider spatial dimensions of conflict. In the introduction of this book, the concept of spatial scale was discussed not as a set of pre-existing containers for human activity but instead as the spatial result of actors engaging in different kinds of relations in particular places. As this discussion suggests, there are many different types of conflict – armed, political, economic, social – and conflict can involve multiple spatial scales as well.

In a critique of the resource conflict literature, O'Lear and Diehl (2007) have noted several limitations that are relevant for how we understand spatial dimensions of resource conflict. They argue that it is important to examine spatial aspects of conflict explicitly as a way to assess multiple factors of a conflict and possible pathways to conflict resolution. One problem is that much of the resource conflict literature adopts a state-centered focus and concentrates on actions taken by states and interactions between or among states. Research on resource abundance and conflict in particular considers themes of disputed state control over environmental resources as a means of economic development (Markandya and Averchenkova 2000), of the "resource curse" experienced by resource rich states (Lujala *et al.* 2005), and on ways that state dependence on resource exports shapes state stability (Dunning 2005; Fearon 2005). Most of these types of studies do not explain why they focus on the state, as opposed to any other scale of activity, or why these issues are only relevant, seemingly, at the state scale. An underlying but mostly unacknowledged assumption of state-centered studies on resource conflict is that the only kind of conflict worth analyzing is that which involves or has the potential to involve state militaries. Other work has examined conflict within a state, but the focus is limited to state governments, militaries, and rebel groups (Buhaug and Gates 2002) without considering other systems or institutions, within or beyond state borders, that shape relations among governments, rebels, and environmental resources. Often these studies are limited by the data set they use and the level of refinement of variables in those datasets. Simon Dalby has made the point that studies applying statistical analyses of state-level aggregated data are "susceptible to what might simply be called the Willie Sutton syndrome, where research is done the way it is because 'that is where the data is'!" (Dalby 2007b, p. 187). Willie Sutton, readers may know, was a bank robber who was once asked why he robbed banks. His response: "Because that's where the money is."

Another shortcoming of a state-centered focus is that it is not clear where the location of conflict is. Studies of water disputes, such as disputes over river water rights or freshwater supplies, have often considered state-to-state interactions over these concerns (Beaumont 1997; Soroos 1997; Toset *et al.* 2000), but it is not always clear how and where those conflicts emerge. This lack of clarity about conflict location results, in part, from identifying environmental conditions at the state level. Environmental resources are not distributed homogeneously across a state, yet some studies utilize variables that imply otherwise. Some studies have considered environmental features such as resource presence or terrain as having a role in civil wars (Collier and Hoeffler 2001; Fearon and Laitin 2003; Ross 2004a), but these features are treated as aggregated at a state level and therefore lead to neither specific nor accurate understanding of the role of environmental elements in conflict. For example, using the percent of land that is forested as a variable may recognize that the entire state is not forested, but it assumes that the effects of forest cover are the same across the whole state. Some studies draw from global scale natural resource databases with information on hydrology, mineral deposits, oil reserves, and so forth and use these pieces of information to create a composite variable to represent "the environment." One study that analyzed contributing factors to conflict used a natural resource variable calculated from datasets on forests, pastures, protected areas, and mineral wealth. These features were quantitatively combined to generate an environmental variable to represent "the net worth of the stock of natural resources of any given country in per capita terms (DeSoysa 2002, p. 407). In such studies:

a single value or meaning of a resource is often assumed to be understood or given, e.g., forest cover means challenges for on-the-ground combat, diamond mines mean access to hard currency, oil means connectivity to world markets, and suitable cropland means adequate food supply. That is, questions such as "for whom is a resource valuable and why?" are rarely considered as useful avenues for understanding conflict or lack thereof.

(O'Lear 2005, p. 300)

Using such aggregated measures of environmental resources at the state level greatly oversimplifies the meaning, value, and influence of environmental features. Such a methodology also limits the opportunity to evaluate specific relationships among people, places, and resources that can lead to conflict. State-level measures of environmental resources are likely to be too general to enable an assessment of the roots of conflict among actors, places, and resource use.

Other analyses of resource conflicts have concentrated their attention on conflicts within states. Two early efforts include The Toronto Group, directed by Thomas Homer-Dixon (1991, 1994, 1999; Homer-Dixon and Blitt 1998) and the Environment and Conflicts Project (ENCOP), directed by Gunther Baechler (1998, 1999a, 1999b). Both of these research efforts acknowledge that resource scarcity, in conjunction with other agitating factors such as ethnic tension, may lead to different types of conflict at the sub-state level. However, they share with state-centered studies the problem of "single-level myopia" (O'Lear and Diehl 2007, p. 173) that only considers one kind of place and a limited selection of types of actors involved in conflict. Identifying the spatial scale of study *a priori* is akin to setting a frame around a study and limiting the potential for creative evaluation of spatial relationships. When the spatial parameters of a study are established, it might not allow for an assessment of how the conflict changes as additional actors become involved. It also constrains any evaluation of relevant interactions across spatial scales such as the influence of international business or the role of traditional, localized power hierarchies. A challenging but perhaps more realistic approach to understanding conflict would do just the opposite: assess processes contributing to conflict and then evaluate their spatial dimensions.

What is the role of environmental resources in conflict?

This chapter began with Peter Gleick's assessment of why the environment is a security concern. His reasons may seem persuasive at first blush, but to gain perspective on them it is helpful to look at Daniel Deudney's (1991) rather different arguments that were published in the same journal. He points out that making the environment a security issue blurs the fact that environmental degradation and natural disasters pose different threats than violence does, and they may not usefully be considered threats to "national security." Environmental degradation is usually not done intentionally whereas acts of violence are usually organized and intentional. Organizations that protect a country from aggression or violence are very different from organizations that protect the environment. Also, state security issues often involve "Us/Them" thinking with clear borders outlining national identity. Environmental issues such as pollution do not necessarily recognize state boundaries and are often most appropriately addressed through collaborative, not competitive, efforts. Deudney further observes that:

> The scope and source of threats to environmental well-being and national security from violence are very different. Nothing about the problem of environmental degradation is particularly national in character. Few environmental threats afflict just one nation, and many altogether ignore national borders. But it would be misleading even to call most environmental problems international, because perpetrators and victims are within the same country. There is nothing distinctively national about the causes, harms, or solutions.
>
> *(p. 24)*

He cautions against looking for simple or direct relationships between environmental features and conflict "In today's world everything is connected, but not everything is tightly coupled" (p. 27).

Ten years after Gleick and Deudney debated the value of linking environmental features to security in the pages of *The Bulletin of Atomic Scientists,*

Michael Klare (2001) published an article in *Foreign Affairs*, a journal widely read by policy makers. The article was titled "The New Geography of Conflict." He includes three attention-grabbing maps to illustrate his discussion of potential hot spots of resource-related conflict. The first map shows major oil and gas deposits indicated by approximately 20 icons clustered in the Middle East, scattered across Africa, and here and there in South America, North America, Central Asia, and Siberia. The second map shows water systems and aquifers of which only five are indicated. All of them are clustered in Northeast Africa, the Middle East, and South Asia. The last map shows the location of major gem and mineral deposits and timber. The icons on this map draw our attention to Central and South America, Central Africa, and Southeast Asia. The message of these maps is clear: Here are places with resource abundance (or scarcity), and many of these places have been, are, or are likely to be sites of conflict. The same cartographic strategy is used on each map (i.e., the location of forests, mines, dams, etc. is generally indicated by oversized icons) suggesting that processes associated with each feature are the same. The scarcity of one resource (water) appears the same as an abundance of another (gems or oil). The correlation between environmental resources and conflict seems immediately convincing since we often hear of war or political instability in the Middle East and in Africa. However, these maps simplify the role of environmental resources as much as they generalize the places where these resources are located. There is no consideration of what conflict over these resources might look like, who it might involve, and what kinds of spaces or places might be implicated. These maps suggest that all environmental features, whether due to abundance or scarcity, lead to conflict in the same way.

So what is it about environmental resources that contributes to conflict? Resource conflict involves more than the mere presence, absence, distribution, or market value of environmental features. Valuing resources or other environmental features along a single dimension limits our understanding of that resource. Philippe Le Billon (2001) has considered how different types of resources tend to be implicated in different types of conflict (see Table 7.1). For instance, conflict associated with a point-source resource, such as an oil field or a dam, that is located at a specific site that could be relatively easily controlled, will involve different actors and objectives than conflict associated with a diffuse resource such as a vast area of forest or agriculturally rich land that would require a different kind of control. Is a resource proximate or distant from sites of conflict, and how does that relative location shape the relationship between the resource and the conflict? Is a resource "lootable" or easily smuggled? In this table from Le Billon's article, he sorts conflicts

Table 7.1. *Relation between the nature/geography of a resource and type of conflict*

	Point	Diffuse
Proximate	*State control/coup d'etat*	*Rebellion/rioting*
	Algeria (gas)	El Salvador (coffee)
	Angola (oil)	Guatemala (cropland)
	Chad (oil)	Israel-Palestine (freshwater)
	Congo-Brazzaville (oil)	Mexico (cropland)
	Iran-Iraq (oil)	Senegal-Mauritania (cropland)
	Iraq-Kuwait (oil)	
	Liberia (iron ore, rubber)	
	Nicaragua (coffee)	
	Rwanda (coffee)	
	Sierra Leone (rutile)	
Distant	*Secession*	*Warlordism*
	Angola/Cabinda (oil)	Afghanistan (opium)
	Caucasus (oil)	Angola (diamonds)
	D.R. Congo (copper, cobalt, gold)	Burma (opium, timber)
	Indonesia (oil, copper, gold)	Caucasus (drugs)
	Morocco/W. Sahara (phosphate)	Cambodia (gems, timber)
	Nigeria/Biafra (oil)	Colombia (cocaine)
	Papua New Guinea/Bouganville (copper)	D.R. Congo (diamonds, gold)
	Senegal/Casamance (marijuana)	Kurdistan (heroin)
	Sudan (oil)	Lebanon (hash)
		Liberia (timber, diamonds, drugs)
		Peru (cocaine)
		Philippines (marijuana, timber)
		Sierra Leone (diamonds)
		Somalia (bananas, camels)
		Tadjikistan (drugs)
		Former Yugoslavia (marijuana, timber)

Source: Le Billon, P. (2001). The political ecology of war: natural resources and armed conflicts. *Political Geography*, **20**, 561–584.

geographically to demonstrate that there is more to resources than absolute location and that different types of conflict emerge around environmental resources.

To understand their role in conflict, we need to understand spatial dimensions of how resources are distributed, controlled, and consumed (see Figure 7.2). Taking Le Billon's observations about resource location one step further, the problem with identifying resources or environmental features with only an absolute location (as in Klare's maps) provides no information about how that resource or feature is situated relative to consumers, borders,

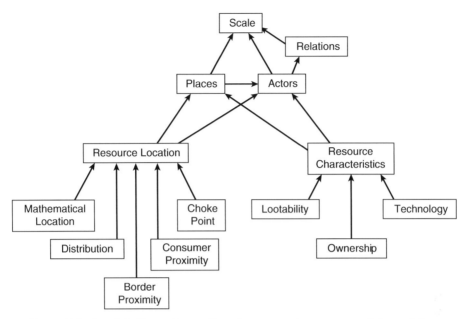

Figure 7.2 Spatial dimensions of environmental resources. Adapted from O'Lear, S. and Diehl, P. F. (2007) A model of scale in environmental conflict. Unpublished manuscript.

or systems of control (O'Lear and Diehl, unpublished data). Is the resource contained by or close to a border? Is the border permeable? Does the resource straddle the border? Is it a chokepoint resource that may be controlled "upstream"? What are the conditions of ownership or control? What kinds of technology or infrastructure are necessary to realize the economic value of the resource? Looking at these aspects of environmental resources helps us to understand power dimensions associated with these resources: How is the resource controlled, valued, or influenced and by whom or by what systems? In much of the resource conflict literature, environmental resources are often valued unproblematically as simple territorial features without adequate assessment of power relations, meanings, or historical contexts and without consideration of how those features are connected to other places.

Critiques of the resource conflict perspective

The literature on resource conflicts, and the way in which people tend to think about resource conflicts, has been critiqued on several points. In much of the literature, including Gleick's piece discussed earlier in this chapter and demonstrated in Klare's maps, resource scarcity is conflated with environmental disturbance. Yet these situations have very different potential routes to resolution. Scarcity can often be addressed through substitution and trade in similar commodities (Simon 1981; Lipschutz and Holdren 1990). Pricing mechanisms may be adjusted to alleviate the scarcity. For example, the Mexican tortilla riots of 2006, discussed in Chapter 3: Oil and energy, could have been avoided through more appropriate conditions in the trade of corn for ethanol production. Scarcities in stock resources such as fish could be addressed through more effective negotiations and agreements in catch limits or fishing technology restrictions. The Kimberley Process for diamond certification is a mechanism that sharply decreases the value of conflict diamonds in order to discourage their production and trade. Economic approaches are limited, however, and cannot address scarcities resulting from degraded soil and water supplies. These kinds of environmental disturbances must be addressed through different means such as changes to resource management practices, land tenure systems, waste management approaches, and industrial accountability. These responses are more political in form and require institutions that are capable of negotiating and implementing sound policy. The point is that lumping all environmental issues together as a category to spark conflict is misleading and blurs the meaning of environmental resources and conditions.

Take, for example, the issue of water conflicts which is increasingly gaining attention. Water is a complex resource in that it is not only vital to human life and ecosystems on which life depends, but it has multiple uses and is also a marketable commodity. There is a large body of research examining the threat of water-related conflict, emphasizing that there are 214 river systems that are shared by at least two countries (Renner 1997, p. 60). Jon Barnett (2000) describes the trend in this water conflict in the literature:

There is a typical pattern to this literature: the geographical misfit between water and national boundaries is explored, then a healthy dose of 'practical geopolitical reasoning' is applied, then, having made much of the prospect of water wars, there is usually a brief discussion of remedial measures, which tends to read like an afterthought or an addendum to the substantive issue of warfare. The usual case is the Middle East, a region already rife with religious, ethnic, and political tensions. For many authors water scarcity will be the proverbial spark that starts the metaphorical Middle East bonfire, which in turn is seen to threaten international security.

(p. 276)

In this literature, conflict looms as a violent threat that could erupt quickly. However, other work has shown that transboundary water systems rarely are the focus of armed or violent conflict. According to one study, out of 1831 state-to-state interactions over shared water systems between 1949 and 1999, only 56 involved hostile acts, and only 37 involved military acts (distinct from military support which involves security provision). None resulted in war (Wolf *et al.* 2008; see also Wolf *et al.* 2003).

Other work has examined social conflicts over water, as opposed to armed conflicts, as worthy of attention:

Amid the talk of looming "water wars," a less dramatic – but more immediate – link between water and violence is often ignored: the violence engendered by poor governance of water resources. Policies to expand water supplies, develop hydroelectric power, alter freshwater ecosystems, or change the terms of access to water can have devastating impacts on the livelihoods, cultures, and human rights of local communities. As these communities learn to voice their grievances, build networks across borders, and connect with human rights and environmental activists, once-local conflicts become international disputes.

(Conca 2006a, p. 76; see also Conca 2006b)

Although these governance conflicts do not necessarily involve military action, they can still be violent and harm people's lives and well-being. Thinking about conflict in this way shifts attention from state-level military or diplomatic acts towards spatial scales and actors beyond the state. Such an approach enables inquiry that considers and addresses multiple social, political, and economic dimensions of water which appropriately reflect the multiple physical attributes, meanings, and uses of this environmental resource.

An example of this kind of work is Kathryn Furlong's (2006) consideration of the shortcomings of using International Relations (IR) theory and International Organization (IO) theory to understand transboundary water management. IR theory focuses on states as the unit of analysis. It interprets state to state interactions through the lens of game theory in an attempt to understand how states behave in order to maximize their own power or promote their own interests. IO theory looks at how institutions such as governing bodies or agreements emerge among states in the pursuit of shared interests. Applying either of these perspectives to a study of transboundary water management certainly enables an assessment of the state-level decision-making process and conflict avoidance at the international level. However, it misses much of the complexity surrounding water as an ecological feature, a basic human need, and a commodity. Furlong argues that theories of political ecology and critical geopolitics are useful in assessing complex human–nature relations involving water because they direct attention to different ways that water is valued, controlled, and attached to multiple dimensions of social and ecological systems:

These are necessary perspectives if the 'flood for the few and the drought for the many' is to be recalibrated to achieve socially just ends. Distributive injustice with respect to water has many implications; basic survival, public health, and economic security are but a few. When water becomes difficult to access, as in rural Lesotho following the development of the LHWP [Lesotho Highlands Water Project] for example, the responsibility for collecting water frequently falls to women and girls, with negative consequences for female education and their income-earning opportunities.

(pp. 453–454)

Acknowledging and understanding these complexities at multiple spatial scales – among states, within states, across boundaries, and even across social groups – allows for a more appropriate understanding of ways in which different forms of power are involved among a broad set of actors associated with water management and distribution. Cooperation and conflict are not locked in to a one-dimensional continuum but may occur in different forms simultaneously at overlapping spatial scales. Clearly, looking at resource conflict only as involving state-to-state military engagement misses much of the story.

Another critique of the resource conflict perspective, in addition to taking a narrow perspective both on environmental resources and on conflict, is that it can miss political, economic, or cultural variables such as social fragmentation that shape conflict or cooperation associated with environmental features (Gleditsch 1998, 2001; see also Gleditsch and Urdal 2002). As Barnett (2000) has noted "The most striking difficulty of water wars thesis is the impossibility of clearly distinguishing among the many factors which contribute to warfare. When one sifts through the hyperbole, it seems that few wars have been induced solely by water shortages" (p. 276). Finally, most studies that have analyzed links between environmental resources or degradation and conflict examine only cases where both features – degradation and conflict – are evident (Hauge and Ellingsen 1998, 2001). Much could be learned by looking at cases where conflict does not emerge as expected despite conditions of resource scarcity, abundance, export dependence, or degradation. Indeed, resource abundance may actually override rather than ignite conflict by enabling the consolidation of power (Englebert and Ron 2004). The next section considers just such a case.

The case of Azerbaijan: Where is the conflict?

What can we learn from looking at a case where the generally accepted conditions for resource conflict exist but such conflict does not occur? To look at this question, we can consider the case of Azerbaijan. Azerbaijan is a small country in the oil-rich Caspian Sea region that was previously a Soviet republic. Its neighbors include Russia, Turkey, and Iran. At the time of the Soviet Union's collapse in 1991, Azerbaijan already had an active oil industry. In fact, Azerbaijan has a long history of producing and exporting oil that goes back to the 1890s. Having suddenly become an independent country, Azerbaijan's economy was cut off from the lifeline of support from the centralized Soviet economy. In 1994, Azerbaijan's President Heidar Aliyev signed what became known as The Contract of the Century which invited international oil companies to invest in Azerbaijan's oil industry. At that time, it was critical for Azerbaijan to secure investment in the development of its oil sector and to take advantage of Western technology in oil extraction and transport. Within a few years of signing these contracts, Azerbaijan's oil production, oil exports, and earnings from oil (not to mention dependency on oil exports) all increased significantly.

Also in the early 1990s as Soviet republics became independent countries, Azerbaijan became embroiled in armed conflict with Armenians over an area within Azerbaijan known as Nagorno-Karabakh or simply, Karabakh. In Soviet times, this area was recognized as a special administrative unit known as an Autonomous Oblast or region. It was populated predominantly by Armenians who did not want to be part of Azerbaijan in the new, post-Soviet political configuration. Violent, armed conflict and displacement of both Azerbaijanis and Armenians from the area have led to the current conditions in which Karabakh and territory surrounding it are now controlled by Armenians, and there are approximately 600 000 internally displaced persons (IDPs) resulting from the conflict. The dispute over Karabakh has yet to be resolved, but it is not directly related to Azerbaijani oil resources. True, there is a small but vocal group of people in Azerbaijan promoting the idea of using oil wealth to strengthen Azerbaijan's military and reclaim Karabakh by force, but economic wealth is not so easily translated in military capacity. Azerbaijan does have resource wealth in the form of oil abundance. It has also had armed, violent conflict within its borders, but these phenomena are not necessarily linked.

A study that has examined the lack of environment-related conflict in Azerbaijan[1] (O'Lear and Gray 2006; O'Lear 2007) aimed to understand why there is not environmental conflict there as we might expect from the literature on resource conflict. Azerbaijan has resource abundance and dependence on its oil exports, and it has resource scarcity experienced by many residents. That scarcity can also be thought of as structural scarcity reflected in uneven access to the benefits of resource wealth (Gleditsch and Urdal 2002). These are underlying features of conflict frequently cited in this area of work.

Starting with the basic premise that conflict involves people, the study used survey and interview methodologies to collect data on public opinion. The objective was to assess points of tension that might be the grounds from which public dissent and conflict might emerge. The study looked at three questions: Are people in Azerbaijan concerned about the environment? What would be the focal point of public dissent about the environment? Are people in Azerbaijan politically active or likely to participate in dissent? These three questions addressed root conditions – concern, a focal point for activism, and an ability to mobilize – that would have to be met in order for widespread public mobilization, dissent, or other initial phases of conflict to emerge.

The study involved data collection through a survey of 1200 adults throughout Azerbaijan. The sample population reflected demographic parameters such as age, ethnicity, gender, internally displaced person status, and location. Population size is not necessarily a factor in determining an appropriate sample size of a study, yet a sample size of 1200 individuals provides sufficient coverage of Azerbaijan's population of approximately 8 000 000 to allow for a 95% confidence level and a minimum 5% confidence interval that the sample population will be suitably reflective of the population of Azerbaijan (Czaja and Blair 1996).

The first question, quite simply, asked whether or not people in Azerbaijan are concerned about the environment. Similar to the discussion about environmental resources in this chapter, the study acknowledged that there are several facets to the environment that people experience in their day to day lives. Of course a key focus for the study was to assess public impressions of impacts of oil in Azerbaijan, but other dimensions of the environment were also considered: environmental degradation, human health risks, agricultural concerns, water and air pollution, and access to environmentally based utilities such as gas, electricity, and water. By expanding the meaning of "environment" beyond a single environmental resource commodity, the study aimed to get a clear picture of people's level of environmental concern.

This question of public concern about the environment draws from work done by David Wheeler and the Infrastructure and Environment Development Research Group at the World Bank (Dasgupta and Wheeler 1997). In their analysis of citizens' environmental complaints in China, they found that people with higher incomes were more likely to complain to officials about environmental conditions such as poor air and water quality. China, another country in economic flux, provides a good comparison for Azerbaijan. Compressed incomes in China's transitional economy appear to generate greater concern with daily, economic survival than with issues of environmental quality or natural resource access. That research suggests that environmental concern, or at least acting on environmental concern, is more closely connected to economic welfare than to exposure to negative environmental impacts. Put another way, wealthier people are more likely to complain about environmental conditions most likely because their basic, economic needs have already been met.

Since environmental concern is likely tied to economic status, the survey in Azerbaijan aimed to collect data on respondents' sense of economic well-being. Although government statistics on incomes, minimum wage, employment levels, etc. might provide some insight into the economic status of a country's population overall, those figures are general, possibly inaccurate,

Table 7.2. *Azerbaijan survey: what is the economic situation in your family?*

	Percentage of respondents ($N = 1200$)
Not enough money for food	20
Difficulties buying clothes	31
Expensive durable goods a problem	29
No car or trip abroad	15
Can afford everything	1
Don't know/refuse to answer	3

and they do not reveal how people themselves perceive their own economic status. Survey data can get around those obstacles, but how the question is asked is key. It is unlikely that people would want to tell a researcher conducting a survey how much they earn, so the question was asked in terms of what people can afford. Asking this question also provides insights into the degree of economic difficulty that people live with daily. The data in Table 7.2 indicate that a significant segment of the population sample has difficulty securing even the most basic necessities – food and clothing – in their families. If environmental concern really is tied to economic well-being, then these data suggest that most people in Azerbaijan are not likely to be concerned about the environment or, if they are concerned, they might be unlikely to take any action on those concerns since they are likely eclipsed by economic issues.

In Table 7.3, we see that a significant percentage of survey respondents actually are concerned with environmental quality and with environment-related utilities. These issues, however, do not outpace their concerns with the frozen conflict in Karabakh, their material well-being, and unemployment.

The second question of the study asked what the focus of public dissent about the environment might be. For example, in Nigeria there has been public outcry against Shell Oil since its oil extraction activities have caused environmental degradation in ethnically cohesive Ogoniland. Shell Oil has been the focal point of environmental activism and ethnic demands for environmental justice (see Watts 2001). Is there similar public sentiment in Azerbaijan against the international oil industry? Several foreign oil companies have been active in exploiting Azerbaijan's oilfields and constructing export pipelines and other infrastructure necessary to expand oil extraction. The involvement of these oil companies has drastically altered Azerbaijan's economy by generating considerable wealth that does not necessarily reach the general population. Additionally, the booming oil industry has affected landscapes along pipeline export routes and has changed the face of the capital city, Baku. Do Azerbaijanis view international oil industry

Table 7.3. *Azerbaijan survey: percentage of respondents in Azerbaijan indicating concern*

	Percentage of respondents ($N = 1200$)
Environmental concerns	
Overall ecological situation	50
Pollution/degradation problems	49
Dissatisfaction with access to:	
Gas	54
Electricity	40
Water	27
Non-environmental concerns	
Nagorno-Karabakh	88
Material well-being	73
Unemployment	66
Access to health care	44
Education	38
Political freedom/democracy	31
Crime	29
Interethnic conflicts	15

Adapted from O'Lear, S. and Gray, A. (2006). Asking the right questions: environmental conflict in the case of Azerbaijan. *Area*, **38** (4), 390–401.

Table 7.4. *Azerbaijan survey: impact of foreign oil contracts on Azerbaijan's economy? (1 = negative, 10 = positive)*

	Percentage of respondents ($N = 1200$)
1–4 (negative)	<10
5–9 (positive)	64
10 (very positive)	21
Don't know	5

involvement in their country as positive or negative? Perhaps they are more concerned with how their government is managing the oil wealth? Without a clear focus, it is unlikely that people would mobilize or be able to focus their activism effectively. Again, recall Mann's (1986) argument that the public is often organizationally outflanked by more powerful actors and institutions. It requires considerable time, energy, and resources such as effective informational networks to bring a group of people together in coordinated action, and having a focal point is key.

An obvious question to ask survey respondents is how they feel about the international oil industry in Azerbajian. Table 7.4 shows how people responded when asked if contracts with foreign oil companies had positive or negative effects on the country's economy. Since we know that most people included in this study face economic difficulty in their family, these views about the international oil industry's involvement in their country probably indicate that people have heightened expectations for how the oil industry might eventually be able to influence their situation.

Additionally, respondents were asked if oil extraction and transport had any negative impacts in the places where they live. This question again recalls the situation in Nigeria where residents living near Shell Oil's oil extraction activities mobilized to protest the resulting environmental damage. In Azerbaijan, however, over half of the respondents thought oil extraction and transport were not harmful at all, about one quarter thought these activities were a little harmful, and just over 10% thought these activities were "harmful" or "very harmful." This low level of concern about environmental impacts of the international oil industry may be partly explained by the fact that respondents from all over the country were included in the survey, but the oil industry only has direct, environmental effects in certain places. Much of the extraction is done around the Absheron Peninsula near the capital city of Baku and along pipeline routes that cross Azerbaijan underground. Much of the country is physically unaffected by oil industry activity. These data suggest, though, that the international oil industry or any of its individual components are unlikely to be the focal point of political dissent.

Could the government be a focal point for public dissent related to environmental quality, environmental utilities, or about oil resources? When asked how satisfied they were with their government's use of oil revenues, just over half of the respondents reported that they were dissatisfied or fully dissatisfied, about 30% said they were neutral, and less than 20% said that they were satisfied or fully satisfied with their government's management of oil revenues. This is not a very good report card. In interviews with Azerbaijani residents, it was clear that the general sentiment towards the international oil industry is favorable. International oil companies are seen as a potential source of positive change since the government is perceived as being locked in the ways of a relatively small and elite group of powerful people. Most people are well aware of the significant boost their country has gotten from its oil exports. Not many people have seen a parallel, significant improvement in their own lives, and they appear to have limited optimism for improvement in the near future (O'Lear 2007).

The third question of the study asked if people in Azerbaijan are politically active and, if so, on what issues? Dissent and political activism do not spontaneously emerge from dissatisfaction. This question aimed to investigate the roots of social mobilization. How does conflict emerge? State-to-state conflict involves state-supported militaries, but who is involved in conflict at other spatial scales? There is a large body of literature on social movements that examines how and why and under what conditions people come together to pursue a shared, political, social, or economic end. Political geographers bring a spatial dimension into a study of social movements by recognizing how the creation of spaces of resistance can be a strategy for local activists to wage struggles that may incorporate or be carried over into other spaces and scales (Lake 1994; Miller 1994, 2000; Staeheli 1994; Staeheli and Cope 1994; Steinberg 1994; O'Lear 1997, 1999; Cox 1998). The third question of this study was intended as a cursory look at what the potential might be for public involvement in political activity such as dissent. Like anywhere else, people in Azerbaijan are likely to prioritize their concerns and be politically active – to the extent that they are politically active at all – on a limited selection of issues. Depending on how environmental or resource concerns measure up to other concerns, patterns of environment-related dissent may not be evident.

It has already been stated that survey respondents in Azerbaijan are concerned with environmental and non-environmental concerns, that they view the influence of the international oil industry favorably, and that there is significant dissatisfaction among them as to how their government is managing oil wealth. Do these trends necessarily lead to public dissent? If a baseline of public participation is not present, it is unlikely that shared sentiments will translate into organizational capacity. Survey respondents were asked if they had been involved in any public activity – which could include attending a meeting or demonstration, signing a petition, distributing information about a particular civic or political issue or event, or even being a member of a social or political organization – in the previous 12 months. Responses suggest that public involvement is very low: over 90% of the respondents said they had not been involved in any such activity. When asked which issue might ever motivate them to join a protest, respondents ranked "dissatisfaction with Nagorno-Karabakh" as first (chosen by 26%) followed by "dissatisfaction with local unemployment conditions" (chosen by 24%). The next most frequently selected response, chosen by 14% of the respondents, was that nothing would motivate them to join a protest.

These survey data suggest that there is unlikely to be a public eruption in response to environmental conditions, even though people have concerns about the environment, or in response to the international oil industry which is generally viewed in a positive light. The trend appears to be that people in Azerbaijan are not happy with their government's handling of oil wealth, but we also see that there is not much experience with or interest in mobilizing to

Figure 7.3 Pope John Paul II's visit to Baku, Azerbaijan in 2002. Photo: Shannon O'Lear.

bring attention to any issue, environment-related or otherwise. These survey data, more importantly, highlight shortcomings of focusing on "resource conflict." Whereas outside perspectives on Azerbaijan tend to prioritize oil as a key concern for the country, these data show that the activities and impacts of the oil industry itself are not a concern for people in Azerbaijan as represented by survey respondents. They do have concerns related to the environment, but for them, the "environment" does not equate with "oil." Their concerns with pollution or environment-related utilities are unlikely to be addressed effectively through dissent. It is important, clearly, to under-stand what "the environment" or what "resources" mean to people. Some studies have argued that environmental or resource-related conditions are not enough in themselves to lead to conflict but that they can combine with ethnic tensions to spark conflict in some form (Baechler 1998, 1999b; Homer-Dixon and Blitt 1998). Although Azerbaijan is home to multiple ethnic groups, these differences have not caused turmoil in the country. In recognition of this

point, Pope John Paul II visited Baku in 2002 and said Mass in a predominantly Muslim country to honor Azerbaijan's stability during turbulent times in
the neighborhood (see Figure 7.3). Furthermore, the survey data suggest a
few reasons why "conflict" or even public dissent is not likely to emerge in
Azerbaijan: most people are not already active or experienced in social mobilization and the focal point for such public involvement is not clear.
Our attention instead turns to questions of how the government is managing
income from oil exports, how it is adjusting the domestic economy, and
the extent to which it is investing in education, health care, physical infrastructure, or other channels that would benefit the populace. Once we understand
more clearly conditions in this place, the focus on "resource conflict" does
not seem very helpful in explaining what is (or what is not) going on in
Azerbaijan.

Conclusion

In a similar vein to the case study of Azerbaijan, Jon Barnett (2000) has
critiqued the scholarly emphasis on resource conflict as being theoretically
rather than empirically driven. He makes the case that the resource conflict
thesis serves the interests of more economically developed and politically
powerful parts of the world which are sometimes referred to as "the North"
or the economic core parts of the world as opposed to the less powerful
"South" or periphery. Governments, businesses, and consumers in more
powerful parts of the world seek to detract attention away from their own
consumption and pollution levels by identifying or dramatizing threats
emerging elsewhere. By creating a narrative about external threats to the
state, including environment- and resource-related threats, attention is shifted
away from the role that politically and economically powerful actors play in
the destruction of the environment within and beyond their own political
borders. The issue of a degraded environment or scarce resources is made into
a threat to "our" security that could negatively influence our way of life (read:
our consumption habits) or require the projection of military capacity to
stabilize the very parts of the world where our demands and influence are
generating strife. Barnett argues that the resource conflict literature perpetu-
ates denial if not ignorance about the role that more powerful actors and
political units play in creating the problems of uneven and unequal use and
enjoyment of the environment. The environment becomes a security issue
which then channels our thinking along the lines of the state and state or
military controls to ensure stability. Barnett points out:

What is to be secured is the modern world order from the threat of change. However, to make the point again, instability, not unlike conflict, does not necessarily imply change for the worse. Indeed, given that the areas where instability is anticipated are all areas where there are numerous and pervasive injustices and deprivation, change and instability are to be welcomed. If . . . environmental security means resisting, avoiding and suppressing change, then it is a vehicle for the continued defense of injustice. Furthermore, given that social changes are inevitable . . . suppression of change is ultimately futile. Instead, change should be welcomed and negotiated to ensure that it is non-violent.

(p. 286)

Change to "our" way of life seems unthinkable even if we know the earth's ecosystems cannot continue to support it. Rather than solidify and strengthen our political borders in the face of potential change, however, a more pro-active approach would be to explore avenues for more equitable distribution of environmental benefits and measures to reduce consumption before crisis conditions severely restrict our options to respond creatively.

A focus on resource conflict can oversimplify the nature of conflict, over-look the types of actors that may be involved, and blur environmental features without fostering an understanding of how those features are distri-buted, used, and valued and by whom. Our spatial understanding of how resources are connected to various forms of conflict tends to be limited. It is helpful to understand that resources themselves are spatially complex. They cannot be understood only as having just absolute, geographical loca-tion because they are associated with human systems of demand and control, channels and networks of processing and exchange, and, ultimately, con-sumption. A more thoughtful appreciation of spatial aspects of environmen-tal features and how those features are connected to other places, in terms of cultural and economic values, could serve to expand our thinking beyond the confines of the state. A focus on resource conflict also blurs economic, political, and military power by making marketable commodities appear as threats to political stability when really what is at the heart of concern is profits. Ideological power is evident in how arguments about resource conflict have emerged in academic and policy circles and moved into public aware-ness. Seeking out conflict-free diamonds, for example, is a positive start, but perhaps there should be more thought given to understanding the drive to purchase diamonds in the first place. That is, a lot could be gained by examining how and why we use resources the way we do. Untangling intertwined dimensions of power as they relate to a specific resource or environmental condition allows us to ask how the valuation of a particular resource is controlled and projected, how a resource or environmental condition may serve the interests of political or economic actors, and how a resource or condition is connected to systems of control, networks of exchange, and processes of refining and marketing. Taking such a critical approach would allow a deeper understanding of complexities of human–environment relationships and how those relationships may either invite or avoid conflict – violent, structural, or otherwise – either in support of the status quo or in support of change.

Endnote

1 This material is based upon work supported by the National Science Foundation under Grant No. 0514229. Any opinions, findings and conclusions or recommendations expressed in this material are those of the author and do not necessarily reflect the views of the National Science Foundation.

8

Conclusion

It has to start somewhere.
It has to start sometime.
What better place than here?
What better time than now?

— *Rage Against The Machine*, Guerilla Radio

This book has covered what might seem to be an eclectic array of topics and information: current thinking on the world's oil supply and why ethanol is a problematic transitional fuel, carbon offset forests as an unrealistic and unfair response to climate change, the influence that a few corporations have over much of our food supply, the volume and effects of e-waste on less economically developed countries, the cocktail of toxins we all carry in our bodies, and limitations of assuming resource scarcity leads to armed conflict to name a few issues. Many of the topics examined in this book spill across the chapter headings. The discussion of plastic water bottles, for instance, is in the chapter on garbage and waste, but it is also relevant for oil and energy as well as toxins. The Mexican tortilla riots were discussed in the chapter on oil and energy and mentioned in the chapter on resource conflicts, but clearly these events pertain to food security as well. Diacetyl, the butter flavoring in microwave popcorn, was discussed in the chapter on toxins, but clearly it is also an issue for food security. The book has demonstrated a two-fold approach that assesses power dimensions shaping the way we think (or do not think) about environmental issues and that focus our attention on (or away from) particular spatial scales. Other concepts have been integrated into these discussions to provide additional ways of understanding how forms of power work. The model for rational decision-making, discussed in Chapter 5, is a template for how policy decisions, for example, "should" work, but it also serves to demonstrate why it is important to know who is involved in the decision-making process, what kinds of data are used, and even how a problem is defined. Risk assessment, discussed in Chapter 6, is another process by which influential decisions are made, but it is important to appreciate that there are many ways to define, measure, and monitor risk.

How can all of these diverse and overlapping stories be neatly tied up in a concluding chapter? It is at this point in the book we resort to the tactic all thoughtful instructors use at critical junctures in a class: Let's watch a video.

This video clip comes from *The Onion*, renowned for its satirical "news" coverage. The scene opens to a daytime talk show "Today Now!" with two perky hosts: Tracy and Jim. Let's watch:

Tracy: It's Green Week on Today Now!, and we're highlighting individuals and companies that are helping the environment.

Jim: And one of those companies is Taco Bell. Starting this week, Taco Bell restaurants are going 100 percent green. Now, they're going to have the same menu items that you've come to know and love, but none of the ingredients are taken from nature.

Tracy: And that means zero environmental impact. So, joining us now, live, is Paul Lancaster, spokesman for Taco Bell. Hi, Paul.

Paul: Hello, Jim. Hello, Tracy,

Jim: Now, Paul, nothing on Taco Bell's new menu uses anything from nature?

Paul: Not a single ingredient. Starting this week, all of the ingredients that we use are going to be produced in labs by special Taco Bell food synthesizers.

Tracy: Wow, and it tastes the same as before, Paul?

Paul: You can't even taste the difference.

Tracy: Wow, the lettuce looks so realistic!

Jim: Now, how hard was it to make the leap into the eco-friendly menu?

Paul: Well, at Taco Bell we have a long tradition of taking as little as possible from the natural world. Our ground beef, for example, has always been fairly eco-friendly. It's 85 percent gluten filler, 8 percent petroleum based grease flavoring, but it's always had 4 percent meat from real livestock.

Jim: And that's bad for the environment.

Paul: Well, exactly right. But with Taco Bell's new green initiative we've actually been able to replace that 4 percent meat with a simple chemical adhesive.

Tracy: So, you're not wasting food or water to feed the cattle!

Paul: That's right.

Jim: And because you're using no natural ingredients whatsoever anymore, I understand you're able to add something you're calling "Super Green Supreme" menu items that you never would have been able to do before.

Paul: Yes. At Taco Bell, Jim, we are changing the definition of food. Starting next month we're introducing the Ultimate Grande Crunchador, which is jam-packed with chunks of an ingredient that has no equivalent in the natural world.

Jim: Wow, that does look filling.
Paul: We also have a new chalupa that removes the carbon dioxide and pollution from the air around it so that it helps reduce global warming.
Tracy: Look at that! So we're eating at Taco Bell; we're cleaning the earth!
Paul: That's right.
Jim: What are those science guys gonna think up next?
Tracy: Amazing! Amazing!
Paul: Plus, in three years we're planning to start melting down all of the lids, the straws, and the wrappers that the food comes in and recycle it into new Taco Bell foods. You will actually be *eating* the garbage you produce.
Jim: Isn't that something? That's quite an inspiration!
Tracy: Yes! Paul, thank you so much for joining us.
Paul: My pleasure.
Tracy: Listen, don't go away, coming up next we're going to show you how to save money by writing your own books! (http://www.theonion.com/content/video/taco_bells_new_green_menu_takes, accessed 13 December 2009)

This "news" clip is clearly exaggerated as far as satire goes, but it is relevant to the objective of this book in a few ways. First, it highlights some of the overlapping issues discussed in this book: Where does our food come from? What are unknown or non-food ingredients in what we eat? How are energy and resource issues implicated in commodity chains? How does our consumption have impacts on climate change, garbage production, and recycling? Second, part of the humor of this spoof is how closely it resembles a talk show. If not for the exaggeration, it is almost believable because we are familiar with this format of "news." This book has repeatedly raised the question of where we get our information and how that shapes our views of particular environmental issues. In this video clip, we see the role of corporate influence appearing as a friendly spokesperson but in actuality slipping in a public relations opportunity (of course, the best PR is that which no one recognizes as such!).

We tend to gather a lot of information passively from mainstream media about world events, consumer items, and environmental issues. We do not necessarily question who or by what process that information is controlled or the extent to which it might serve particular interests. Information is rarely ever complete, but it can certainly be incomplete and present a selective picture. For example, in the analysis of the ground beef ingredient list, the components are quantified as we learn that the unsightly 4% meat will be replaced with 4% of a "simple chemical adhesive." Quantifying an argument tends to boost its perceived legitimacy, but rarely do we question what the numbers mean or where they came from. Recall the critique of global climate models in Chapter 2 or the discussion of Table 6.2: Acceptable levels of natural food defects in Chapter 6. Mainstream media, such as television, newspapers, magazines, billboards, and even Google ads, are not the only sources of information. As Chapter 7 demonstrates, even scholarly literature goes through trends of popular topics which may or may not actually be the most pressing issues in reality. Different topics capture academic attention depending on current events and funding priorities of research institutions and government agencies. For example, following the bombing of Pan Am flight 103 over Lockerbie, Scotland in December 1988, which resulted in the deaths of all 259 people in the aircraft plus 11 people on the ground, there was a surge of academic interest in terrorism for some years and justifiably so. The events of September 11 2001 led to another surge of academic interest in terrorism. The discussion in Chapter 7, however, questions if academic attention is focused at times more by trends in funding and government interest rather than by empirical realities of real world needs.

This over-the-top news spoof brings us back to the overarching aim of the book: to encourage readers to think critically about dominant narratives on various environmental issues – narratives such as those presented in mainstream media, public discussions, and even scholarly literature. The objective of the book is to demonstrate how an understanding of different forms of power – political, economic, ideological, and military – shape the way we tend to think about environmental issues and the spatial scales at which we understand these issues. The examination of specific cases and examples has shown how our appreciation of environmental issues, human–environment relationships, and connections among places can be deepened by looking at spatial dimensions of power. Climate change is not necessarily best viewed at a global scale, energy issues are closely related to issues of food supply and waste, and toxins are a real threat at the scale of the body and are not particularly well controlled at government levels. The topics in this book are demonstrative but by no means exhaustive. The same approach could be applied to water issues, endangered species, environmental law, land use, nuclear energy, environmental disasters, and other environment-related concerns that societies face today.

In addition to power and scale, there is another component that is useful in clarifying how we think about environmental issues. In a short article titled "In praise of clumsiness," Michael Thompson and Martin Price (2002) discuss how we tend to think of change in ecosystems and in social systems as moving from state A to state B. Different social theories have been promoted to explain these shifts. Marx argued that capitalistic societies are driven by internal contradiction to move towards communism, and Weber promoted the idea that traditional societies move towards modernity through rationalization. Thompson and Price observe:

These transitions, whether ecological or socio-cultural, are all in the direction of more orderliness, more differentiation, more connected, and more consistency, and once they have gone as far as they can go in that direction, that is that. In other words, these models of change end up making change impossible. Of course something on the outside may intervene and mess things up, thereby setting the whole thing in motion once more. Left to themselves, these models get ecosystems and socio-cultural systems from A to B and then stop. Change, these models tell us, is a temporary phenomenon. . . There is clearly something less than satisfactory about these models. They explain change by getting rid of it . . .

(p. 14)

The authors then turn to vignettes of two societies, villagers in the Himalayas and villagers living in the Swiss Alps. In each instance, we are told a story about how these longstanding societies make decisions about their transactions with the environment based on shifting economic conditions, resource issues, and seasonality. How Himalayan villagers manage their agricultural plots differs from how they view trade expeditions to India. These stories highlight the importance of flexibility in making decisions regarding human interactions with the environment. We already know that different people have different views about the environment. What the stories about Himalayan and Swiss villagers illustrate, however, is that an individual's views about the environment can (and perhaps should) adjust in response to external conditions, new information, and societal values and power structures. The title of the article "In praise of clumsiness," captures the idea that change is not a predetermined process that follows a linear path. The article suggests that it is a mistake to believe we can determine an absolutely correct and permanent way to engage with the environment. Instead, the authors suggest that we should monitor social and environmental changes and let that information guide our interactions.

One way to summarize different views towards the environment comes from Schwarz and Thompson (1990, see also Holling 1986 and Timmerman 1986) in their Myths of Nature. Figure 8.1 shows these four myths as a ball in a landscape to represent human–environment relationships. In the lower left quadrant, *Nature benign* captures the attitude that the earth is forgiving. Humans can kick our ball around, using the environment however we see fit, and everything will settle back into a stable situation. This is the view promoted by segments of the Wise Use Movement arguing that humans learn by making mistakes (see Chapter 5: Garbage and waste). In the lower right quadrant, *Nature ephemeral* is just the opposite view. It depicts the view that humans' relationship to the environment is fragile. If we move much in any direction, overusing resources or pushing ecosystems beyond their capacity for resilience, we will "fall off" the slope and face untold dangers. In the top

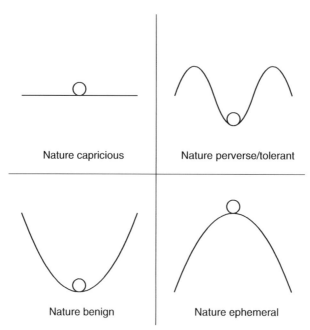

Figure 8.1 Four myths of nature. Adapted from Schwarz and Thompson (1990), p. 5.

right quadrant, *Nature perverse/tolerant* is the view that the environment will fall back into balance within limits, but we must be careful not to go past identifiable thresholds. This view is adopted by those individuals and institutions, such as the Environmental Protection Agency, working to identify and establish thresholds of safety or "bright lines" (see Chapter 6: Toxins). Finally, the top left quadrant, *Nature capricious* reflects the view that nature is random and that there is not much that we can do to alter it for better or worse. Here, the view is that we can neither manage nor learn from our engagement with the environment; we "just cope with erratic events" (Schwarz and Thompson 1990, p. 5).

We can look at these four myths of nature – four ways of approaching our interactions with the physical environment – as reflecting effects of different forms of power. That is, we can aim to understand how forms of power shape our understanding of and attitude towards environmental issues. Where do we get our information about environmental issues? Who or what forms of power influence our understanding of spatial dimensions of those issues? What is the resulting myth we formulate in response to that understanding? There is not necessarily one "right" way to approach the environment at all times and in all cases, and indeed this book has illustrated how even "the environment" can be interpreted differently according to context. The point, however, is that if we can understand more clearly why we believe what we believe, or why we do what we do, it is likely that we will make and encourage better choices in our interactions with the environment. If we can assess environmental issues as involving multiple and perhaps even competing dimensions of power as well as overlapping and intersecting spatial aspects, we will appreciate the complexity of human–environmental interactions and not accept the first, simplified explanation that comes along.

A person may not be equally concerned about all of the issues in this book (and beyond). As humans, we can only care about so many things. For those issues we do care about, whether it is political views on climate change or consumer safety issues or ways in which our consumption contributes to social and environmental decline elsewhere, we can (and should) be informed enough to delve beyond simple narratives ("Diamonds are forever!" "Energy independence is good for national security!" "Buying a hybrid car is better for the environment!" "If they sell it, it must be safe!") to explore the complexity of environmental issues. This book suggests a starting point for that exploration: an attentiveness to less obvious spatial aspects of environmental issues, an assessment of forms of power, and clearer understanding of our many relationships to the environment.

References

Adger, W. N., Arnell, N. W. and Tompkins, E. L. (2005). Successful adaptation to climate change across scales. *Global Environmental Change*, **3**, 77–86.

Agarwal, A. and Narain, S. (1991). *Global Warming in an Unequal World: a case of Environmental Colonialism*. New Delhi: Centre for Science and Environment.

Agarwal, A. and Narain, S. (1998). Global warming in an unequal world: a case of environmental colonialism. In *Green Planet Blues*, eds. K. Conca and G. D. Dabelko. Boulder, CO: Westview Press, pp. 157–60.

Agnew, J. (1994). The territorial trap: the geographical assumptions of international relations theory. *Review of International Political Economy*, **1**, 53–80.

Allen, J. (2003). *Lost Geographies of Power*. Malden, MA: Blackwell Publishing.

Amuzegar, J. (1982). Oil wealth: a very mixed blessing. *Foreign Affairs*, **60**, 814–35.

Arda, M. (2007). Food retailing, supermarkets, and food security: highlights from Latin America. In *Food Security: Indicators, Measurement, and the Impact of Trade Openness*, ed. B. Guha-Khasnobis, S. S. Acharya, and B. Davis. Oxford, UK: Oxford University Press, pp. 322–44.

Arnold, R. (1996). Overcoming ideology. In *A Wolf in the Garden: The Land Rights Movement and the New Environmental Debate*, eds. P. D. Brick and R. McGreggor Cawley. Lanham, MD: Rowman & Littlefield Publishers, Inc., pp. 15–26.

Ascher, W. (1999). *Why Governments Waste Natural Resources: Policy Failures in Developing Countries*. Baltimore, MD: The John Hopkins University Press.

Ascher, W. (2000). Understanding why governments in developing countries waste natural resources. *Environment*, **42**, 8–18.

Auty, R. M., ed. (2001a). *Resource Abundance and Economic Development*. New York, NY: Oxford University Press.

Auty, R. M. (2001b). Reforming resource-abundant transition economies: Kazakhstan and Uzbekistan. In *Resource Abundance and Economic Development*, ed. R. M. Auty. New York, NY: Oxford University Press, pp. 260–76.

Auty, R. and De Soysa, I., eds. (2006). *Energy, Wealth and Governance in the Caucasus and Central Asia*. London, UK: Routledge.

Auty, R. M. and Mikesell, R. F. (1998). *Sustainable Development in Mineral Economies*. Oxford, UK: Clarendon Press.

Ayers, E. and French, H. (1996). The refrigerator revolution. *World Watch*, **9** (5), 15–21.

Bacher, J. (2000). *Petrotyranny*, Toronto: Dundurn Press.

Baechler, G. (1998). Why environmental transformation causes violence: a synthesis. *Environmental Change and Security Project Report*, **4**, 24–44.

Baechler, G. (1999a). *Violence Through Environmental Discrimination: Causes, Rwanda Arena, and Conflict Model*. Dordrecht: Kluwer Academic Publishers.

Baechler, G. (1999b). Environmental degradation and violent conflict: hypotheses, research agendas and theory-building. In *Ecology, Politics and Violent Conflict*, ed. M. Suliman. New York, NY: Zed Books, pp. 76–114.

Baev, P. K. (2008). *Russian Energy Policy and Military Power: Putin's Quest for Greatness*. London: Routledge.

Baev, P. K. (2009). Gazprom's war has damaged Russian interests. *Eurasia Daily Monitor*, **6** (11), January 19. Online at http://www.jamestown.org.

Baker, N. (2008). *The Body Toxic: How the Hazardous Chemistry of Everyday Things Threatens Our Health and Well-being*. New York, NY: North Point Press.

Ball, J. (2005). Companies try keeping ice cream frozen, emissions down. *Wall Street Journal*, 4 May 2005, p. B1.

Barber, C. V. (1998). Forest resource scarcity and social conflict in Indonesia. *Environment*, **40** (4), 4–37.

Barkenbus, J. N. (2006). Putting energy efficiency in a sustainability context. *Environment*, **40**, 10–20.

Barnett, J. (2000). Destabilizing the environment-conflict thesis. *Review of International Studies*, **26**, 271–88.

Barnett, J. (2001). *The Meaning of Environmental Security: Ecological Politics and Policy in the New Security Era*. New York, NY: Zed Books.

BBC News (2007). *Russia Plants Flag Under N. Pole*. 2 August. Online at http://news.bbc.co.uk/2/hi/europe/6927395.stm#arctic, accessed 30 January 2009.

Beaumont, P. (1997). Water and armed conflict in the Middle East – fantasy or reality? In *Conflict and the Environment*, ed. N. P. Gleditsch. Dordrecht: Kluwer Academic Publishers, pp. 355–74.

Beck, U. (1992). *Risk Society: Towards a New Modernity*. London: Sage Publications.

Benbrook, C. (2001). Do GM crops mean less pesticide use? *Pesticide Outlook* (October), 204–7.

Benjamin, D. (2007). The benefits of recycling are a myth. In *Garbage and Recycling*, ed. M. Young. Detroit, MI: Greenhaven Press, pp. 76–83.

Bird, L., Parsons, B., Gagliano, T., Brown, M., Wiser, R. and Bolinger, M. (2003). Policies and market factors driving wind power development in the United States. *Energy Policy*, **33** (11), 1397–407.

Blaikie, P. (1985). *The Political Economy of Soil Erosion in Developing Countries*. New York, NY: Longman.

Blaikie, P. and Brookfield, H. (1987). *Land Degradation and Society*. New York, NY: Methuen.

Blatt, H. (2008). *America's Food: What You Don't Know About What You Eat*. Cambridge, MA: The MIT Press.

Bodley, J. H. (2008). *Anthropology and Contemporary Human Problems*, 5th edn. Lanham, MD: Altamira Press.

Bolinger, M. and Wiser, R. (2008). *Annual Report on U.S. Wind Power Installation, Cost, and Performance Trends, 2007*, Lawrence Berkeley National Laboratory.

Borgström, G. (1965). *The Hungry Planet: The Modern World at the Edge of Famine*. New York, NY: The Macmillan Company.

Bouzarovski, S. and Konieczny, M. (2010). Landscapes of paradox: Public discourses and policies in Poland's relationship with the Nord Stream Pipeline. *Geopolitics*, **15** (1), 1–21.

Boykoff, M. T. (2007). From convergence to contention: United States mass media representations of anthropogenic climate change science. *Transactions of the Institute of British Geographers*, **32**, 477–89.

Boykoff, M. T. (2008). Fight semantic drift!? Mass media coverage of anthropogenic climate change. In *Contentious Geographies: Environmental Knowledge, Meaning and Scale*, eds. M. K. Goodman, M. T. Boykoff and K. T. Evered. Burlington, VT: Ashgate, pp. 39–57.

Brenner, N. (2001). The limits to scale: methodological reflections on scalar structuration. *Progress in Human Geography*, **25** (4), 591–614.

Bridge, G. (2001). Resource triumphalism: postindustrial narratives of primary commodity production. *Environment and Planning A*, **33**, pp. 2149–73.

Bridge, G. and Jonas, A. E. G. (2002). Governing nature: the reregulation of resource access, production, and consumption. *Environment and Planning A*, **34**, 759–66.

Brodie, B. (1972). The impact of technological change on the international system. In *Change and the Future of the International System*, eds. D. S. Sullivan and M. L. Sattler. New York, NY: Columbia University Press, pp. 1–15.

Bryce, R. (2009). Opinion: Let's get real about renewable energy. *The Wall Street Journal*, 5 March 2009. Online at http://online.wsj.com/article/SB123621221496034823.html, accessed 5 March 2009.

Bryson, C. (2004). *The Fluoride Deception*. New York, NY: Seven Stories Press.

Buhaug, H. (2007). The future is more than scale: a reply to Diehl and O'Lear. *Geopolitics*, **12** (1), 192–9.

Buhaug, H. and Gates, S. (2002). The geography of civil war. *Journal of Peace Research*, **39**, 417–33.

Bulkeley, H. and Betsill, M. M. (2003). *Cities and Climate Change: Urban Sustainability and Global Environmental Governance*. London and New York: Routledge.

Butts, K. H. (1993). *Strategic Minerals in the New World Order*. Report ACN 93049. Strategic Studies Institute, U.S. Army War College, Carlisle Barracks, PA. Online at http://www.dtic.mil/cgi-bin/GetTRDoc?AD=ADA274394&Location=U2&doc=GetTRDoc.pdf, accessed 13 December 2009.

Caraher, M. and Coveney, J. (2004). Public health nutrition and food policy. *Public Health Nutrition*, **7**, 591–8.

Carson, R. (1962). *Silent Spring*. Boston, MA: Houghton Mifflin Company.

Caulfield, L. E., *et al.* (2004). Undernutrition as an underlying cause of child deaths associated with diarrhea, pneumonia, malaria, and measles. *American Journal Clinical Nutrition*, **80**, 193–8.

Cavalcanti, H. B. (2005). Food Security. In *Human and Environmental Security: An Agenda for Change*, eds. F. Dodds and T. Pippard. Sterling, VA: Earthscan, pp. 152–65.

Clapp, J. (2001). *Toxic Exports: The Transfer of Hazardous Wastes from Rich to Poor Countries*. Ithaca, NY: Cornell University Press.

Clarke, L. (2006). *Worst Cases: Terror and Catastrophe in the Popular Imagination*. Chicago, IL: The University of Chicago Press.

Clement, D. (2007). Flexibility is the key to efficient waste disposal practices. In *Garbage and Recycling*, ed. M. Young. Detroit, MI: Greenhaven Press, pp. 84–92.

Cohen, S. D., Demeritt, J. R. and Rothman, D. (1998). Climate change and sustainable development: towards dialogue. *Global Environmental Change*, **8**, 431–71.

Colborn, T., Dumanoski, D. and Myers, J. P. (1996). *Our Stolen Future: How We Are Threatening Our Fertility, Intelligence and Survival – A Scientific Detective Story*. New York, NY: Dutton.

Coleman, K. (2005). *A History of Chemical Warfare*. New York, NY: Palgrave Macmillan.

Collier, P. and Hoeffler, A. (2001). *Greed and Grievance in Civil War*. Policy research working paper 2355. Development Research Group, Washington, DC:World Bank.

Conca, K. (2006a). The new face of water conflict. *Environmental Change & Security Program Special Report*, **13** (3), 76–9.

Conca, K. (2006b). *Governing Water: Contentious Transnational Politics and Global Institution Building*. Cambridge, MA: The MIT Press.

Copeland, B. R. and Taylor, M. S. (2004). Trade, growth and the environment. *Journal of Economic Literature*, **42**, 7–71.

Cox, K. R. (1998). Spaces of dependence, spaces of engagement and the politics of scale, or: looking for local politics. *Political Geography*, **17** (1), 1–23.

Crutzen, P. J. (2002). Geology of mankind. *Nature*, **415** (6867), 23.

Crutzen, P. J. and Stoermer, E. F. (2000). The "Anthropocene." *Global Change News Letter* **41** (May), 17–18.

Czaja, R. and Blair, J. (1996). *Designing Surveys: a Guide to Decisions and Procedures*. Thousand Oaks, CA: Pine Forge Press.

Dalby, S. (1992). Security, modernity, ecology: the dilemmas of post-Cold War security discourse. *Alternatives: Social Transformation and Humane Governance*, **17** (1), 95–134.

Dalby, S. (1996). Environmental security: geopolitics, ecology and the new world order. In *Environmental Policy with Political and Economic Integration: The European Union and the United States*, eds. J. B. Braden, H. Folmer, and T. Ulen. Cheltenham, UK: Edward Elgar, pp. 452–75.

Dalby, S. (2002). *Environmental Security*. Minneapolis, MN: University of Minnesota Press.

Dalby, S. (2007a). Anthropocene geopolitics: globalization, empire, environment and critique. *Geography Compass*, **1** (1), 103–18.

Dalby, S. (2007b). Geopolitical knowledge: scale, method and the "Willie Sutton Syndrome." *Geopolitics*, **12** (1), 183–91.

Dasgupta, S. and Wheeler, D. (1997). *Citizen Complaints as Environmental Indicators: Evidence from China* (Working Paper 1704), Infrastructure and Environment Development Research Group, Washington, DC: World Bank. Online at http://ideas.repec.org/p/wbk/wbrwps/1704.html, accessed 13 December 2009.

Dasgupta, S. L., Laplante, B., Wang, H. and Wheeler, D. (2002). Confronting the environmental Kuznets curve. *Journal of Economic Perspectives*, **19**, 147–68.

Davies, A. R. (2008). *The Geographies of Garbage Governance: Interventions, Interactions and Outcomes*. Burlington, VT: Ashgate Publishing Company.

Davis, M. (1998). Utah's toxic heaven. *Capitalism, Nature, Socialism*, **9** (2), 35–9.

De Soysa, I. (2002). Paradise is a bazar? Greed, creed and governance in Civil War, 1989–1999. *Journal of Peace Research*, **39** (4), 395–416.

DeBardeleben, J. and Hannigan, J., eds. (1995). *Environmental Security and Quality after Communism: Eastern Europe and the Soviet Successor States.* Boulder, CO: Westview Press.

Deffeyes, K. S. (2005). *Beyond Oil: The View From Hubbert's Peak.* New York, NY: Hill and Wang.

Demeritt, D. (2001). The construction of global warming and the politics of science. *Annals of the Association of American Geographers,* **91** (2), 307–37.

Deudney, D. H. (1991). Environment and security: muddled thinking. *Bulletin of the Atomic Scientists,* **47** (3), 22–9.

Deudney, D. H. and Matthew, R. A. (1999). *Contested Grounds: Security and Conflict in the New Environmental Politics.* Albany, NY: State University of New York Press.

Deutsch, C. H. (2007). Mum's the word: we found a greener gas. *The New York Times,* **7** November, p. H8.

Dhillon, A. and Harnden, T. (2006). How Coldplay's green hopes died in the arid soil of India. *Telegraph* 29 April 2006 and 12 January 2009. Online at http://www.telegraph.co.uk/news/worldnews/asia/india/1517031/How-Coldplay%27s-green-hopes-died-in-the-arid-soil-of-India.html, accessed 28 February 2010.

Dienes, L. (2002). Reflections on a geographic dichotomy: Archipelago Russia. *Eurasian Geography and Economics,* **43,** 443–58.

Dietz, T., Ostrom, E. and Stern, P. C. (2003). The struggle to govern the commons. *Science,* **302** (5652), 1907–12.

Dovers, S., Bammer, G. and Smithson, M. *et al.* (2008). Uncertainty complexity and the environment. In *Uncertainty and Risk: Multidisciplinary Perspectives,* eds. G. Bammer and M. Smithson. Sterling, VA: Earthscan, pp. 245–60.

Dow, K. and Downing, T. E. (2007). *The Atlas of Climate Change: Mapping the World's Greatest Challenge.* Berkeley and Los Angeles, CA: University of California Press.

Downie, D. L. and Fenge, T., eds. (2003). *Northern Lights Against POPs: Combatting Toxic Threats in the Arctic.* Montreal: McGill-Queen's University Press.

Dunning, T. (2005). Resource dependence, economic performance and political stability. *Journal of Conflict Resolution,* **49** (4), 451–82.

Dunning, T. and Wirpsa, L. (2004). Oil and the political economy of conflict in Colombia and beyond: A linkages approach. *Geopolitics,* **9** (1), 81–108.

Durning, A. T. and Ayres, E. (1994). The history of a cup of coffee. *World Watch,* **7** (5), 20.

Easterling, W. E. and Polsky, C. (2004). Crossing the divide: linking global and local scales in human-environment systems. In *Scale and Geographic Inquiry: Nature, Society and Method,* eds. E. Sheppard and R. B. McMaster. Malden, MA: Blackwell Publishing, pp. 66–85.

Ebbesmeyer, C. and Scigliano, E. (2009). *Flotsameterics and the Floating World: How One Man's Obsession with Runaway Sneakers and Rubber Ducks Revolutionized Ocean Science.* New York, NY: Smithsonian Books.

Echeverria, J. and Eby, R. B., eds. (1995). *Let the People Judge: Wise Use and the Private Property Rights Movement.* Washington, DC: Island Press.

Eckley, N. (2001). Traveling toxics: the science, policy and management of persistent organic pollutants. *Environment,* **43** (7), 24–36.

Edkins, J. (1999). *Poststructuralism and International Relations: Bringing the Political Back in.* Boulder, CO: Lynne Rienner Publishers.

Ellis, D. M. (2003). Changing earth and sky: movement, environmental variability, and responses to El Nino in the Pio-Tura Region of Papua New Guinea. In *Weather, Climate, Culture,* eds. S. Strauss and B. Orlove. New York, NY: Berg, pp. 161–80.

Englebert, P. and Ron, J. (2004). Primary commodities and war: Congo-Brazzaville's ambivalent resource curse. *Comparative Politics*, **37** (1), 61–81.

Environment News Service (2008). *Climate-friendly greenfreezers come to the United States*. Online at http://www.ens-newswire.com/ens/oct2008/2008–10–01–092. asp, accessed 27 October 2008.

Ettlinger, S. (2007). *Twinkie, Deconstructed: My Journey to Discover How the Ingredients Found in Processed Foods Are Grown, Mined (Yes, Mined), and Manipulated into What America Eats*. New York, NY: Hudson Street Press.

Falk, R. (1971). *This Endangered Planet*. New York, NY: Random House.

Falola, T. and Genova, A. (2005). *The Politics of the Global Oil Industry: An Introduction*. Westport, CT: Praeger.

Farber, D. and Weeks, J. (2001). A graceful exit? Decommissioning nuclear power reactors. *Environment*, **43** (6), 8–21.

Farrell, A. E., Plevin, R. J., Turner, B. T., *et al.* (2006). Ethanol can contribute to energy and environmental goals. *Science*, **311**, 506–8.

Faustman, E. M. and Omenn, G. S. (2008). Risk assessment. In *Casarett and Doull's Toxicology: The Basic Science of Poisons*, 7th edn, ed. C. D. Klaassen. New York, NY: McGraw Hill Medical, pp. 107–28.

Fearon, J. (2005). Primary commodities exports and civil war. *Journal of Conflict Resolution*, **49** (4), 451–82.

Fearon, J. D. and Laitin, D. D. (2003). Ethnicity, insurgency and civil war. *American Political Science Review*, **97**, 75–90.

Felgenhauer, P. (2009). A restart of U.S.-Russian relations. *Eurasia Daily Monitor*, **6** (9), 15 January. Online at http://www.jamestown.org.

Fisher, E., Jones, J. and von Schomberg, R., eds. (2006). *Implementing the Precautionary Principle: Perspectives and Prospects*. Cheltenham, UK: Edward Elgar.

Flannery, T. (2005). *The Weather Makers: How Man is Changing the Climate and What it Means for Life on Earth*. New York, NY: Atlantic Monthly Press.

Fogel, C. (2004). The local, the global, and the Kyoto Protocol. In *Earthy Politics: Local and Global in Environmental Governance*, eds. S. Jasanoff and M. L. Martello. Cambridge, MA: The MIT Press, pp. 103–25.

Food and Agricultural Organization (FAO) (1996). *Rome Declaration on World Food Security and World Food Summit Plan of Action*. World Food Summit, 13–17 November, Rome, Italy. Online at http://www.fao.org/docrep/003/ w3613e/ w3613e00.HTM, accessed 7 December 2009.

Frank, M. V. (2008). *Choosing Safety: A Guide to Using Probabilistic Risk Assessment and Decision Analysis in Complex, High-Consequence Systems*. Washington, DC: Resources for the Future.

Franke, A., ed. (2006). *B-Zone: Becoming Europe and Beyond*. Berlin: Actar/ Kunst-Werke.

Friedman, T. L. (2008). *Hot, Flat, and Crowded: Why we Need a Green Revolution – and How it Can Renew America*. New York, NY: Farrar, Straus, and Giroux.

Furedi, F. (2005). *The Culture of Fear Revisited: Risk-taking and the Morality of Low Expectation*. New York, NY: Continuum.

Furlong, K. (2006). Hidden theories, troubled waters: international relations, the 'territorial trap', and the Southern African Development Community's transboundary waters. *Political Geography*, **25** (4), 438–58.

Gattuso, D. J. (2007). The dangers of e-waste are exaggerated. In *Garbage and Recycling*, ed. M. Young. Detroit, MI: Greenhaven Press, pp. 127–34.

Gelb, A. (1986). Adjustment to windfall gains: a comparative analysis of oil-exporting countries. In *Natural Resources and the Macroeconomy*, eds. J. P. Neary and S. Van Wijnbergen. Oxford, UK: Basil Blackwell, pp. 54–92.

Gelb, A. (1988). *Oil Windfalls: Blessing or Curse?* New York, NY: Oxford University Press.

Glantz, M. H. (1994). *Drought Follows the Plow*. Cambridge, UK: Cambridge University Press.

Gleditsch, N. P. (1998). Armed conflict and the environment: a critique of the literature. *Journal of Peace Research*, **35**, 381–400.

Gleditsch, N. P. (2001). Armed conflict and the environment. In *Environmental conflict*, eds. P. F. Diehl and N. P. Gleditsch. Boulder, CO: Westview Press, pp. 251–72.

Gleditsch, N. P. and Urdal, H. (2002). Ecoviolence? Links between population growth, environmental scarcity and violent conflict in Thomas Homer-Dixon's work. *Journal of International Affairs*, **56**, 283–302.

Gleick, J. (1988). *Chaos: Making a New Science*. New York, NY: Penguin Books.

Gleick, P. H. (1991). Environment and security: the clear connections. *Bulletin of the Atomic Scientists*, **47** (3), 16–21.

Golding, D. (1992). A social and programmatic history of risk research. In *Social Theories of Risk*, eds. D. Golding and S. Krimsky. Westport, CT: Praeger, pp. 23–52.

Goolsby, D. A. and Battaglin, W. A. (2000). Nitrogen in the Mississippi Basin – estimating sources and predicting flux to the Gulf of Mexico. USGS Kansas Water Center. http://ks.water.usgs.gov/pubs/fact-sheets/fs.135-00.html, accessed 4 December 2009.

Greim, H. and Snyder, R. (2008). Introduction to the discipline of toxicology. In *Toxicology and Risk Assessment: A Comprehensive Introduction*, eds. H. Greim and R. Snyder. West Sussex, UK: John Wiley & Sons Ltd., pp. 1–18.

Grossman, E. (2006). *High Tech Trash: Digital Devices, Hidden Toxics, and Human Health*. Washington, DC: Island Press.

Grossman, E. (2007). Electronics recycling is a thriving, environmentally sound business. In *Garbage and Recycling*, ed. M. Young. Detroit, MI: Greenhaven Press, pp. 107–15.

Guha-Khasnobis, B. and Hazarika, G. (2007). Women's status and children's food security in Pakistan. In *Food Security: Indicators, Measurement, and the Impact of Trade Openness*, eds. B. Guha-Khasnobis, S. S. Acharya and B. Davis. Oxford, UK: Oxford University Press, pp. 95–108.

Hauge, W. and Ellingsen, T. (1998). Beyond environmental scarcity: causal pathways to conflict. *Journal of Peace Research*, **35**, 299–317.

Hauge, W. and Ellingsen, T. (2001). Causal pathways to conflict. In *Environmental Conflict*, eds. P. F. Diehl and N. P. Gleditsch. Boulder, CO: Westview Press, pp. 36–57.

Hawkins, G. (2006). *The Ethics of Waste: How We Relate to Rubbish*. Lanham, MD: Rowman & Littlefield Publishers, Inc.

Heinberg, R. (2005). *The Party's Over: Oil, War and the Fate of Industrial Societies*. Gabriola, BC: New Society Publishers.

Heller, M. C. and Keoleian, G. A. (2000). *Life Cycle-Based Sustainability Indicators for Assessment of the US Food System*, The Center for Sustainable Systems, Report No. CSS000–04. Online at http://www.umich.edu/~ css.

Helvarg, D. (1994). *The War Against the Greens: The "Wise-Use" Movement, the New Right, and Anti-Environmental Violence*. San Francisco, CA: Sierra Club Books.

Herod, A. (2003). Scale: the local and the global. In *Key Concepts in Geography*, eds. S. L. Holloway, S. P. Rice and G. Valentine. London, UK: Sage Publications, pp. 229–47.

Herrmann, M. (2007). Agricultural support measures of developed countries and food insecurity in developing countries. In *Food Security: Indicators, Measurement, and the Impact of Trade Openness*, ed. B. Guha-Khasnobis, S. S. Acharya and B. Davis. Oxford, UK: Oxford University Press, pp. 206–38.

Heynen, N. and Robbins, P. (2005). The neoliberalization of nature: governance, privatization, enclosure and valuation. *Capitalism, Nature, Socialism*, **16**, 5–8.

Hill, J., Nelson, E., Tilman, D., Polasky, S. and Tiffany, D. (2006). Environmental, economic and energetic costs and benefits of biodiesel and ethanol biofuels. *Proceedings of the National Academy of Sciences of the United States of America*, **103**, 11206–10.

Hiro, D. (2007). *Blood of the Earth: The Battle for the World's Vanishing Oil Resources*, New York, NY: Nation Books.

Holling, C. S. (1986). The resilience of terrestrial ecosystems: local surprise and global change. In *Sustainable Development of the Biosphere*, eds. W. C. Clark and R. E. Munn. Cambridge, UK: Cambridge University Press, pp. 292–317.

Homer-Dixon T. (1991). On the threshold: environmental changes as causes of acute conflict. *International Security*, **16** (2), 76–117.

Homer-Dixon T. (1994). Environmental scarcities and violent conflict: evidence from cases. *International Security*, **19** (1), 5–40.

Homer-Dixon, T. (1999). *Environment, Scarcity, and Violence*. Princeton, NJ: Princeton University Press.

Homer-Dixon, T. and Blitt, J., eds. (1998). *Ecoviolence: Links Among Environment, Population, and Security*. Lanham, MD: Rowman and Littlefield.

Howitt, R. (1998). Scale as relation: musical metaphors of geographical scale. *Area*, **30** (1), 49–58.

Hubbert, M. K. (1969). Energy resources. In *Resources and Man*, ed. P. Cloud. San Francisco, CA: W. H. Freeman, pp. 157–242.

Huish, R. (2008). Human security and food security in geographical study: Pragmatic concepts or elusive theory? *Geography Compass* **2**, 1386–403.

Hulme, M. (2008a). Geographical work at the boundaries of climate change. *Transactions of the Institute of British Geographers*, **35**, 5–11.

Hulme, M. (2008b). Governing and adapting to climate: a response to Ian Bailey's commentary on 'Geographical work at the boundaries of climate change.' *Transactions of the Institute of British Geographers*, **33**, 424–7.

Human Rights Watch (2009). Diamonds in the rough: human rights abuses in the Marange Diamond Fields of Zimbabwe. Online at http://www.hrw.org/en/reports/2009/06/26/diamonds-rough, accessed 26 October 2009.

Hunt, S. C., Sawin, J. L. and Stair, P. (2006). Cultivating renewable alternatives to oil. In *The State of the World 2006: A Worldwatch Institute Report on Progress Toward a Sustainable Society*, ed. L. Starke. New York, NY: W.W. Norton & Company.

International Boundaries Research Unit. (2008). Maritime jurisdiction and boundaries in the Arctic Region. Durham, UK: Durham University. Online at http://www.dur.ac.uk/ibru/resources/arctic/, accessed 4 December 2009.

IPCC (2007). Summary for policymakers. In *Climate Change 2007: Impacts, Adaptation and Vulnerability. Contribution of Working Group II to the Fourth Assessment Report of the Intergovernmental Panel on Climate Change*, eds.

M. L. Parry, O. F. Canziani, J. P. Palutikof, P. J. van der Linden and C. E. Hanson. Cambridge, UK: Cambridge University Press, pp. 7–22.

Janney, A. (2007). Curbside recycling wastes environmental and economic resources. In *Garbage and Recycling*, ed. M. Young. Detroit, MI: Greenhaven Press, pp. 93–9.

Jasper, J. M. (1990). *Nuclear Politics: Energy and the State in the United States, Sweden and France*. Princeton, NJ: Princeton University Press.

Jonas, A. E. G. (1994). The scale politics of spatiality. *Environment and Planning: Society and Space*, **12**, 257–64.

Juhasz, A. (2008). *The Tyranny of Oil: The World's Most Powerful Industry – and What we Must Do to Stop it*. New York, NY: Harper Collins Publishers.

Kamieniecki, S. (2006). Navigating the maze: corporate influence over federal environmental rulemaking. *Environment*, **48** (5), 9–20.

Kandiyoti, R. (2008). *Pipelines: Flowing Oil and Crude Politics*. New York, NY: I. B. Taurus.

Kapuściński, R. (1985). *Shah of Shahs*. San Diego, CA: Harcourt Brace Jovannovich.

Karl, T. L. (1997). *The Paradox of Plenty: Oil Booms and Petro-States*. Berkeley, CA: University of California Press.

Karl, T. L. (2000). Crude calculations: OPEC lessons for the Caspian region. In *Energy and Conflict in Central Asia and the Caucasus*, eds. R. Ebel and R. Menon. Lanham, MD: Rowman & Littlefield, pp. 29–54.

Kasperson, R. E. (2008). Coping with deep uncertainty: challenges for environmental assessment and decision-making. In *Uncertainty and Risk: Multidisciplinary Perspectives*, eds. G. Bammer and M. Smithson. Sterling, VA: Earthscan, pp. 337–47.

Kigotho, A. W. (1997). World Bank oil-pipeline project designed to prevent HIV transmission. *The Lancet* (29 November).

Klare, M. T. (2001). The new geography of conflict. *Foreign Affairs*, **80** (3), 49–61.

Klare, M. T. (2004). *Blood and Oil: The Dangers and Consequences of America's Growing Petroleum Dependency*. New York, NY: Metropolitan Books.

Klare, M. T. (2008). *Rising Powers, Shrinking Planet: The New Geopolitics of Energy*. New York, NY: Metropolitan Books.

Kupchinsky, R. (2009). The 18-day gas war – Why was it fought? Who won? *Eurasia Daily Monitor*, **6** (12), 20 January. Online at http://www.jamestown.org/.

Kuzio, T. (2009). Russian-Ukrainian gas crisis fueled by national identity. *Eurasia Daily Monitor*, **6** (12), 20 January. Online at http://www.jamestown.org/.

Kuznets, S. (1955). Economic growth and income inequality. *American Economic Review*, **45**, 1–28.

Lake, R. W. (1994). Negotiating local autonomy. *Political Geography*, **13** (5), 423–42.

Lal, R. (2005). Climate change, soil carbon dynamics, and global food security. In *Climate Change and Global Food Security*, eds. R. Lal, B. A. Stewart, N. Uphoff and D. O. Hansen. New York, NY: Taylor & Francis, pp. 113–43.

Lal, R., Stewart, B. A., Uphoff, N., and Hansen, D. O., eds. (2005). *2005 Climate Change and Global Food Security*. New York, NY: Taylor & Francis.

Lam, N. S. and Quattrochi, D. A. (1992). On the issues of scale, resolution, and fractal analysis in the mapping sciences. *Professional Geographer*, **44** (1), 88–98.

Lang, T. (1997). Going public: Food campaigns during the 1980s and early 1990s. In *Nutrition in Britain: Science, Scientists and Politics in the Twentieth Century*, ed. D. F. Smith. London, UK: Routledge, pp. 238–60.

Layzer, J. A. (2002). *The Environmental Case: Translating Values into Policy*. Washington, DC: CQ Press.

Layzer, J. A. and Moomaw, W. R. (2007). Afterword. In *What We Know About Climate Change*, ed. K. A. Emanuel. Cambridge, MA: The MIT Press, pp. 71–85.

Le Billon, P. (2001). The political ecology of war: natural resources and armed conflicts. *Political Geography*, **20** (5), 561–84.

Leech, G. (2006). *Crude Interventions: The United States, Oil, and the New World (Dis)order*. London, UK: Zed Books.

Levkoe, C. Z. (2006). Learning democracy through food justice movements. *Agriculture and Human Values*, **23**, 89–98.

Lieven, D. (2002). *The Russian Empire and Its Rivals*. New Haven, CT: Yale University Press.

Lipschutz, R. D. (2004). *Global Environmental Politics: Power, Perspectives and Practice*. Washington, DC: CQ Press.

Lipschutz, R. D. and Conca, K., eds. (1993). *The State and Social Power in Global Environmental Politics*. New York, NY: Columbia University Press.

Lipschutz, R. and Holdren, J. (1990). Crossing borders: resource flows, the global environment and international stability. *Bulletin of Peace Proposals*, **21**, 121–33.

Lipsett, C. H. (1963). *Industrial Wastes and Salvage: Conservation and Utilization*. New York, NY: The Atlas Publishing Co., Inc.

Litfin, K. T. (1997a). Sovereignty in world ecopolitics. *International Studies Quarterly*, **41** (2), 167–204.

Litfin, K. (1997b). The gendered eye in the sky: a feminist perspective on earth observation satellites. *Frontiers*, **18** (2), 26–47.

Liu, X., Vedlitz, A. and Alston, L. (2008). Regional news portrayals of global warming and climate change. *Environmental Science & Policy*, **11**, 379–93.

Liverman, D. (2004). Who governs, at what scale, and at what price? Geography, environmental governance, and the commodification of nature. *Annals of the Association of American Geographers*, **94**, 734–8.

Loh, J., ed. (2008). *2010 and Beyond: Rising to the Biodiversity Challenge*. Gland, Switzerland: World Wide Fund for Nature.

Lohman, L. (Forthcoming). Climate crisis: social science crisis. In *Der Klimawandel: Sozialwissenschaftliche Perspektiven*, ed. M. Voss. Berlin: VS-Verlag. Online at http://www.thecornerhouse.org.uk/pdf/document/SocSci.pdf, accessed 7 December 2009.

Lohman, L., ed. (2006). *Carbon Trading: A Critical Conversation on Climate Change, Privatization and Power*. Uppsala: Dag Hammarskjold Foundation.

Loos, A. (1992). *Gentlemen Prefer Blondes: The Illuminating Diary of a Professional Lady*. New York and London: Penguin Books.

Løvendal, C. R. and Knowles, M. (2007). Tomorrow's hunger: a framework for analysing vulnerability to food security. In *Food Security: Indicators, Measurement, and the Impact of Trade Openness*, eds. B. Guha-Khasnobis, S. S. Acharya, and B. Davis. Oxford, UK: Oxford University Press, pp. 62–94.

Lujala, P., Gleditsch, N. P. and Gilmore E. (2005). A diamond's curse? Civil war and a lootable resource. *Journal of Conflict Resolution*, **49** (4), 538–62.

Maathai, W. (2005). Why a Nobel Peace Prize for environmental activism? *New Perspectives Quarterly*, **22** (2), 16–19.

Maathai, W. (2008). An unbreakable link: peace, environment, and democracy. *Harvard International Review*, **29** (4), 24–7.

Mamadouh, V., Kramsch, O. and Van Der Velde, M. (2004). Articulating local and global scales. *Tijdschrift voor Economische en Sociale Geografie*, **95** (5), 455–66.

Mann, M. (1986). *The Sources of Social Power Volume 1: A History of Power from the Beginning to A.D. 1760*. Cambridge, UK: Cambridge University Press.

Mann, M. (1993). *The Sources of Social Power Volume 2: The Rise of Classes and Nation States, 1760–1914*. Cambridge, UK: Cambridge University Press.

Mann, M. (2003). The autonomous power of the state: its origins, mechanisms and results. In *State/Space: A Reader*, eds. N. Brenner, B. Jessop, J. Martin and G. MacLeod. Malden, MA: Blackwell, pp. 53–64.

Manning, R. (2004). The oil we eat: following the food chain back to Iraq. *Harper's* (February), pp. 37–45.

Margonelli, L. (2007). *Oil on the brain: Adventures from the pump to the pipeline*. New York, NY: Doubleday.

Markandya, A. and Averchenkova, A. (2000). Transition and reform: what effect does resource abundance have? *Environment and Planning B: Planning and Design*, **27** (3), 349–64.

Marsden, T., Munton, R., Ward, N. and Whatmore, S. (1996). Agricultural geography and the political economy approach: A review. *Economic Geography*, **72**, 361–75.

Marston, S. A. (2000). The social construction of scale. *Progress in Human Geography*, **24** (2), 219–42.

Maxwell, J. W. and Reuveny, R. (2000). Resource scarcity and conflict in developing countries. *Journal of Peace Research*, **37**, 301–22.

Mayor, A. (2003). *Greek Fire, Poison Arrows, and Scorpion Bombs: Biological and Chemical Warfare in the Ancient World*. Woodstock, CT: Overlook Duckworth.

McAllister, D. M. (1988). *Evaluation in Environmental Planning: Assessing Environmental, Social, Economic, and Political Trade-offs*. Cambridge, MA: The MIT Press.

McCarthy, J. and Prudham, S. (2004). Neoliberal nature and the nature of neoliberalism. *Geoforum*, **35**, 275–83.

McDonough, W. and Braungart, M. (2002). *Cradle to Cradle: Remaking the Way We Make Things*. New York, NY: North Point Press.

McLuhan, M. (1964). *Understanding Media: The Extensions of Man*. New York, NY: McGraw-Hill Book Company.

Mearns, L. O. (2003). *Issues in the Impacts of Climate Variability and Change on Agriculture* (reprinted from Climatic Change volume 60, nos. 1–2) Dordrecht: Kluwer Academic Publishers.

Melis, A. and Happe, T. (2001). Hydrogen production: green algae as a source of energy. *American Society of Plant Biology*, **127**, 740–8.

Melis, A., Zhang, L., Forestier, M., Ghirardi, M. L. and Seibert, M. (2000). Sustained photobiological hydrogen gas production upon reversible inactivation of oxygen evolution in the green alga Chlamydomonas reinhardtii. *Plant Physiology*, **122** (1), 127–36.

Michaels, D. (2008). *Doubt is Their Product: How Industry's Assault on Science Threatens Your Health*. New York, NY: Oxford University Press.

Miller, B. A. (1994). Political empowerment, local–central state relations, and geographically shifting political opportunity structures: strategies of the Cambridge, Massachusetts, peace movement. *Political Geography*, **13** (5), 393–406.

Miller, B. A. (2000). *Geography and Social Movements: Comparing Antinuclear Activism in the Boston Area*. Minneapolis, MN: University of Minnesota Press.

Miller, N., ed. (2009). *Cases in Environmental Politics: Stakeholders, Interests and Policymaking*. New York, NY: Routledge.

Mol, A. P. (2007). Boundless biofuels? Between environmental sustainability and vulnerability. *Sociologia Ruralis*, **47**, 297–315.

Moody, S. (2006). *Washed Up: The Curious Journeys of Flotsam and Jetsam*. Seattle, WA: Sasquatch Books.

Moore, M. (2008). Political practice: uncertainty, ethics and outcomes. In *Uncertainty and Risk: Multidisciplinary Perspectives*, eds. G. Bammer and M. Smithson. Sterling, VA: Earthscan, pp. 171–82.

Morgan, K., Marsden, T. and Murdoch, J. (2006). *Worlds of Food: Place, Power, and Provenance in the Food Chain*. New York, NY: Oxford University Press.

Naylor, R. L., Liska, A. J., Burke, M. B., *et al.* (2007). The ripple effect: biofuels, food security, and the environment. *Environment* **49** (9), 30–43.

Ndumbe, J. A. (2002). The Chad-Cameroon Oil Pipeline – Hope for poverty reduction? *Mediterranean Quarterly* **13** (4), 74–87.

Nuclear Waste Update (2009). Yucca mountain project: is it dead or alive? **14** (2), 1–2. Online at http://www.yuccamountain.org/pdf/summer_2009.pdf, accessed 28 February 2010.

Ó Tuathail, G., Dalby, S. and Routledge, P. (2006). *The Geopolitics Reader*. New York, NY: Routledge.

O'Brien, M. (2008). *A Crisis of Waste?: Understanding the Rubbish Society*. New York, NY: Routledge.

O'Lear, S. (1996). Using electronic mail (e-mail) surveys for geographic research: lessons from a survey of Russian environmentalists. *Professional Geographer*, **48** (2), 213–22.

O'Lear, S. (1997). Electronic communication environmental policy in Russia and Estonia. *Geographical Review*, **87** (2), 275–90.

O'Lear, S. (1999). Networks of engagement: electronic communication and grassroots environmental activism in Kaliningrad. *Geografiska Annaler*, **81**, 165–78.

O'Lear, S. (2005). Resource concerns for territorial conflict. *GeoJournal*, **64** (4), 297–306.

O'Lear, S. (2007). Azerbaijan's resource wealth: political legitimacy and public opinion. *The Geographical Journal*, **173** (3), 207–23.

O'Lear, S. and Diehl, P. F. (2007). Not drawn to scale: research on resource and environmental conflict. *Geopolitics*, **12** (1), 166–82.

O'Lear, S. and Gray, A. (2006). Asking the right questions: environmental conflict in the case of Azerbaijan. *Area*, **38** (4), 390–401.

O'Neill, K. (2000). *Waste Trading among Rich Nations: Building a new Theory of Environmental Regulation*. Cambridge, MA: The MIT Press.

O'Rourke, M. (2007). Society must address the potential dangers of e-waste. In *Garbage and Recycling*, ed. M. Young. Detroit, MI: Greenhaven Press, pp. 120–6.

Oldfield, J. D. (2005). *Russian Nature: Exploring the Environmental Consequences of Societal Change*. Burlington, VT: Ashgate Publishing Company.

Olson, M. (1963). Rapid economic growth as a destabilizing force. *Journal of Economic History*, **23**, 529–52.

Olson, R. D. (2008). NAFTA's food and agricultural lessons. *Peace Review: A Journal of Social Justice*, **20**, 418–25.

Onuf, N. (2007). Forward. In *The Social Construction of Climate Change: Power Knowledge, Norms, Discourses*, ed. M. E. Pettenger. Burlington, VT: Ashgate, pp. xi–xv.

Ostrom, E., Burger, J., Field, C. B., Norgaard, R. B. and Policansky, D. (1999). Revisiting the commons: local lessons, global challenges. *Science*, **284** (5412), 278–82.

Packard, V. (1963). *The Waste Makers*. New York, NY: Pocket Books, Inc.

Paolisso, M. (2003). Chesapeake Bay watermen, weather and blue crabs: cultural models and fishery policies. In *Weather, Climate, Culture*, eds. S. Strauss and B. Orlove. New York, NY: Berg, pp. 61–81.

Parry, M. L., Rosenzweig, C., Iglesias, A., Livermore, M. and Fisher, G. (2004). Assessing the effects of climate change on global food production under socio-economic scenarios. *Global Environmental Change*, **14** (1), 53–67.

Paterson, M. and Stripple, J. (2007). Singing climate change into existence: on the territorialization of climate policymaking. In *The Social Construction of Climate Change: Power Knowledge, Norms, Discourses*, ed. M. E. Pettenger. Burlington, VT: Ashgate, pp. 149–72.

Pearce, J. (2007). Oil and armed conflict in Casanare, Colombia: Complex contexts and contingent moments. In *Oil Wars*, eds. M. Kaldor, T. L. Karl and Y. Said. Ann Arbor, MI: Pluto Press, pp. 225–73.

Pegg, S. (2005). Can policy intervention beat the resource curse? Evidence from the Chad-Cameroon Pipeline Project. *African Affairs*, **105**, 1–25.

Peltonen, M., ed. (1996). *The Cambridge Companion to Bacon*. Cambridge, UK: Cambridge University Press.

Peterson, D. J. (1993). *Troubled Lands: The Legacy of Soviet Environmental Destruction*. Boulder CO: Westview Press.

Pettenger, M. E. (2007). Introduction: power, knowledge and the social construction of climate change. In *The Social Construction of Climate Change: Power Knowledge, Norms, Discourses*, ed. M. E. Pettenger. Burlington, VT: Ashgate, pp. 1–19.

Pfeiffer, D. A. (2006). *Eating Fossil Fuels: Oil, Food and The Coming Crisis in Agriculture*. Gabriola Island, BC: New Society Publishers.

Pimentel, D. (2003). Ethanol fuels: energy balance, economics, and environmental impacts are negative. *Natural Resources Research*, **12**, 127–34.

Pinchot, G. (1947). *Breaking New Ground*. Covelo, CA: Island Press.

Pinstrup-Andersen, P. and Herforth, A. (2008). Food security: achieving the potential. *Environment*, **50** (5), 49–60.

Pollan, M. (2006). *The Omnivore's Dilemma: A Natural History of Four Meals*. New York, NY: Penguin.

Ponte, L. (1976). *The Cooling*. Englewood Cliffs, NJ: Prentice Hall.

Porter, R. C. (2002). *The Economics of Waste*. Washington, DC: Resources for the Future.

Rae, I., Thomas, J. and Vidar, M. (2007). The right to food as a fundamental human right: FAO's experience. In *Food Security: Indicators, Measurement, and the Impact of Trade Openness*, eds. B. Guha-Khasnobis, S. S. Acharya and B. Davis. Oxford, UK: Oxford University Press, pp. 266–85.

Ramachandran, N. (2007). Women and food security in South Asia: current issues and emerging concerns. In *Food Security: Indicators, Measurement, and the Impact of Trade Openness*, eds. B. Guha-Khasnobis, S. S. Acharya and B. Davis. Oxford, UK: Oxford University Press, pp. 219–40.

Rathje, W. and Murphy, C. (2001). *Rubbish!: The Archaeology of Garbage*. Tucson, AZ: The University of Arizona Press.

Rayner, S. (2008). Get serious about climate change. *Wired Magazine*, **16** (10), 176.

Rayner, S. and Malone, E. L. (1997). Zen and the art of climate maintenance. *Nature*, **390** (6657), 332–4.

Renner, M. (1997). *Fighting For Survival: Environmental Decline, Social Conflict and the New Age of Insecurity*. London, UK: Earthscan.

Renting, H., Marsden, T. K. and Banks, J. (2003). Understanding alternative food networks: exploring the role of short food supply chains in rural development. *Environment and Planning A*, **35**, 393–411.

Roberts, P. (2004). *The End of Oil: On the Edge of a Perilous New World*. Boston, MA: Houghton Mifflin Company.

Rogers, H. (2005). *Gone Tomorrow: The Hidden Life of Garbage*. New York, NY: The New Press.

Roncoli, C., Ingram, K., Jost, C. and Kirshen, P. (2003). Meteorological meanings: farmers' interpretations of seasonal rainfall forecasts in Burkina Faso. In *Weather, Climate, Culture*, eds. S. Strauss and B. Orlove. New York, NY: Berg, pp. 181–200.

Rosenbaum, W. A. (2005). *Environmental Politics and Policy*, 6th edn. Washington, DC: CQ Press.

Rosenbaum, W. A. (2008). *Environmental Politics and Policy*, 7th edn. Washington, DC: CQ Press.

Rosenzweig, C. and Hillel, D. (2005). Climate change, agriculture, and sustainability. In *Climate Change and Global Food Security*, eds. R. Lal, B. A. Stewart, N. Uphoff and D. O. Hansen. New York, NY: Taylor & Francis, pp. 243–68.

Ross, M. L. (2004a). How do natural resources influence civil war? Evidence from thirteen cases. *International Organization*, **58**, 35–67.

Ross, M. L. (2004b). What do we know about natural resources and civil war? *Journal of Peace Research*, **41**, 337–56.

Rosset, P. M. (2006). Genetically modified crops for a hungry world: how useful are they really? *Tailoring Biotechnologies*, **2** (1), 79–94.

Royte, E. (2005). *Garbage Land: On the Secret Trail of Trash*. New York, NY: Little, Brown and Company.

Royte, E. (2008). *Bottlemania: How Water Went On Sale and Why we Bought it*. New York, NY: Bloomsbury.

Runge, C. F. and Senauer, B. (2007). How biofuels could starve the poor. *Foreign Affairs*, **86** (3), 41–53.

Rutledge, I. (2005). *Addicted to Oil: America's Relentless Drive for Energy Security*. New York, NY: I. B. Tauris.

Sachs, J. D. and Warner, A. M. (2001). The curse of natural resources. *European Economic Review*, **45**, 827–38.

Sack, R. D. (1986). *Human Territoriality: Its Theory and History*. Cambridge, UK: Cambridge University Press.

Sack, R. D. (2001). The geographic problematic: empirical issues. *Norsk Geografisk Tidsskrift*, **55**, 107–16.

Sandalow, D. (2008). *Freedom from Oil: How the Next President Can End the United States' Oil Addiction*. New York, NY: McGraw Hill.

Sarewitz, D. (2004). How science makes environmental controversies worse. *Environmental Science & Policy*, **7**, 385–403.

Sarewitz, D. and Pielke, R. Jr. (2000). Breaking the global-warming gridlock. *The Atlantic Monthly*, **86**, 54–64.

Scanlon, J. (2005). *On Garbage*. London, UK: Reaktion Books.

Schapiro, M. (2007a). Toxic inaction: why poisonous, unregulated chemicals end up in our blood. *Harper's Magazine* (October), 78–83.

Schapiro, M. (2007b). *Exposed: The Toxic Chemistry of Everyday Products and What's at Stake for American Power*. White River Junction, VT: Chelsea Green Publishing.

Schill, S. R. (2007). Ethanol lobbying dwarfed by oil industry. *Ethanol Producer Magazine*, November. Online at http://www.ethanolproducer.com/article.jsp?article_id=3404, accessed 26 February 2009.

Schmidt, C. W. (2006). Unfair trade: e-waste in Africa. In *Environmental Health Perspectives*, **114** (4), A232–5.

Schwartz, B. (2005). Le Désordre est Général: An assessment of the socio-economic impacts of the Chad-Cameroon Pipeline in the villages of Bélel and Djertou, unpublished thesis.

Schwarz, M. and Thompson, M. (1990). *Divided we Stand: Redefining Politics, Technology and Social Choice*. Philadelphia, PA: University of Pennsylvania Press.

Seager, J. (1993). *Earth Follies: Coming to Feminist Terms with the Global Environmental Crisis*. New York, NY: Routledge.

Searchinger, T., Heimlich, R., Houghton, R. A., *et al.* (2008). Use of US croplands for biofuels increases greenhouse gases through emissions from land-use change. *Science*, **319**, 1238–40.

Sen, A. (1981). *Poverty and Famines*. New York, NY: Oxford University Press.

Service, R. F. (2005). Is it time to shoot for the sun? *Science*, **309**, 548–51.

Sheppard, E. and McMaster, R. B. (2004). *Scale and Geographic Inquiry: Nature, Society and Method*. Malden, MA: Blackwell Publishing.

Shiva, V. (2008). *Soil Not Oil: Environmental Justice in a Time of Climate Crisis*. Cambridge, MA: South End Press.

Simmons, C. S. (2004). The political economy of land conflict in the Eastern Brazilian Amazon. *Annals of the Association of American Geographers*, **94** (1), 183–206.

Simon, J. (1981). *The Ultimate Resource*. Princeton, NJ: Princeton University Press.

Sissell, K. (2007). Nations agree to accelerate HCFC phaseout. *Chemical Week*, **169** (32), 51.

Slade, G. (2006). *Made to Break: Technology and Obsolescence in America*. Cambridge, MA: Harvard University Press.

Slocum, R. (2004). Polar bears and energy-efficient light bulbs: strategies to bring climate change home. *Environment and Planning D: Society and Space*, **22**, 413–38.

Slovic, P. (2000a). Perceived risk, trust and democracy. In *The Perception of Risk*, ed. P. Slovic. Sterling, VA: Earthscan Publications Ltd, pp. 316–26.

Slovic, P. (2000b). Trust, emotion, sex, politics and science: surveying the risk-assessment battlefield. In *The Perception of Risk*, ed. P. Slovic. Sterling, VA: Earthscan Publications Ltd, pp. 390–412.

Smil, V. (2003). *Energy at the Crossroads: Global Perspectives and Uncertainties*. Cambridge, MA: The MIT Press.

Smil, V. (2008). *Energy in Nature and Society: General Energetics of Complex Systems*. Cambridge, MA: The MIT Press.

Smith, H. A. (2007). Disrupting the global discourse of climate change: the case of indigenous voices. In *The Social Construction of Climate Change: Power Knowledge, Norms, Discourses*, ed. M. E. Pettenger. Burlington, VT: Ashgate, pp. 197–215.

Smith, K. (2007). The carbon neutral myth: offset indulgences for your climate sins. In *Carbon Trade Watch*. Amsterdam, The Netherlands: Transnational Institute.

Smith, N. (1992). Contours of a spatialized politics: homeless vehicles and the production of geographic scale. *Social Text*, **33**, 54–81.

Snitow, A., Kaufman, D. and Fox, M. (2007). *Thirst: Fighting the Corporate Theft of Our Water*. San Francisco, CA: John Wiley & Sons, Inc.

Socor, V. (2009a). Germany vulnerable to Russian energy supply manipulation. *Eurasia Daily Monitor*, **6** (5), 9 January. Online at http://www.jamestown.org/.

Socor, V. (2009b). Russia hiding gas shortfall by touting multiple export routes. *Eurasia Daily Monitor*, **6** (7), 13 January. Online at http://www.jamestown.org/.

Socor, V. (2009c). Hungary to host Nabucco summit in a reshaped strategic context. *Eurasia Daily Monitor*, **6** (14), 22 January. Online at http://www.jamestown.org/.

Socor, V. (2009d). Russia strengthening its monopoly on Uzbek gas. *Eurasia Daily Monitor*, **6** (16), 26 January. Online at http://www.jamestown.org/.

Solar Energies Technologies Program. Online at http://www1.eere.energy.gov/solar/, accessed 28 February 2010.

Solomon, B. D. and Lee, R. (2000). Emissions trading systems and environmental justice. *Environment*, **42** (8), 32–45.

Soroos, M. W. (1997). The Turbot War: resolution of an international fishery dispute. In *Conflict and the Environment*, ed. N. P. Gleditsch. Dordrecht: Kluwer Academic Publishers, pp. 235–52.

Souder, W. (2000). *A Plague of Frogs: Unraveling an Environmental Mystery*. Minneapolis, MN: University of Minnesota Press.

Souder, W. (2006). It's not easy being green: are weed-killers turning frogs into hermaphrodites? In *Harper's Magazine* (August), 59–66.

Staeheli, L. A. (1994). Empowering political struggle: spaces and scales of resistance. *Political Geography*, **13** (5), 387–91.

Staeheli, L. A. and Cope, M. S. (1994). Empowering women's citizenship. *Political Geography*, **13** (5), 443–60.

Steinberg, P. E. (1994). Territorial formation on the margin: urban anti-planning in Brooklyn. *Political Geography*, **13** (5), 461–76.

Stern, D. I. (2004). The rise and fall of the environmental Kuznets curve. *World Development*, **32** (8), 1419–39.

Strauss, S. and Orlove, B. (2003). Up in the air: the anthropology of weather and climate. In *Weather, Climate*, eds. S. Strauss and B. Orlove. New York, NY: Berg, pp. 3–14.

Tabor, D. (2009). Swept away: Tracing the origins of debris. *Wired Magazine* vol. **17**, no. 4 (April). Online at http://www.wired.com/special_multimedia/2009/st_infoporn_1704, last accessed 18 June 2009.

Takada, J. (2005). *Nuclear Hazards in the World*. Berlin, Germany: Springer-Verlag.

Talberth, J., Wolowicz, K., Venetoulis, J., *et al.* (2006). *The Ecological Fishprint of Nations: Measuring Humanity's Impact on Marine Ecosystems*. Oakland, CA: Redefining Progress.

Tennberg, M. (1995). Risky business: defining the concept of environmental security. *Cooperation and Conflict*, **30** (3), 239–58.

The Economist (2007). *Tortilla blues*. 1 February.

The Economist (2008a). *Ethanol and water don't mix*. 28 February.

The Economist (2008b). *The starvelings*. 24 January.

The Economist (2009a). *No more fish in the sea*. 2 March.

The Economist (2009b). *Depths of bounty*. 2 March.

The Economist (2009c). *You are what you throw away*. 28 February, 4.

The Economist (2009d). *Down in the dumps*. 28 February, 3–5.

The Economist (2009e). *Talking rubbish*. 28 February, 3–5.

Thompson, M. (1979). *Rubbish Theory: The Creation and Destruction of Value*. New York, NY: Oxford University Press.

Thompson, M. and Price, M. F. (2002). In praise of clumsiness: understanding man and nature as a single but complex system. *IHDP [International Human Dimensions Programme]* Newsletter UPDATE (January), Bonn, Germany, pp. 14–16.

Tietz, J. (2006). Pork's dirty secret: the nation's top hog producer is also one of America's worst polluters. *Rolling Stone*, December. Online at http://www. rollingstone.com/politics/story/12840743/porks_dirty_secret_the_nations_top_ hog_producer_is_also_one_of_americas_worst_polluters, accessed 13 December 2009.

Timmerman, P. (1986). Mythology and surprise in the sustainable development of the biosphere. In *Sustainable Development of the Biosphere*, eds. W. C. Clark and R. E. Munn. Cambridge, UK: Cambridge University Press, pp. 435–54.

Tirman, J. (2006). *100 Ways America is Screwing Up the World*. New York, NY: Harper Perennial.

Torbakov, I. (2009). The Russia-Ukraine gas crisis: the big picture. *Eurasia Daily Monitor*, **6** (11), 19 January. Online at http://www.jamestown.org/.

Toset, H. P. W., Gleditsch, N. P. and Hegre, H. (2000). Shared rivers and interstate conflict. *Political Geography*, **19**, 971–96.

Treehugger (2005). *Jake Gyllenhaal and Future Forests*. Online at http://www. treehugger.com/files/2005/01/jake_gyllenhaal.php, accessed 28 February 2010.

Trenin, D. (2002). *The End of Eurasia: Russia on the Border Between Geopolitics and Globalization*. Washington, DC: Carnegie Endowment for International Peace.

Trenin, D. (2007). *Getting Russia Right*. Washington, DC: Carnegie Endowment for International Peace.

Tulloch, J. (2008). Culture and risk. In *Social Theories of Risk and Uncertainty: An Introduction*, ed. J. O. Zinn. Malden, MA: Blackwell Publishing, pp. 138–57.

Tweeten, L. (1999). The economics of global food security. *Review of Agricultural Economics*, **21** (2), 473–88.

Tweeten, L. (2005). Confronting the twin problems of global warming and food insecurity. In *Climate Change and Global Food Security*, eds. R. Lal, B. A. Stewart, N. Uphoff and D. O. Hansen. New York, NY: Taylor & Francis, pp. 657–78.

Tweeten, L. and Zulauf, C. (2008). Farm price and income policy: lessons from history. *Agribusiness*, **24** (2), 145–60.

Tyner, J. (2010). *Military Legacies: A World Made by War*. New York, NY: Routledge.

Ullman, R. (1983). Redefining security. *International Security*, **8** (1), 129–53.

UNDP, UNEP, OSCE. (2004). *Environment and Security Transforming Risks into Cooperation: The Case of the Southern Caucasus*. Switzerland: United Nations Development Program.

UNEP, UNDP, OSCE. (2003). *Environment and Security Transforming Risks into Cooperation: The Case of Central Asia and Southeastern Europe*. Switzerland: United Nations Development Program.

US Department of Energy (2008). 20% *Wind Energy by 2030: Increasing Wind Energy's Contribution to U.S. Electricity Supply, Energy Efficiency and Renewable Energy, Executive Summary*. Oak Ridge, TN: US Department of Energy. Online at http://heller.brandeis.edu/myHeller/heller_academics/readings/HS259f-Abt/ Rec_Reading_USDE_I.pdf, accessed 28 February 2010.

US Department of Energy (2009). Strategic Petroleum Reserve website. Online at http://www.fossil.energy.gov/programs/reserves/, accessed 22 January 2009.

Varady, R., Lankao, P. R. and Hankins, K. (2001). Managing hazardous materials along the U.S.–Mexico border. *Environment*, **43** (10), 22–36.

Vick, B. D., Nolan Clark, R. and Carr, D. (2007). *Analysis of Wind Farm Energy Produced in the United States*, Canyon, TX West Texas A & M University – Alternative Energy Institute. Online at http://www.cprl.ars.usda.gov/wmru/ pdfs/awea07bv.pdf, accessed 28 February 2010.

Visser, M. J. (2007). *Cold, Clear, and Deadly: Unraveling a Toxic Legacy.*
    East Lansing, MI: Michigan State University Press.
Watts, M. (1983). *Silent Violence: Food, Famine and Peasantry in Northern Nigeria.*
    Berkeley, CA: University of California Press.
Watts, M. (1994). Oil as money: the devil's excrement and the spectacle of black gold.
    In *Money, Power and Space*, eds. R. Cordridge, R. Matrin, and N. Thrift.
    Oxford, UK: Blackwell, pp. 406–46.
Watts, M. (2001). Petro-violence: community, extraction, and political ecology of a
    mythic commodity. In *Violent Environments*, eds. N. L. Peluso and M. Watts.
    Ithaca, NY: Cornell University Press, pp. 189–212.
Watts, M. J. (2003). Development and governmentality. *Singapore Journal of Tropical
    Geography*, **24**, 6–34.
Watts, M. J. (2004). Antinomies of community: some thoughts on geography, resources
    and empire. *Transactions of the Institute of British Geographers*, **29**, 195–216.
Webb, P. and Thorne-Lyman, A. (2007). Entitlement failure from a food quality
    perspective: the life and death role of vitamins and minerals in humanitarian
    crises. In *Food Insecurity, Vulnerability and Human Rights Failure*, eds.
    B. Guha-Khasnobis, S. S. Acharya and B. Davis. New York, NY: Palgrave
    MacMillan, pp. 243–65.
Welch, D. (2007). A buyer's guide to offsets. *Ethical Consumer*, **106**, May/June.
Werkle, G. R. (2004). Food justice movements: policy, planning and networks.
    Journal of Planning, Education and Research, **23**, 378–86.
Westing, A. (1984). *Environmental Warfare: A Technical, Legal and Policy Appraisal.*
    Philadelphia, PA: Taylor & Francis.
Wilbanks, T. J. (2003). Integrating climate change and sustainable development in a
    place-based context. *Climate Policy*, **3** (1), 147–54.
Wilbanks, T. J. and Kates, R. T. (1999). Global change in local places: how scale
    matters. *Climatic Change*, **43**, 601–28.
Wilbanks, T. J., Lankao, P. R., Bao, M., *et al.* (2007). "Industry, settlement and
    society" Climate Change 2007. Impacts, Adaptation and Vulnerability.
    *Contribution of Working Group II to the Fourth Assessment Report of the
    Intergovernmental Panel on Climate Change*, eds. M. L. Parry, O. F. Canziani,
    J. P. Palutikof, P. J. van der Linden and C. E. Hanson. Cambridge, UK:
    Cambridge University Press, pp. 357–90.
Williams, A. (2008). *Fungi discovered in patagonia rainforest could be used to make
    biodiesel.* Gas2.org (3 November). Online at http://gas2.org/2008/11/03/fungi-
    discovered-in-patagonia-rainforest-could-be-used-to-make-biodiesel/, accessed
    15 January 2009.
Wilson, J., Low, B., Costanza, R. and Ostrom, E. (1999). Scale misperceptions and
    the spatial dynamics of a social-ecological system. *Ecological Economics*, **31**,
    243–57.
Wolf, A. T., Yoffe, S. and Giordano, M. (2003). International waters: identifying
    basins at risk. *Water Policy*, **5** (1), 31–62.
Wolf, A. T., Kramer, A., Carius, A. and Dabelko, G. D. (2008). Water can be a
    pathway to peace, not war. *Environmental Change and Security Program Report*,
    13, 66–70.
Wood, R. (2007). *Ronnie.* New York, NY: St. Martin's Press.
World Health Organization (2003). *World Health Report 2003.* Online at http://www.
    who.int/whr/2003/en/index.html, accessed 4 December 2009.

World Wildlife Fund International (2005). *Generations X: Results of WWF's European Family Biomonitoring Survey*. Brussels, Belgium: WWF EPO. Online at http://assets.panda.org/downloads/generationsx.pdf, accessed 21 September 2009.

Worldwatch Institute (2007). *Biofuels for Transport: Global Potential and Implications for Sustainable Energy and Agriculture*. Sterling, VA: Earthscan.

Yergin, D. (1992). *The Prize: the Epic Quest for Oil, Money and Power*. New York, NY: Simon & Schuster.

Zakrezewski, S. F. (2002). *Environmental Toxicology*, 3rd edn. New York, NY: Oxford University Press.

Zimmerman, C. (2008). *Ethanol Provisions in Farm Bill*. Domesticfuel.com (8 May). Online at http://domesticfuel.com/2008/05/08/ethanol-provisions-in-farm-bill/, accessed 26 February 2009.

Zinn, J. O. (2008). Introduction: the contribution of sociology to the discourse on risk and uncertainty. In *Social Theories of Risk and Uncertainty: An Introduction*, ed. J. O. Zinn. Malden, MA: Blackwell Publishing, pp. 1–17.

Index

9216870R00132

Printed in Great Britain
by Amazon.co.uk, Ltd.,
Marston Gate.